Bienstock, Gregory
The struggle for the Pacific.

THE STRUGGLE
FOR THE
PACIFIC

Gregory Bienstock

THE STRUGGLE FOR THE PACIFIC

KENNIKAT PRESS
Port Washington, N. Y./London

THE STRUGGLE FOR THE PACIFIC

First published in 1937
Reissued in 1970 by Kennikat Press
Library of Congress Catalog Card No: 76-115199
ISBN 0-8046-1092-4

Manufactured by Taylor Publishing Company Dallas, Texas

PREFACE

I FINISHED writing this book about a year ago, and I have made a few additions to it which are relatively unimportant. Since I completed my task the evolution in the Far East has continued. The Japanese offensive in North China has increased both its scope and its tempo; the Nanking Government has successfully pursued its cautious policy of consolidation, and after a brief intermezzo of a "civil war" between Canton and Nanking, has brought practically the whole of South China into its sphere of influence; the tension existing between Japan and the Soviet Union has entered a new phase. The events inside Japan itself—the "putsch" of February 16, 1936, the resignation of the Okada Cabinet and the formation of the Hirota Cabinet—have no doubt given Far Eastern affairs in some respects a new aspect. But fundamentally the situation has not changed. The pieces on the Far Eastern chessboard are still pretty much where they were, although one or two of them may have slightly altered their places. It is clear that the two protagonists, Japan and the Soviet Union, have strengthened their positions. In particular the Soviet Union has strongly consolidated its defensive position on the Manchurian–Korean–Mongolian frontier. It is already true to say that the fortified area of Vladivostok is now one of the most important bastions of the Russian line of defence. The Japanese, too, have greatly strengthened their political and strategic positions in North China and Inner Mongolia. But the stronger the positions of these protagonists become, the greater for each becomes the risk of war. The war which may possibly break out later in the Far East will be on a far greater scale than if it had come two years ago; it will now undoubtedly be really a "great war." The chances of peace or war are at the moment about equal, apparently for no other reason than that the risk involved in going to war is to-day much greater both for Russia and for Japan.

No doubt Japan has made up her mind to use the present difficult situation in which the European States find themselves to secure her hegemony in North China or perhaps in the whole continent of Asia. Against this effort on the part of Japan, the Nanking Government opposes its old policy of waiting and manœuvring. The Chinese have behind them the experience of the Mongol and Manchu conquests; they feel they can afford to wait a couple of decades until the Japanese wave ebbs or the forward effort is exhausted. That Britain and America should adopt a similar policy may be comprehensible from a wide, historico-philosophical point of view, but it is very questionable if it is really a shrewd policy. If Japan really extends her hegemony over China, then Japan is undoubtedly mistress of the Western Pacific. I have fully set forth in my book what such a domination would mean for the Anglo-Saxon Powers and particularly for the British Empire.

The onward march of man's history never halts. The present division of the world's raw materials and of the world's population among the individual States is not a permanent division. It seems likely that the world to-day is on the eve of great mass movements which will change the whole aspect of our planet and will certainly change the actual division of raw materials. Here we must reckon with the ambition of the Japanese nation to secure a position of predominance in the Far East. The only question is how far and in what way that ambition will be realized. The Anglo-Saxon Powers, the Soviet Union, and doubtless even China, will have to recognize Japan's claim to such predominance, simply because Japan has already won it by her economic, cultural, political, and military achievements. What the other Powers with interests in the Western Pacific cannot, however, admit—and not for reasons of prestige but simply as a matter of their own security and as a condition of their existence as Great Powers—is the hegemony of Japan over the Far East as a whole and therefore over the Pacific. That this has nothing at all to do with an inter-racial struggle between yellow and white is evident simply from the fact that among the opponents of Japanese hegemony is—China.

Europe to-day is definitely inclined to devote herself to her own difficulties, those *querelles Européenes*, and to neglect all the rest of the world. But the *status quo* in Europe depends on the "balance of power" in Africa and Asia—Africa, which had been of little real interest to public opinion in Europe since the Morocco crisis of 1911 and Italy's war in Tripoli of 1911–12, has suddenly and forcibly called itself to the attention of Europe's statesmen. The disturbance of the balance of power in Africa as a result of Italy's victory in Ethiopia must alter the balance in Europe itself. But the development of the political situation in the Far East, a development increasing steadily in importance and affecting ever wider spheres, has for Europe and for America a far greater significance than have events in Africa. To prove to people living on either Atlantic coast that they are seriously affected by what happens in the Western Pacific and that they may be decisively affected —that is the real purpose of this book.

It is my duty—a very pleasant one—to return thanks here to all those who have been so good as to lend me their help in my work. The great kindness of the Director of the Oriental Institute in Prague, Dr. Karel Haltmar, enabled me to use its valuable library, and I owe a similar debt to Prof. Dr. Jan Slavik, A. F. Iziumov, and S. F. Postnikov, who are in charge of the Russian archives at the Ministry of Foreign Affairs of Czechoslovakia; to Dr. Hartl and Dr. Bystrov, of that Ministry's library, and to the librarian of the Statistical Office in Prague. My friend, Colonel Emanuel Moravec, of the General Staff, was kind enough to read in manuscript my third chapter, which deals with problems of strategy, and to give me valuable guidance. The maps were drawn to my instruction by the artist, Georg H. Trapp, and I should like here to express my warmest thanks to him. I have also to thank Mr. R. T. Clark and my friend W. A. Tyrmos, who have been of such help in preparing the English translation.

And finally I should like to express my deep gratitude to my wife, Maria Bienstock, who from first to last has been my valuable collaborator and counsellor.

September 1936

CONTENTS

LIST OF MAPS

All at the end of the book

CHAPTER I

THE PACIFIC WORLD IN THE MAKING

THE history of mankind is now entering the Pacific era: that is to say, it is within the Pacific region that the great historical events of the next hundred years will take place. The greater becomes the concern of Europe with the conflicts in the Pacific, the more fateful are the two fundamental misconceptions which, from the European point of view, are entertained about the Pacific area. The first is seen in the tendency to consider political events in the Pacific as isolated events which are said to have no direct connection with the political development in Europe. Only during the last twenty years has Europe begun to realize that the events in the Pacific region are decisive for the destinies of the West. This realization comes, however, more by instinct as a result of the tremendous experiences of the last twenty-five years than from a sociological and political comprehension of the interconnection of historical events. The "man in the street" in Europe is still very far from being aware of the fact that during the last six hundred years there has been scarcely any development of general importance in the sphere of Western politics which has not been directly or indirectly connected with contemporary events in the Pacific world. No *world* policy in the general sense of the term is possible unless the continuous action and reaction of events in the West and in the Pacific upon each other is fully recognized, and such recognition becomes a definite element in policy.

The second misconception is seen in the prevailing tendency in Europe to view political events in the Pacific solely from the angle of the recurrent sharpening of the conflicts between the various Pacific Powers, as though these conflicts, e.g. that between the United States and Japan, or between Japan and Russia, were not the result of a general development which is going on in the whole Pacific region. This view takes no account of the long evolution of the different forces which are at work to-day in the Pacific region, nor of the history of their mutual interrelations, and makes impossible any attempt to judge the present position in the light of history.

Much has been written about the significance of great rivers and inland seas for the development of the different civilizations. The importance of the oceans equally was early recognized, but their influence has been less studied. Their importance for the growth of civilization has been recognized only in recent times. That is because it was only through the development of modern means of transport that the part played by oceans as creative factors could be realized. In the nineteenth century the chief factor in economic-political development was the action and reaction on one another of the two cultural spheres on the Atlantic—Western Europe and Eastern America. In that century three-quarters of the whole world traffic used the Atlantic route. The colonization of the eastern shores of America created a new Europe on the other side of the Atlantic, which has since had a decisive influence on the history of the mother continent. During the same century the African continent was occupied by the European Powers. As a result the Atlantic-Mediterranean sphere of culture was enlarged and advanced into the Pacific. Holland and England founded Indian empires, and thus came into direct touch with China from the Indian Ocean. It was only by transocean traffic that the European West was able to come once again into direct contact with the Asiatic East, into a contact much closer and more productive of results than the earlier contact, which had been based in the Middle Ages on the overland route.

The European settlement of North America from the Atlantic side was necessarily followed by the transcontinental colonization of the New World. The waves of European migration rushed forward one after another until they reached the shores of the Pacific. In the middle of the last century the wave of European-American colonization finally reached the Pacific.

That was a second channel, a second stream of European culture flowing into the Pacific Ocean. The first one was the Dutch-English colonization of the Indies.

Much earlier still another colonization wave from Europe had reached the Pacific—the Russian colonization. In their flight from the intolerable oppression of Muscovite rule, Russian peasants, Cossacks, adventurers, bandits, and refugees passed the Ural Mountains in the middle of the sixteenth century, and in an irresistible, almost incredible, advance reached the most eastern frontier of Siberia, the Pacific, a century later. In 1638 the Russians reached the Sea of Okhotsk. The eighteenth and the beginning of the nineteenth century witnessed an amazing activity on the part of Russian merchants and soldiers on the western shores of the Pacific. The geopolitical pressure went on, and at the end of the eighteenth century the Russians had reached the North American continent (Alaska). Russian factories were also being opened on Hawaii, and Russian ships sailed into Japanese ports.

About the middle of the nineteenth century the clash proper between the Western and the Eastern Asiatic spheres of culture began, and the field for this clash could only be the Pacific. It was France who between the years 1840 and 1860 was the first to wrest its eastern provinces from the Chinese Empire and found an Indo-Chinese Colonial Empire. In the same period England forced by war the surrender of the most important commercial positions of Southern China and since has been the predominant commercial Power in the Yang-tse valley. In 1853 Commodore Perry appeared off the Japanese islands with an American squadron demanding that the Japanese ports should be opened to European-American trade. The West was storming at the gates of Eastern Asia.

§ 1. THE ATLANTIC AND THE PACIFIC

Are we entitled to-day to state that the Pacific Ocean has become the political focal point of our planet, as more than some twenty years ago Theodore Roosevelt declared it was?[1] From the standpoint of traffic, the Atlantic Ocean is still the main channel of world trade, the most important part of which is that between Western Europe and the Eastern States of America, by the North Atlantic route. Even to-day transatlantic trade is about seven-tenths of world trade. Of 68 million gross tons of the world's merchant fleet, about 42 million tons, or rather less than two-thirds, is registered in Europe.[2] The States on the North Sea alone account for about 35 million tons, and to-day Europe still accounts for more than half of the whole world's trade turnover. To-day still, world economy is a European-American concern, and generally speaking is based on North-West Europe and Eastern America. Even the World War brought no change whatever in this respect.

But what has changed in our time is the importance of the Pacific in world trade. There is no direct data here, and the fact of change can be established only indirectly.

In the first place, the share of Asia and Australia in world trade has increased, while Europe's has fallen. When we speak of Asia and Australia, we mean those countries which are either actually in the Pacific or in the Pacific region (the Indian Ocean).

SHARE OF EUROPE, ASIA, AND AUSTRALIA IN WORLD TRADE[3] AS PERCENTAGE OF TOTAL TURNOVER

Year	Europe	Asia	Australia	Asia and Australia Total
1900	65·9	9·5	2·3	11·8
1913	61·2	11·4	2·5	13·9
1933	56·3	15·6	2·7	18·3

The well-known tendency towards what is called "counter-colonization," which is really nothing but the result of the industrialization and commercialization of the world outside Europe, is also seen in the slackening of the rate at which European trade increases, while the foreign trade of the world outside Europe is progressively increasing.

TOTAL FOREIGN TRADE TURNOVER OF THE MOST IMPORTANT ATLANTIC AND PACIFIC COUNTRIES IN 1913 AND 1929 (IN MILLIARDS OF DOLLARS)[4]

	1913	1929	Percentage Rise, 1929, as compared with 1913
1. *Atlantic Countries*			
Great Britain and Northern Ireland	5·8	9·0	55·2
Norway	0·2	0·5	150·0
Belgium	1·6	1·9	18·7
France	3·0	4·2	40·0
Germany	5·0	6·4	28·0
United States (Atlantic trade)..	3·8	7·6	100·0
Total	19·4	29·6	52·6
2. *Pacific Countries*			
Japan	0·7	2·0	188·8
China (Manchuria included) ..	0·7	1·5	114·2
Australia	0·8	1·3	62·5
New Zealand	0·2	0·5	150·0
Chile	0·3	0·5	66·6
Peru	0·07	0·2	185·7
United States (Pacific trade) ..	0·4	1·9	375·0
Total (without United States)..	2·8	6·0	114·2
Total (United States included)	3·2	7·9	146·8

The most striking feature here is the general increase of world trade in 1929 as compared with pre-War times. But we ought not to forget that the purchase value of the dollar in 1929 was one-third lower than in 1913. The wholesale trade index in 1929 (1913 = 100) gives the figure of 137 in the United States, and the same figure for England. The rise in the gold value of overseas trade in no way means an equal rise in its volume. A rise in the volume of the overseas trade of such Atlantic countries as Great Britain, France, and to a still higher degree Germany and Belgium, is distinctly doubtful. Except for the United States and Norway, which, for particular reasons, saw a very rapid increase in their overseas trade, we may affirm, as far as the most important Atlantic countries are concerned, that their overseas trade is stabilized.

The Pacific countries offer a very different picture. Here we

SHARE OF PACIFIC AND ATLANTIC COUNTRIES IN THE TOTAL OVERSEA TRADE TURNOVER IN PERCENTAGE OF THE TOTAL WORLD TRADE TURNOVER, 1913 AND 1929[5]

	1913	1929
1. *Atlantic Countries*		
Great Britain and Northern Ireland ..	15·24	13·04
Norway	0·65	0·70
Belgium	4·22	2·73
France	7·80	6·19
Germany	13·12	9·34
United States (Atlantic trade)	10·03	11·07
Total	51·06	43·07
2. *Pacific Countries*		
Japan	1·79	2·87
China (Manchuria included)	1·88	2·13
Australia	1·99	1·89
New Zealand	0·54	0·72
Chile	0·71	0·70
Peru	0·19	0·30
United States (Pacific trade)	1·12	2·76
Total	8·22	11·37

have to do with a fundamental structural change; we may say, with a revolution in foreign trade.

Except, possibly, Australia and Chile, we find not only a rise in gold value but also a tremendous increase in the volume of the foreign trade of the Pacific countries.

In the Atlantic sphere we see stagnation, in the Pacific region a violent rise in overseas trade; that is only a phase of the general tendency of the present dynamic state of world economy.

The "commercialization" of the Pacific Ocean is, besides, evident from the fact that the share of the Pacific countries in world trade is growing very rapidly, while that of the Atlantic countries remains at the pre-War level, or even falls below it. (See table page 22.)

The same picture is got by a comparison of the development of the merchant marines. Here, too, except in Australia, we

GROSS TONNAGE (STEAM AND MOTOR SHIPS OVER 100 TONS)[6]

(*In Thousands of Tons*)

	June 30, 1913	June 30, 1932	Percentage Increase
1. *Atlantic Countries*			
Great Britain and Northern Ireland	18,274	19,562	7·1
France	1,793	3,507	105·8
Holland	1,287	2,957	130·7
Norway	1,871	4,164	121·0
Total	23,225	30,190	30·1
2. *Pacific Countries*			
Japan	1,500	4,255	180·0
China (Manchuria included)	87	370	325·2
Australia and New Zealand*	672	640	−4·7
Chile	108	174	61·1
Total	2,367	5,439	125·0

* June 30, 1921.

find in the Pacific countries a great development in the merchant marine. In the Atlantic group Holland, Norway, and France also show an exceptional increase of tonnage, while the merchant marine of Great Britain has risen only very slightly. In 1933 Germany showed a decrease of tonnage as compared with the pre-War tonnage. We have chosen only the four most representative countries in the Atlantic and in the Pacific to show the general trend of development here.

Though the development of the Panama route has certainly

favoured the development of the Atlantic traffic, its chief result has been an increase in Pacific traffic. Traffic via Panama, as compared with traffic via Suez, which is the chief sea route of the Old World, is still to-day lower. It is impossible to state precisely for what part of the Suez traffic the Pacific or the Indo-Pacific coast regions are responsible. But the most important traffic through this canal consists of the exchange of goods between England (which was responsible in 1928 for 57·1 per cent of the total traffic) and the other great industrial countries of North-Western Europe, Germany, Netherlands, France, etc., on the one hand, and the Indo-Eastern-Asian world on the other. From north to south the following goods are shipped via the Suez route: machinery, engines, iron goods, railway material (to Eastern India, the Malay States, and China), fertilizers (to Japan, Java, etc.), coal (to Colombo, India, and the East Indies, etc.). From south to north or east to west come via the Suez canal such important raw materials and foodstuffs as soya beans (from Manchuria), cereals (from Australia), cotton (from India), sugar (from the Dutch East Indies), and rubber (from the Malay States).

From this survey, then, we may see that most of these goods are going either from or to the Pacific-Indian region. So we may say that the development of traffic via the Suez canal in post-War times is a sign of the growth of the trade of the Pacific area. Here the following table is of interest:

TRAFFIC VIA THE SUEZ CANAL AND VIA THE PANAMA CANAL[7]

(Warships not included. For the Panama canal (first fiscal year) 1915; for Suez 1913

Year	Suez Canal		Panama Canal	
	Number of Ships	Tonnage in 1,000 net tons	Number of Ships	Tonnage in 1,000 net tone
1913	4,979	16,200	1,075	3,034
1933	5,322	23,514	4,939	18,148

The Suez canal traffic thus increased during the last twenty years by about 30 per cent; that of the Panama canal by about 500 per cent.

It is significant of the tendency for the centre of gravity of world trade to shift from the Atlantic to the Pacific that between 1913 and 1928 (taking 1928 as the last normal, i.e. pre-crisis, year) the traffic at the chief Pacific ports shows a greater increase than does that at the chief Atlantic ports. The following table presents a comparison between the seven most important ports of the Atlantic and of the Pacific.

OVERSEAS TRAFFIC OF THE ATLANTIC AND PACIFIC PORTS, 1913–28[8]

(In Thousands of Registered Tons)

	1913	1928
Atlantic Ports		
London	10,002	14,657
Liverpool	9,462	9,960
Rotterdam	9,073	16,355
Antwerp	12,017	20,302
New York	15,595	23,170
Montevideo	9,438	11,001
Hamburg	13,038	19,333
Total	78,625	114,778
Percentage Increase: 46·1.		
Pacific Ports		
San Francisco	1,428	2,047
Shanghai	9,321	17,293
Kobe	6,939	14,393
Osaka	459	5,452
Yokohama	4,443	10,295
Sidney	5,278	7,600
Vancouver	1,778	5,414
Total	29,646	62,494

Percentage Increase: 113·8.

The difference in the increase of traffic of the Pacific and Atlantic ports consists first of all in the fact that the Atlantic traffic has attained a certain stability in spite of the changes brought about by the World War, whereas there are great structural trade changes in the Pacific Ocean. There we find as everywhere else where the clash of the Atlantic and the Pacific worlds is visible, that the West, once revolutionary and expanding, which in its effort at world conquest had finally roused the slumbering East, is being overtaken and forced into second place by the East.

§ 2. RAILWAYS IN THE FAR EAST

For the development of traffic on any sea, the construction and condition of trade routes of any kind on the adjoining mainland is of the highest importance. In its origins, sea traffic is a mere continuation of land traffic; sea trade is first of all coastal trade, linked up with the great caravan roads. Later, however, sea traffic in its turn creates a whole network of land routes, so that land routes, especially the railways, but also motor roads and air routes, seem to be designed merely to complement the sea routes.

In the post-War period the various means of transport are gradually being unified and made to constitute a world traffic system in which each particular kind of transport has more or less equal rights.[9]

The construction of railways on the Pacific area has been greatly speeded up during the post-War period. On the western coast of the Pacific the total length of railways in China (without Manchuria) increased between the years 1913 and 1932 by 73·5 per cent; in Japan (including Korea and Formosa but excluding Manchuria) has almost doubled between 1913 and 1930. The highest rate of development was in Manchuria itself, where the length of railway line more than doubled.

The development of railway construction on the Chinese mainland during the nineteenth century was the result of foreign influence. The Chinese inland trade, besides the most ancient means of transport, that by man himself, was carried on by means of caravan and river routes. The isolated agrarian economies of the various provinces did not stimulate the development of transport. The national economy of China was in the main satisfied with a highly developed system of waterways, which, including the Great Imperial canal, was about 68,500 km. in length.

The initiative to railway construction came from abroad, and the railway concessions became the main object of a fierce international struggle for spheres of influence in China. During the nineteenth century England and France were the chief rivals in railway construction here. The English construction plans (the Macdonald-Stephenson plan of 1864) from the beginning were intended to link up the English sphere of influence in the Yang-tse valley with Northern India. A direct connection of Shanghai with Calcutta over Northern Yün-nan and Burma was planned. England, which in the 'forties of last century had established its power at the mouth of the Yang-tse river and in Hong-Kong, which in 1842, by the Treaty of Nanking, passed into the permanent possession of England, sought through this line to envelop China simultaneously from the ocean as well as from India and Tibet. The French were approaching South China as a result of their conquest of Cambodia and Cochinchina (1861–63). It was at this time that France attempted, through the construction of a Suez canal, to enter the Indian and Pacific Oceans without having to go by the English Capetown. These far-reaching French plans in the Indo-Pacific area were wrecked by the defeat in Europe in 1870–71. In 1875 England acquired a dominating influence in the management of the Suez canal. Nevertheless, France did not cease her struggle for Southern China, nor in part her equally far-reaching plans for supremacy in the Pacific. In 1884 she annexed Annam and Tonkin.

The French sphere of influence thus interposed between British India and the Yang-tse valley. Simultaneously France sought to gain access to the Pacific Ocean by means of a Panama canal. The direct rivalry between London and Paris ceased in the 'nineties, but efforts to paralyse indirectly the influence of the other in the Chinese Empire lasted till the World War and even afterwards. England did not drop the scheme to connect the Yang-tse valley with India by rail, but neither did the French effort to wreck the English railway plans by cross lines stop.

At the end of the last and the beginning of this century Paris supported the Russian railway policy in Manchuria, which was being carried out by Belgo-French capital; France dreamed of a junction of the Russian railways in Northern China with the French railway in Southern China, which was to be pushed from Tonkin to Yün-nan. The builder of the Suez canal, Lesseps, planned a railway across Russian Turkestan to the Indian frontier (see Map 5).

The period from the Boxer revolution to the World War is a long struggle for railway concessions; here the Anglo-German competition for the moment occupied the foreground. The competitors to-day are England, France, and Japan, for the Russian influence in Manchuria has vanished completely, and Germany appears in South China only as a competitor of minor importance. Direct American competition is visible only in the province of Shen-hsi, where the Americans have considerable interests in oil-fields as well. A short railway line from the Ping-Hsiang (Chiang-hsi) mines to Hunan-fu has been constructed by American capital. In addition, American capital shares in the construction of the great railway line Canton–Hankow. Manchuria apart, where the whole railway system is actually under direct Japanese control, Japanese railway interests lie partly in Northern China and Inner Mongolia, where new lines would connect with the Manchurian railways, partly in the province of Shan-tung where since the World War Japan has vast economic and political interests, and partly because of Shan-tung in the Huang-ho valley and farther west. The Japanese railway plans in Inner Mongolia, in Shan-tung, in the valley of the Huang-ho, in the provinces of Shan-hsi, Shen-hsi, and Kan-su, which will be discussed in more detail in the next chapter, interpose between Southern and Northern China and, apart from their economic importance, they are of extreme strategical importance, for they bring support to the defence of the entrances to Manchuria on the west and north-west.

The construction of railways in China is passing more and more into Chinese hands, and the Government of Nanking not only controls railway construction but also the management of the lines already working. At present 74 per cent of the railways are in the hands of the Government. Chinese capital is gradually getting a firm foothold in railway construction, and thus foreign influence, at least within the area controlled by the Nanking Government, has, during the last years, been driven out. But this conquest of the railways of Central China by Chinese influence has not yet altered the general character of the system. The railway map remains to-day very like what it was in 1912; there has certainly been a lot of construction, but essentially this was merely addition to the great lines already built. Even to-day the interior of China, as well as its western provinces, has scarcely any railway communications, for these are concentrated chiefly on the coast and in the immediately adjacent provinces. The Chinese national economy is, moreover, less interested in the further development of the railway system in the eastern part of China, which is so rich in waterways—the eastern system was chiefly built by foreign capital—than in the construction of railways in the western colonial regions, which lack any modern means of transport, and in connecting them by rail with Eastern China. Here little has been done up to the present; the great railway plans of Sun-Yat-Sen, as well as those worked out later by the Ministry of Railways at Peiping (1927), and those of the National Government (Sung-fo plan, 1928), have been left unrealized because of the unrest in the interior.[10]

During the last few years, and particularly since October 16

1931, the construction of railways in Manchuria has proceeded at top speed. Until Manchukuo was declared a separate State, Chinese and Japanese projects mutually paralysed each other and so hampered the development of railway construction. The Chinese were endeavouring to build competing railway lines east and west of the Dairen–Harbin line, which was under Japanese control. It was probably this Chinese competition which hastened the events of September 1931. To-day railway construction in Manchuria is directed by onc unifying will concentrated in the management of the South Manchurian Railway. After the sale of the Chinese Eastern Railway by the Russians, there has been nothing to oppose it. On January 1, 1934, according to official statements, the length of the Manchurian railways amounted to 3,600 miles, of which 660 miles belongs to the South Manchurian Railway, 1,020 miles to the Chinese Eastern Railway, and the remaining 1,860 miles to the State railways of Manchukuo. This railway system is to be extended in the next few years on a unified, comprehensive, economic, and strategic plan which we shall explain later in another connection. During the next ten years about 2,500 miles of line are to be constructed, and in the not-too-distant future it is hoped that the Manchurian system will be 15,000 miles in length. We may point out here that the Korean railway system increased in length by 30 per cent during the five years 1927–31.

Thus the territory on the continent opposite the Japanese Islands is being transformed by Japanese capital and under the Japanese control into a Japanese outpost as far as economic, military, and transport policy is concerned.[11]

Here we have left out of consideration the development in the Western States of Canada and Mexico. In Colombia, in the north-western corner of South America there has, in in the post-War period, been intense activity in the construction of railway communications between the rich Cauca valley and the central part of the country on the one hand, and the Pacific coast on the other. The length of the railways of Colombia has doubled. This is connected with the opening up of an exceedingly rich farming and mining (platinum) region, as big as Germany and France put together. Other railway lines in the Andes, too, which are the highest railways in the world, reaching sometimes the height of 4,500 m. above sea-level, will be of great importance in the commercialization and industrialization of the Pacific countries.[12]

In Africa, too, the network of railways increased during this period by 50 per cent, whereas the length of the European

DEVELOPMENT OF THE RAILWAY SYSTEMS IN IMPORTANT[13] PACIFIC COUNTRIES DURING THE POST-WAR PERIOD (IN KM.)

	1913*	At the End of 1931†	Percentage Increase
China (without Manchuria) ..	6,053	10,501	73·5
Manchuria	3,480	6,987	100·7
Japan (Korea and Formosa included)	10,986	20,501	86·7
Chile	6,370	8,919	40·0
Peru	2,766	4,522	63·4
Australia and New Zealand ..	35,510	49,197	38·5
Total	65,165	100,627	54·4

*For China and Manchuria, 1912. † Ibid., 1930.

railways during the same period increased only by 11·4 per cent, and in the United States railway construction stopped almost entirely. This does not mean, however, that the countries where capitalism is highly developed are lagging behind as far as traffic is concerned. Traffic in such densely populated and industrial countries to-day makes use of other means of communication. We need only consider the development of motor and air traffic, which no doubt, to a certain extent, limits railway construction. None the less, the fact remains that it is the countries on the Pacific and Indian Oceans in which after the War an especially intense phase of traffic development is visible. This is not only evident in the field of railway construction but also in that of those modern means of communication which compete most seriously with the railways.

It is difficult to state definitely how great in the Pacific countries the development of motor transport has been, but it is sufficient to point out that during the period 1926–30, Japan has more than doubled the number of motor cars on her roads, while China has increased it by about 86 per cent.[14]

But it is aircraft which is of the highest importance for the development of traffic in the Pacific regions. Any comparison here with pre-War times is impossible. Civil aviation is essentially a post-War achievement. Aircraft will play a very special rôle in the Pacific countries. For this means of communication will be more advantageous because, on the one hand, of the tremendous distances and lack of roads, and on the other because the railway system is so little developed that aviation has to fear no competition from the railway in its development and no obstacles placed in its way by railway interests. The development of air traffic in the Pacific countries puts all the problems of traffic in the Pacific region in a new light.

§ 3. AIR DEVELOPMENTS IN THE FAR EAST

In China air transport may become of special importance, because first of all the railway system there is as yet very little developed and, secondly, the lack of native capital and the meagre support of foreign investment is much hampering the further development of the railway network.

LENGTH OF THE RAILWAYS PER 100 SQ. KM. AND PER 10,000 INHABITANTS IN THE MOST IMPORTANT ASIATIC COUNTRIES[15]

	To 100 sq. km. of Area	To 10,000 Inhabitants
	km.	km.
China	0·2	0·3
Indian Empire	1·4	1·9
Japan	4·3	3·1
Dutch East Indies ..	0·3	0·9

It is obvious that this meagre railway development is extremely favourable to the development of air traffic as there is complete lack of competition. Actually, the development of air transport may greatly stimulate and promote the development of the whole Chinese transport system, for air lines may serve as complements to the railways as well as to the waterways, by making transport possible where the use of other means is hopeless.

There is no satisfactory data available from Chinese sources about the development of air traffic. So far, private traffic is forbidden by law, that is to say, the whole of civil aviation is in the hands of concessionaire companies, in which the Government owns the majority of the shares. Three large aviation companies share the total Chinese air transport.

The China National Aviation Corporation (C.N.A.C.) began its activity on July 8, 1929. On October 20th of that year the first machine left from Shanghai for Hankow.

Of its 10,000,000-dollar capital, 55 per cent is held by the Nanking Government. The rest was originally held by the well-known American Curtis American Aviation Co., but that company ceded it in the spring of 1933 to the Panamerican Airways Co. The board of C.N.A.C. is composed of three Chinese and two American directors.

Its fleet consists exclusively of American machines, and it is said to have acquired recently ten modern planes with a cruising speed of 240–320 km. an hour. The staff consists of eleven Americans, twelve Chinese, and one German, all of whom are thoroughly trained and experienced.

The starting-point for the C.N.A.C. traffic is naturally Shanghai, the capital of the Yang-tse valley. From here the first line was naturally that up the river Yang-tse; starting from Shanghai, it touched such important points as Hankow, Chungking, and Cheng-tu (in the province of Szu-chuan). Until then one was obliged to travel for four days by steamer and railway from Shanghai to Hankow, and for fifteen to twenty days to Cheng-tu. By air the journey from Shanghai to Hankow takes seven hours and to Cheng-tu sixteen hours. The coastal service, which was inaugurated later, goes in a wide sweep along the coast from Peiping, via Shanghai to Canton. Here, too, there has been a great saving in travelling time. By rail it took forty-five hours to get from Shanghai to Peiping; by air it takes nine hours, with stops at Haichow, Tsingtau, and Tientsin. There is still greater saving in time between Shanghai and Canton; to-day by air the journey takes eight hours fifteen minutes. And a further saving in time, on the average 70 per cent, will, it is hoped, soon be made on all air lines. Besides, the development of other lines is being considered, and has partly been decided in part by C.N.A.C. The most important new service will be the service from Chung-king to Yün-nan-fu. The importance of this is well shown by the following figures: by caravan, a difficult and toilsome twenty-four days' journey; by air, a three-hours' flight.

While the China National Aviation Corporation is developing service by air in Eastern China, particularly in a north-westerly direction along the coast and up the Yang-tse river valley, i.e. following the line of the old waterways and railways, the activities of the German-Chinese aviation company, the Eurasia Aviation Corporation, founded in the spring of 1931, are directed to serve the needs of the vast transcontinental traffic. "Eurasia" dreams of nothing less than an air line Berlin–Shanghai. The first step to the opening of Central China, untouched so far by railways and on none of the great waterways, is to be taken by including these vast areas in the air-traffic system. Of this grandiose scheme, only the line Shanghai–Chugu-chak is in operation so far. The distance of 4,500 km. between these, which formerly meant several months' journey by a dangerous camel caravan route, is now covered in a flight of two and a half days. This line, which runs in a north-westerly direction from Shanghai via Lanchow–Suchow–Hami–Urumtchi to Chugu-chak comes at the Tarbagatai mountains very close to the Russian frontier. Chugu-chak by air is about 250 km. from Sergějopol, the great railway station of Turksib on the great railway line from Semipalatinsk to Alma-ata-Frunse, which has lately been opened to traffic. Here the Trans-China air line could easily be linked up with the Russian air services in Western Turkestan and Usbekistan.

"Eurasia" also operates a branch line Lanchow–Paotow on the upper Huang-ho in the province of Sui-jüan, and the great north-south line Peiping–Chenchow–Canton. This last line runs parallel to the C.N.A.C. coast line Peiping–Canton, or rather it is, as it were, the chord of the arc of the C.N.A.C. line. The Eurasia Aviation Corporation was created by the German Lufthansa and the Chinese Ministry of Transport; the German investment amounts to one-third and the Chinese to two-thirds of the share capital. It is hoped to bring both lines managed by "Eurasia" into connection with the Russian air lines and the Russian railways, and so to complete the Eurasian air system.

The Canton Government has with purely Chinese capital, as it seems, founded yet another aviation company, the China South-West Aviation Corporation. This company hopes to open up Southern China. At the end of August 1934 the Canton–Lui-chow–Kung-chow service of this company was opened.

"Eurasia" showed for 1931 a passenger figure of 300,000 km.; for 1933 the figure rose to 771,520 km.; and for 1934 it was estimated at about 900,000 km. C.N.A.C.'s record is as follows:

Year	Miles Flown	Passengers	Mail (in kg.)
1929	57,893	354	3,932
1933	636,900	3,050	49,246
1934	932,100	5,160	70,104

The immense increase in China's air traffic is still more evident if we remember that at the end of 1924 there was only 5,860 km. of air line in service throughout the whole of Asia. For China the development here described means a complete revolution of the whole transport system.

So far we have dealt with Chinese aviation from the standpoint of transport service to the Pacific Ocean. We may say that, although the number of passengers transported and the amount of mail carried are not in themselves important, the mere fact that such vast areas of the Chinese continent are being opened up by aviation is of the highest importance for the life of the Pacific world. It means first of all the bringing of vast and impassable regions of the continent, which so far have lacked any modern means of transport, into some connection with the Pacific coast. The aeroplane renders here invaluable pioneer service, but we must never fail to remember that a real opening up of the Chinese continent can be effected only by means of the development of great transcontinental railways in an east-westerly direction, as well as by the modernization and improvement of the inland waterways, which run essentially in the same direction. To-day the whole of the Chinese inland traffic follows a north-south direction, and is mostly confined to the eastern coastal districts. Up to the present the Chinese railway and air traffic has found here its centre of gravity. But the traffic is tending to acquire far more than its old inland economic significance, and in China it is the most modern means of traffic, the aeroplane, which has brought into favour the conception of a transcontinental international traffic which seeks to pass the frontiers of its own country.

Preparations are already made to open China from at least three sides to international aviation, as the forerunner of other transcontinental routes. On the continental side we have the plans already mentioned of the Eurasia Aviation Corporation, which is under German influence; the scheme to extend the air line Shanghai–Chugu-chak in a north-westerly direction would mean linking it to the air routes in inner Asia of the official Russian "Aeroflot," and so to the great Transsiberian route, Moscow–Omsk–Vladivostok, which is more than 8,000 km. in length. "Eurasia" tries, also, to link up with the Transsiberian route from the north-eastern side by the Transmanchurian air line (running east and west) Manchouli–Harbin–Kirin. In the spring of 1931, in collaboration with the German-Russian Aviation Corporation ("Deruluft"), the line Canton–Peiping, operated by "Eurasia," has been extended to Manchouli on the Manchurian-Russian frontier, via Linsi in Western Manchuria, and thus again the Russian Trans-siberian line is brought within reach of the Chinese internal air service. But the events in Manchuria, the consequence of which was less friendly relations between Manchuria and Russia on the one hand, and between Germany and Russia on the other, has temporarily interrupted this development.

At the beginning of November 1934 a preliminary agreement was reached between the Nanking Government and the United States for the opening of a regular air service between the Pacific coast of America and China. By that agreement the Government of the United States is responsible for the technical development of the scheme, i.e. provides the planes, the flying personnel, and the technical materials. The Nanking Government has to provide the working capital and the preparation of landing places in China. The participation of the greatest American aviation company, the Panamerican Airways Co., seems to have been secured. This American company is, as already stated, an influential partner in the China National Aviation Co., but it is not yet clear whether the Transpacific lines will be managed by C.N.A.C. or by a corporation specially formed for that purpose. The greatest air liner in the world has been built in the famous Glenn-Martin Aeroplane works in Baltimore for the Panamerican Airways Co., for a regular air service across the Pacific from America to China. The weight of the air liner at full load is 22,950 kg., and it is able to take, besides its staff, fifty passengers and also a certain amount of mail and goods.

The schemes for the Transpacific air service are not yet definitely completed. A certain amount of preparatory work is still necessary on both sides of the Pacific, before a regular service can be started. It is clear, however, that in the present state of technical development, and considering the minor extent to which the routes to be used by the air liners have been organized, air traffic across the Pacific with its immense distances is a far more difficult problem than air traffic across the Atlantic Ocean. Of decisive importance for air traffic across the Pacific is the question of midway stops, for a non-stop flight across the Pacific by the route San Francisco–Honolulu–Shanghai or Canton means a flight of something between 6,000 and 7,000 sea miles (the North Atlantic air-crossing is between 3,500 and 3,700 sea miles long). With the problem of midway stops the problem of the route to be taken is closely related, and this latter problem is intimately connected with the problem of strategic safety. From the technical standpoint the route Honolulu–Yap or Honolulu–Guam would be the most suitable, if the American landing stations were used. This route, however, brings the air line into Japan's sphere of influence, the islands under mandate, and so is hardly likely to be approved by the Americans for reasons of military policy. To adopt the roundabout Southern Transpacific route would raise other political and technical problems, as well as make the journey longer. For the moment, however, the chief significance of air traffic development has been the fact that the coastal region is now less important in the opening up of China than the inland regions, just as long ago the caravan route—the great "Silk Road"—to the Middle Kingdom became less important as a result of the traffic by sea to the Pacific ports of China.

To no other country in the Pacific, except perhaps Australia, can air traffic mean even approximately so much as it does to China, and especially to the mountainous inaccessible provinces in the West. As far as Eastern Asia is concerned, the Manchurian air traffic possibly is next to that of China proper. In Manchuria, too, we are confronted with the problem of the conquest of vast spaces. Here, too, the railway system is weakly developed, though relatively much less so than in China, while the waterways here are very far below the standard of the Chinese system in importance. The Manchurian air lines follow mainly the line of the railways and, to a certain extent, go beyond them, so that from the point of view of political and traffic geography there is little to say of Manchuria's air system. Its management is in the hands of a semi-official company which is completely under Japanese influence. The Manchukuo Koku Yuso K.K. (abbreviated M.K.K.), that is the Manchurian Airways Corporation, founded October 26, 1932, is a limited company with a capital of 3·85 million yen, the shareholders being the Manchurian Government, the South Manchurian Railway Company, and the great Japanese company Sumitomo. The Manchurian air system is one of about 5,100 km.; during 1933 it carried 9,605 passengers, 17,248 kg. of mail, and 14,038 kg. of expressed goods.

Apart from their importance for inland transport, the Manchurian airways may play a great rôle as intermediary in air traffic between China and the Soviet Union on the one hand, as linking up with the Transsiberian air line—this is to some extent the part it will play on the continent—and on the other hand, as terminus stations for air service to and from Japan. This has indeed been achieved by the opening of the air line Harbin–Hsinking–Mukden–Shingishu (in the most north-western corner of the Manchurian-Korean frontier)–Korea (cross line running north-south-east through Shingishu–Hejo–Keijo (Seoul)–Urusan on the Straits of Korea)–Fukuoka, a line 1,630 km. in length. Through it the iron industrial region in Southern Japan, in the north of her most southerly island Kyû-shû, is connected with the important raw material area on the Asiatic mainland. Moreover, the Japanese province of Korea, which lies between Japan and Manchuria, as well as the Kwantung region, which is strategically so important, are brought by this line into the Japanese-Manchurian airways system.

The other route connecting Manchuria with the Japanese islands, which is still at the trial stage, will go directly across the Sea of Japan. Here it is a question of extending the already existing line Harbin–Kirin–Tunhua–Tumen (on the north-eastern corner of the Manchurian-Korean frontier) to the important North Korean port Rashin (which has just been finished), and thence in the south-eastern direction to Nü-gata, which is already directly connected by air with Tokio. Apart from the strategic importance of that line, which directly connects the north-eastern Manchurian province of Kirin, situated close to the Vladivostok district, with the centre of government, the connection it gives between the northern provinces of Manchuria, which are now being opened up economically and—a fact of especial importance—to colonization and the important industrial area Tokio–Yokohama–Nagoya is economically of very great value.

Although the air traffic inside Manchuria and from Manchuria to Russia, to China—air traffic to China has not been developed for political reasons—and to Japan is not so important as China's, the Manchurian air traffic is highly important for the life of the northern part of the Pacific and the adjoining seas.

The Japanese internal air system is closely connected with the well-developed railway system, and works in the main in a north-south cross direction, connecting the four main industrial regions of the Island Empire by the line Sapporo (Hokkaido)–Aomori–Sendai–Tokio–Nagoya–Fukuoka. This last city, one of the great ports in the most important heavy industries area, is also a point of departure for the service connecting the Japanese islands with the Chinese continent, Korea, and Manchuria, in a westerly and south-westerly direction, and also with Formosa, which is also part of the Japanese Empire. The connection of Fukuoka with Manchuria has been already mentioned. The other oversea lines contemplated, the Fukuoka–Shanghai line (distance by air 900 km.) and the Fukuoka–Taihoku (Formosa) line (by air, 1,250 km.) have not yet been put in regular operation because of political and technical difficulties. The same is true of the line Nügata–Rashin, which has been already mentioned.

The most important Japanese aviation company is the Nippon Koku Yuso Ken Kyujo (the Japan Air Transport Co.), founded in October 1928. Its share capital amounts to 10,000,000 yen, and heavy holdings belong to the famous Japanese companies, Mitsui, Mitsubishi, Sumitomo, and Yasuda. This company receives regular subsidies from the Government, and is under State control. But the State is not directly concerned either as a shareholder or through representation on the board of directors.

The Chinese, Manchurian, and Japanese air systems form part of the North Pacific traffic system. From the point of view of air traffic the Japanese islands are simply a continuation of the Chinese–Manchurian mainland, which for its part belongs with Russia to the great traffic system of North Eurasia. The South Pacific, with the East Indies and the Australian continent, belongs from the point of view of air traffic to the South Asiatic-Indian system which is directly connected with the two great colonial capitals of Western Europe, London and Amsterdam.[16]

The importance of aviation within the Dutch colonial empire in the Indies itself is rather limited, because of the relatively highly developed railway system in Java and the very highly developed sea traffic between its most important ports. The large, sparsely populated islands of Borneo and Celebes, as well as the Molucca islands, lie at the moment entirely off any air route. It is very probable that later they will be included in the cross lines, going in a north-southern direction from the Philippines and connecting the Northern Pacific with the Southern Pacific, roughly the line Fukuoka (Kyû-shû)–Taihoku–Takao (Formosa)–the Philippines (the air line Baguilo–Manilla–Iloilo is planned or is possibly now in use)–North Borneo. At the moment only a line running across Sumatra and Java is in use, as a section of the great European-Dutch-Indian transcontinental air service Amsterdam–Batavia.

The Australian air system, on the other hand, has to some extent a specifically continental importance of its own. The

Western Australian system looks rather like an irregular half-circle in the sparsely populated west part of the continent, running directly along the coast, with landing places at Wyndham (Kimberley county), Derby (Tasman Land), Perth and Adelaide. This line is operated by the West Australian Airways Ltd., which already pays its way and no longer requires a Government subsidy. Corresponding to this great western arc, there is along the coast in the east a much shorter line: Rockhampton (Queensland)–Brisbane–Sydney, worked by two companies. In the south, Melbourne is the starting-point of a network of air lines of local importance, as well as for air traffic with the islands in the south, and with Tasmania.

From the standpoint of transcontinental air traffic, much greater importance is attached to the line Brisbane–Charleville–Camooweal–Birdum Creek, operated by the great Queensland and Northern Territory Aerial Services Ltd. (Quantas) and by another less important company. The importance of this line, apart from its inland traffic service, lies in the fact that it is actually the nucleus of a future transcontinental air line on a large scale, connecting Brisbane, the capital of Queensland, with Port Darwin in the north, which is already regarded as the port of entry for air traffic from England. Every new line planned is connected with it.

Australian air development has now passed completely out of the conservative stage, which was exclusively continental. The interests of Australian airmen is now concentrated on transcontinental-transoceanic traffic with England—the significance of which is political even more than economic. The question here is one of binding more closely the most important part of the British Empire to the mother country.

As early as 1932 the Commonwealth Government began to investigate the conditions for opening this great air service. One great difficulty was the number of large and small independent aviation companies, which made the carrying out of a great unitary air policy impossible. But not only unity in operation but a unified system of landing places and of new line construction is an absolute necessity if a transcontinental air service is to be the basis of a great overseas service. This multiplication of operating interests had to be got rid of and a good start has been made by the granting of a monopoly for transoceanic service to a semi-official company. The Imperial Airways Ltd., which has a monopoly for imperial services in England, and Quantas combined in 1934 to form the Quantas Empire Airways Ltd., which will take over the overseas service at the Australian end. The route of this great line, 15,000 km. in length, which connects London with Port Darwin and so with the south-east of the Australian continent, has not yet been definitely settled, although a mail service has been in operation since 1934 and a passenger service since the spring of 1935. So far Imperial Airways have used a route which is essentially the same as that of the Amsterdam–Batavia line run by the Dutch company, Royal Dutch Airlines; but there were some not unimportant deviations from the Dutch route caused by the desire to fly over British possessions if possible, or at least territories friendly to England, if not actually under English influence. The Dutch air line Amsterdam–Batavia ran a regular fortnightly service from the autumn of 1930 and on October 1, 1931, turned it into a weekly one. The journey was cut down from twelve to nine days, and since the summer of 1934 the journey has been done in seven and a half days from Amsterdam to Batavia. The total length of the Dutch route is 14,650 km. It runs from Amsterdam via Marseilles–Rome–Athens–Marsa Matruk (Egypt)–Cairo–Gaza (Southern Palestine)–Bagdad–Bushire–Djysk (Persia)–Karachi (Northwest India) – Jodhpur – Allahabad – Calcutta – Rangoon (Burma)–Bangkok–Alor Star (British Malaya)–Medan (North Sumatra)–Singapore–Palembang–Batavia (Bandoeng).

Of the 14,600 km, only 3,500 in Europe and about 1,000 km. in the Dutch East Indies, i.e. less than one-third of the whole line, lies in non-British regions or regions not under British influence.

It is significant of the tenseness of the present international situation that the British Air Ministry in conjunction with Imperial Airways Ltd., in the plans recently worked out for the development of the air traffic within the Empire, contemplates changing routes so as, as far as possible, to pass over British territory or at least territory which is within the British sphere of influence. The air correspondent of the *Evening Standard*, at any rate, stated that on the route from London to Australia, Gibraltar was to be the first landing station, and then Malta, Alexandria, and the other stations on the route to India. Gibraltar was to become a first-class central point of aerial traffic, the port of departure for the South Atlantic, South Africa, and the Far East.

According to the very important statements made by Sir Philip Sassoon, the Under-Secretary of State for Air, on December 20, 1934, to the House of Commons, the Air Ministry intended to construct a much denser air-line net within the Empire. The whole of the important mail for the various countries in the Empire would be carried solely by aeroplane or seaplane. The travelling time to the various parts of the Empire would be considerably cut down. The journey from London to India will take just over two days, to East Africa two and a half days, to Cape Town or Singapore four days, and to Australia seven days. There would be two services a week to Australia and three to Singapore. The postage for letters within the Empire would not exceed 2d., and the writer of a letter living within the Empire could send his letter on a week's journey half round the world for so trifling a sum.

The high importance of the Russian Transsiberian air line, Moscow–Vladivostok, 8,000 km. in length, and going via Omsk–Novosibirsk–Irkutsk–Chita and Habarovsk, as far as the North Pacific system is concerned, is not only in the considerable saving in travelling time, as compared with the railway, but also to the fact that the Transsiberian line, which runs parallel to the great railway, is more and more becoming the backbone of a widely spread network of air lines, which open up regions which so far have been without any modern means of communication, vast regions difficult of access which until lately it took many weeks and even months to reach. In Siberia, just as in China, the aeroplane has revolutionized an absolutely primitive traffic system. Herein lies the importance of the line Irkutsk–Yakutsk (2,750 km.), by which one may reach the capital of Northern Siberia in two days instead of in two to three weeks. Another branch (500 km.) of the Transsiberian air line connects Verkhne–Udinsk (in Transbaikalia) with Ulan-Bator (Urga) in the north of Outer Mongolia. Of great importance for Pacific traffic are the branch lines from Habarovsk (on the Amur) which connect this important economic and strategic central point with several important places on the Tatar Sound and the Sea of Okhotsk. Especially important is the line (3,500 km.) Vladivostok–Habarovsk–Nikolajevsk (in the delta of the Amur)–Petropavlovsk (Kamchatka). Here it is a matter of making accessible the regions which cannot be reached with any comfort by any other means of communication. We shall discuss in a later chapter the strategic importance of the Okhotsk–Kamchatka air line and its relation to the strategic position in the Northern Pacific. We shall merely point out here that by this line the rich fur areas on the Sea of Okhotsk and the great oil deposits in North Sakhalin have now a regular mail connection with the Russian coast provinces.

The line planned to link Habarovsk across the Sea of Okhotsk to Uelen (on the Behring Straits not far from Cape Deshnev) will be of great military importance. The distance from Uelen to Nome, the main port of Alaska, is only 250 km. Thus a direct connection between the Russian and the American air lines is possible (see Map 1).

As far as air traffic is concerned, the countries on the Western Pacific, that is, the region between the line Okhotsk–Petropavlovsk in the north and the line Batavia–Port Darwin in the south, are linked on three sides with the world system. The development of the most modern means of transport, the aeroplane, reminds us of similar happenings in the history of transport. Originally, the whole traffic—and it was not a negligible traffic—between Eastern China and the West was developed along the great transcontinental caravan roads in a west-south-east and a west-north-east direction. Since the beginning of the modern age, and especially since the sixteenth century, this transcontinental land traffic has been entirely superseded by the Pacific sea trade.

The railways on the Chinese continent developed first of all as adjuncts to the great ports of Eastern China, situated at the mouths of the great Chinese inland waterways. But it was the Transsiberian and Transmanchurian railways, finished at the beginning of this century, which were a complete and bold solution to the problem of transcontinental traffic by means of a modern method of communication—the railway. The considerable saving in travelling time—the sea journey Hamburg–Shanghai took 56 days; the railway journey Berlin–Shanghai took fourteen and a half days—was not in itself sufficient to give the transcontinental railway traffic supremacy over the Pacific sea traffic. Besides, the Transsiberian line was rather off the line of the great traffic system of the Western Pacific.

Naturally, there can be no question of transcontinental air traffic competing with maritime transport, as the railways in the long run would have done. As has been said, at the present stage of technical development we need not expect the earlier means of communication to be superseded, but rather to be complemented by air traffic.

But as to the importance of every particular direction of the air lines, the transcontinental air traffic in all its three aspects has to-day, and will have in the near future at any rate, considerably greater hopes of development than has the Transpacific traffic. Eastern Asia will not continue to be opened up solely from the eastern ocean side, as happened during the last four centuries, in the maritime period, but will be opened up also from the west—from Europe and not from America.

After the detailed picture we have given of the West Pacific air traffic, we need only summarize thus: the three transcontinental routes—the Transsiberian-Manchurian or the North-Asiatic route, the Central Chinese or the Middle Asiatic route, and, finally, the South-east Asiatic route in its two variants, the British and the Dutch—are still in the initial stage and depend for their further development on various economic, political, and military considerations, so that it is not possible yet to give any final verdict on the chances of the various transcontinental lines. Still less certain can be any judgment as to the Transpacific route. Here we are dealing only with schemes. Two of the Transpacific routes are now, however, more or less settled; the plan of a regular air service from San Francisco to Shanghai, i.e. the Mid-Pacific route, and the plan of a Russian-American service, Habarovsk–Uelen–Nome, across the extreme north of the Pacific, both of which have already been described. Whether the European-Australian transcontinental air line in its British variant will find an Australian continuation to the remoter islands of the Southern Pacific, it is impossible yet to say.

§ 4. THE ADVANCE OF THE YELLOW RACES

The radical change in the traffic of the countries on the Pacific presents naturally an important feature in the general change in the geopolitical situation in those regions. It is the modernization of means of communication, the supersession of the ricksha and of the junk by the railway, the motor car, the steamer, and the aeroplane, which is the real basis of the radical change in the economy, the policy, and the entire culture of those countries. Simultaneously with this revolution in traffic, and partly as its consequence, modern colonization goes on, which is the force which has given the Pacific sphere its present aspect, just as the colonization of the western shores of the Atlantic in the nineteenth century created from the geopolitical point of view the Atlantic sphere as we know it to-day. When we come to the investigation of the colonization of the Pacific coasts, we must distinguish two epochs; first, the colonization of the eastern coast of China, the Japanese islands, the East Indies, and the Australian islands, which goes back as far as the prehistoric period—and the colonization of the Pacific shores in modern times. As far as the policy of China is concerned right up to the latest period, it is of fundamental importance that the Chinese have always been an inland people who received nothing or relatively nothing from overseas, and who have never had any interest in oceanic affairs. The original area of Chinese colonization was the middle Huang-ho valley, roughly the present provinces Shen-hsi, Shan-hsi, and Ho-nan. From these colonization spread in prehistoric times eastward down the Huang-ho and into the other valley, near to the north, in the direction of T'ai-yüan-fu, a town which is still to be found on the railway line between Peiping and Hankow, about 400 km. south of Peiping—and to the south in the direction of the Han, a tributary of the Yang-tse river. The Yang-tse valley, which to-day is politically and economically the heart of China, does not belong to the original Chinese colonization area. Even in the period of the Chou dynasty, the later epoch of which begins about 800 B.C., neither the Yang-tse river nor the Ocean coast were directly part of Chinese history. The mountainous region in the south-west was finally conquered only under the Mongol Yüan dynasty, i.e. in the thirteenth and fourteenth centuries.

Even after the Chinese had reached the sea coast they showed no special interest in the ocean-world. The Chinese had for long no idea that the Japanese islands existed. Later on they made contact with the Japanese via the landbridge of Korea. Even under the Yüan dynasty, which on the whole was on the offensive, the attitude to the Japanese seamen and pirates was purely defensive. An exception is formed by the three campaigns of the Mongol emperor Hubilai (Hu-pi-lieh), 1274–84, against the Japanese islands, but these are, however, to be considered as a mere episode. At this first serious clash of the continental people with the seafaring Japanese, the victory was easily won by the latter.[17]

The earliest continental colonization by the Chinese, of which we know very little but which most probably moved east from their centre in the Middle Huang-ho to the Pacific, was undoubtedly the main factor in the colonization of the Pacific shores. But, as we have already pointed out, the ocean is never more than a negative factor in Chinese pre-history; the Pacific, above all, cuts off the Chinese from the outside world.

The original colonization of the Japanese took just the opposite form. Here, too, we know very little about its oldest period. But we may suppose, with some certainty, that the main direction of colonization was from south to north, and that the creator of this colonization was one of the seafaring tribes which came across the ocean in the prehistoric period, most probably from the Malay islands. Besides this oceanic invasion from the south Pacific the "Mongol" immigration from the mainland via Korea plays only a rôle of secondary importance.

In 1450 the northern end of the main island, Hon-do, was conquered after a hard fight with the original inhabitants, the Ainu. The occupation of the most northern island Yezo came only in the eighteenth century (1767). Advances south to the Ryû-Kyû islands and further to Tai-wan (Formosa), parallel with an invasion of the continent in the direction of Korea, go on throughout the whole of Japanese history, and show the two tendencies which are most characteristic of Japanese foreign policy in modern times.[18]

Modern China has been created by internal colonization over a period of thousands of years. Until the first five centuries of the Christian era, the Chinese, as an inland race, were busy with the colonization of the fertile valleys of the great Chinese rivers. But in the seventh century the Chinese oversea emigration was already beginning.

The Chinese migration from Southern China in an eastern and south-eastern direction to the Pacific islands falls into several periods. As early as the seventh century Chinese historical sources mention the occasional colonization of Formosa and the Pescadores. Much later the Chinese stream of migration begins to flow to the Straits Settlements, Malaya, the Dutch Indies, and the Philippines.

The most remarkable feature of the millennial history of China is this migration which led the Chinese people from their original homeland in the Huang-ho valley over immense distances. As a result of their long wanderings, the Chinese early developed that extraordinary faculty of theirs of acclimatization which is the main factor in the later colonization of foreign countries by the Chinese.[19]

Under the rule of the Mongol emperor Hubilai (Kublai Khan, Shih-tsu) the conquest of Java is recorded. From that time, too, we may speak of the Sunda islands as being part of the Chinese Empire. When the Dutch in the seventeenth and eighteenth centuries conquered the largest part of the Sunda islands, a fierce and bloody struggle began between the old and new owners. The third period of intense Chinese migration overseas begins in the middle of the nineteenth century, when the plantations founded by Europeans needed cheap and suitable labour.

The Emperor Kan-si in the eighteenth century formulated the real motive of Chinese emigration as follows: "The soil does not increase but the population does." The oversea migration of the Chinese in the nineteenth century came from the southern provinces of Kuang-tung, Fu-chien, and Chiang-hsi, where by the middle of the previous century the over-populating of the villages and the division of land had attained an extraordinary development.

Here we have to do with a colonial activity which, although in extent it lags behind the other great migrations of world history, is nevertheless of very great importance for the shaping of the Pacific world, and even for the Indian and the Atlantic spheres. There are no precise data on the number of Chinese resident abroad. The figure, indeed, as compared with the total population of China, is negligible—something about 2 to 3 per cent, but the importance of this "China outside China" is of extraordinary importance in the development of the Pacific world.

The *China Yearbook, 1921–22*, and the *Transpacific* of May 3, 1924, give the following figures which, though they are out of date, yet for want of later figures will give some idea of the extent of the Chinese diaspora.[20]

CHINESE LIVING OUTSIDE CHINA (1924)

Annam	197,300
Australia	35,000
Brazil	20,000
Burma	130,000
Canada	12,000
Cuba	90,000
British India	1,030,000
Europe (without Russia)	1,760
Formosa	2,500,000[21]
Hawaii	27,179[22]
Hong-Kong	444,644
Japan	17,700
Java	1,825,700
Korea	15,000
Macao	74,500
Mexico	3,000
Peru	45,000
Philippines	55,212
Siam	1,500,000
Siberia	37,000
European Russia	71,000
Malayan States	903,000
South Africa	5,000
Continental United States	150,000
New Zealand	2,500
Indo-China	250,000
Total about	10,500,000

Chinese emigration in the course of the nineteenth and twentieth centuries till the present time was, in spite of all efforts made by Chinese Governments, assisted to a certain extent by the European Powers, a mild form of "contract slavery." Only after the World War was there any essential change in favour of the coolie emigrants (*Labour Emigration Law of China* and *Labour Recruiting Agency Regulations of China*, both dated April 21, 1918).

The Chinese emigrants, 90 per cent of whom at least are workers of various types—land workers, miners, and hand workers—have in the course of the last decades completely changed the economic and social structure of the Southern Pacific world. The richness of British Malaya, the exploitation of the tin mines in Bangka and Billiton, the plantations in Sumatra, the rubber industry, indeed the whole progress of the Dutch East Indies, Siam, and the Philippines, is based mainly on the patient toil of the Chinese coolie and the enterprise of the Chinese capitalist. Neither the native nor the Indian emigrant can compete here with the Chinese workers. What is happening here is simply the return to the old routes whereby the Chinese cultural and political influences travelled. Many regions of Chinese colonization to-day were centuries ago vassal States of the Chinese Empire. To-day the bearers of Chinese influence both cultural and political are those coolies who, because of the cheapness of their labour in the last decade, gave Malaya and the Dutch East Indies their supremacy in rubber and sugar production.

One-third of the rubber plantations and two-thirds of the tin mines in the Malay States are owned by Chinese. In the Dutch East Indies, too, the Chinese business man plays an outstanding part. Moreover, Chinese capitalism in those countries to which the Chinese emigrate, develops from below; the capitalist mostly is an ex-coolie who started a small business of his own on his savings, and then gradually as a result of hard work and care developed it into a big business. So the enterprising Chinese as banker, manufacturer, or merchant acts as middleman to the native population.

In Siam the Chinese constitute at the least a quarter of the whole population, control practically the whole internal trade and a great part of the foreign trade. In French Indo-

China the Chinese are the most prosperous section of the population, and practically have a monopoly of the national trade. To Australia and New Zealand Chinese immigration practically ceased at the beginning of this century (*Immigration Restriction Act, 1901*, and *Contract Immigrants Act, 1905*, in Australia). As a result of the scarcity of labour Australia's sugar-cane industry has never been able to develop. The immigration of the Chinese to Hawaii, where agriculture has been so largely dependent upon Chinese labour, had been restricted since the early 'eighties of last century and since the annexation of Hawaii by America (in 1898) the American ban on Chinese labour has been extended to these islands.[23]

The most westerly goal of Chinese emigration is the Transvaal, whereto 55,000 coolies were imported for employment in the gold mines and in road construction within the period 1904 and 1910 (see Map 2).

The island world of the Pacific is economically, racially, and politically waking to new life, and that new life is reaching the Southern Pacific through two agencies: first, the colonial capitalism of the white races and secondly its consequence, Asiatic immigration.

Not for the first time has the Pacific world undergone radical economic and political change as a result of immigration from the big Asiatic mainland. For many centuries, until the fourteenth century of our era, waves of conquerors had poured from the continent over the whole Pacific area. During these centuries that blend of races was achieved which the Europeans found when they first appeared in those waters and also those political cultures in the form of a solid organization of the State which ever and anon the conquerors had given. There was at that time no isolation of the island groups. The Polynesians particularly, the Phoenicians of the Pacific, were a seafaring race.[24] They were sailing the ocean, as says De Quatrefages, when the European had not got beyond coastal navigation in the Mediterranean. In their "great canoes," occasionally as long as 118 ft., with a hundred men aboard, they made little of the distance between Tahiti and New Zealand, although it is some 4,000 km. These sea expeditions of conquering peoples constantly maintained a supply of fresh blood, and as a result constant renewal of culture and race regeneration. They ceased two hundred years before the appearance of the Europeans, and it is from that time that the period of stagnation and degeneration begins. When the European conquerors in the sixteenth century (Magellan's journey across the Atlantic and the Indian Ocean and across the Western Pacific from Cape Horn to the Marianne islands took place in 1520) appeared in the Southern Pacific, the population was already degenerate and in process of dying out.

The arrival of the Europeans meant the acceleration of that process. In 1823, soon after the arrival of the first American missionaries (in 1820), there were 142,000 inhabitants in Hawaii. In 1836 there were only 108,579. Sixty years later (in 1896) there were only 39,504 natives and in 1930 only 22,636; there are, however, also 28,224 Hawaiian half-castes. Cook's estimate (in 1773) of 400,000 natives in Hawaii is certainly exaggerated, but there is no doubt that in his day there was a numerous population in these islands which was decimated in the course of the century and a half which followed. There is practically no native population left in the French Marquesas Island (in 1924 1,200 souls), although at the beginning of the nineteenth century it numbered 50,000. This is probably the most obvious instance of the dying out of a flourishing race within so short a period. Since the end of the nineteenth century, as a result of the protective measures taken by the various Governments, the native population has been to some degree stable. It is almost a general phenomenon in the Pacific islands generally. But even the best colonial administration cannot bring in fresh blood.

A new feature has been added to the racial composition in the Pacific by the new immigration from the Asiatic continent which began to assume serious proportions during the last quarter of the nineteenth century. There were serious economic reasons why the colonial administrations were induced to try to attract Asiatic labour to the islands of their Pacific empires. All over the Southern Pacific labour is scarce. That is true also of the British, French, and American colonies, and the Germans had to face the same problem in Kaiser Wilhelm's Land (New Guinea) and Samoa when they possessed these. Everywhere there is the same problem and everywhere the same attempt at solution has been made. In New Caledonia the French tried first to solve the problem by bringing in deported criminals, but this system failed completely, and the attempt to settle white Australians in the New Hebrides failed just as signally.

Natives were, of course, unfit for work either in the cobalt and nickel mines or on the plantations. There was no alternative but to draw on the Asiatic labour market. It was the Chinese who came at the period of the Civil War in America, when the French capitalists were trying to revive cotton-growing in their Pacific colonies. Soon, however, there came the notorious scare of the "Chinese peril," and in the period preceding the World War it was considered politically dangerous to permit the further immigration of Chinese and Japanese to the French colonies in the Pacific.

After the War, when we began to hear of "Awakening Asia" on the one hand, and when on the other a new boom period began in colonial economy, the problem became still more acute. The hunt for raw materials revealed clearly the wealth of the French colonies in the Pacific. There were nickel and cobalt mines in New Caledonia, cotton and cocoa plantations in the New Hebrides, copra, vanilla, and mother-of-pearl in Tahiti. But there was no labour to win these treasures. The native population (130,000) of the French islands was quite unsuited to such work. No one wanted a new influx of Chinese or Japanese labour. There was no other solution than to organize a system of immigration from French Indo-China. The immigration, or rather the import of these Tonkinese and Annamese workers, is estimated to-day at 5,000 persons a year. This is that scheme for the political and economic consolidation of the French position in the Southern Pacific which is styled "entre-aide colonial," for the carrying out of which France must thank the Colonial Minister Albert Sarraut, and the deputy Léon Archimbaud. But, by doing so, the French colonial administration has risked the "Asiatization" of their southern Pacific dominions. A somewhat similar development is seen in the British Fiji Isles. Here, too, there is a considerable possibility of building up a prosperous plantation industry (sugar), but here, too, the native population is unfit for plantation work, and so here, too, the same solution is imposed: to try to meet the scarcity of native labour by the importation of suitable labour from other British colonies. That is why, since the early 'eighties, the Fiji administration concluded agreements with the Government of India regulating the import of Indian labour to the Fiji islands, agreements which were modified by later legislation and by the introduction of Indian officials. It must be recognized that as a rule from this "contract slavery" (the indenture system) there developed a free peasantry which lost all ties with its Indian home and lived under much better conditions than in India. The Indians now constitute about one-third of the population (190,000) of the Fiji group. Here, too, there is a clear tendency towards the predominance of the continental Asian element.

The Hawaiian islands were united at the end of the eighteenth century under one rule by King Kameha-meha I, one of the most outstanding monarchs and organizers in the history of Polynesia. Here Japanese and American interests came into conflict, and in 1898 the group was annexed by America. In Hawaii there has been a notable mixture of races which is characteristic of the Pacific islands generally, but is seen here in a particularly crude form. The Hawaiian islands were colonized in turn by the Chinese (Chinese immigration reached its height from 1878 to 1884), the Portuguese, the Japanese (1884–1896), the Koreans, and the Filipinos. The following table shows how the composition of the population has changed throughout the last twenty years according to the official census.[25]

	1910		1920		1930	
		per cent		per cent		per cent
Total	191,909		255,912		368,336	
Hawaiians ..	26,041	13·6	23,723	9·2	22,636	6·1
Part Hawaiians ..	12,506	6·5	18,027	7·0	28,224	7·6
White	44,048	22·9	54,742	21·4	80,373	21·7
Chinese	21,674	11·4	23,507	9·0	27,179	7·3
Japanese	79,675	41·6	109,274	42·6	139,631	37·9
Filipino	2,361	1·2	21,031	8·2	63,052	17·1
Korean	4,533	2·1	4,950	2·1	6,511	2·1
Negro	695	0·7	348	0·5	513	0·3
Others	376		310		217	

The most striking feature revealed by this table is the sharp decline of the number of full-blood natives, while Hawaiian half-castes, i.e. descendants of mixed marriages mostly with Chinese, increase absolutely as well as proportionately. The white population, as compared with the total, is proportionately stable. Absolutely the white population is steadily increasing. Except for the Portuguese, the increase of whom is due to a high birth-rate, it is immigration that accounts for the increase in the white population, particularly white immigrants from America. Most interesting is the fact of the absolute increase in the Japanese population, but the fall in the Japanese proportion and the rapid decline in the Chinese percentage. We find here the same tendency as in the French and British colonies: the Filipinos, who are the latest comers, are rapidly increasing. The Asiaticizing of Hawaii is proceeding apace, but at least by means of "our own" Asiatics in the sense that the Filipino comes from American territory—a consolation that is hardly valid to-day.

In Hawaii, too, it is the Chinese who of all the Asiatic immigrants are most inclined to intermarry with the natives. Out of 740 marriages entered into by Hawaiian Chinese between July 1, 1920, and June 3, 1924, 114 were marriages with Hawaiian natives or half-caste women, i.e. 15·4 per cent of all Chinese marriages. The corresponding numbers for the Japanese during the same period were 3,450 marriages, of which in 3,399 cases both parties were Japanese. Thus in Hawaii as elsewhere it is the Chinese who appear as the most active agents of race-mixture.

The table shows, too, that the alleged "Japanese danger" in Hawaii has been greatly exaggerated. Although the number of the Japanese is increasing, the percentage of Japanese is falling. It is interesting to note that of all the races in Hawaii, the Japanese have the lowest birth-rate.

If we take as the birth-rate not that more or less deceptive relation between the yearly figure of living children born and the population figure of the race under consideration, but the relation—this indicates relatively clearly the measure of fertility—between the yearly numbers of births and the number of women of child-bearing age, the description of the Japanese as a race whose birth-rate is likely to rise rapidly in the ten to twenty years needs correction. In Hawaii it is clear that in comparison with the other colonizing peoples of the Pacific the Japanese have no pre-eminence in vitality.

One of the best-known experts on the demographical problems of the Pacific, Stephen H. Roberts, from whom we have taken the essential data for what is said above, thus states the whole problem of the Pacific islands, as far as population is concerned: "Either the islands must stagnate or obtain a preponderatingly Asiatic population; there is no middle course, no alternative."

It must be admitted that in the situation as it is to-day and as it is likely to continue, there is no possibility of checking the process of the Asiaticizing of the Pacific islands. The only question to be settled is which of the Asiatic peoples will gain the upper hand and what attitude it will adopt towards the supremacy of the white race in the Pacific. On the answer depends the issue of the struggle for the Pacific.[26]

The extreme limits of the overseas Chinese emigration from the southern provinces of China may be shown as a half-circle, whose centre is in Canton, with a radius (11,000 km.) running from Hawaii to the Transvaal (see Map 2).

Of no less importance is the Chinese emigration from the northern provinces of Chih-li and Shan-tung north-eastward, to Russia's Far Eastern provinces, and later to Manchuria. The Chinese immigration to Russia's Far Eastern provinces is already visible in the 'seventies of last century, and as always the cause of Chinese emigration to regions occupied by Europeans, was the result of the economic development of a land in which native labour was much lacking. By 1870 the number of Chinese immigrants in the Ussuri province was 10,000.

They were for the greater part seasonal workers who after the harvest period or after finishing the work they had been brought to do, used to return to their own country. A considerable number of the Chinese labourers from the northern provinces of China had been attracted to the Russian coast provinces by the construction of the Transsiberian railway, but this wave of immigration equally was not an immigration of settlers. In 1910 the number of the Chinese in the Russian Far-Eastern provinces was estimated at 92,000, who gained their living mostly as labourers, but also as hawkers and as domestic servants. During the Great War, when after mobilization the Russian Far East had been deprived almost entirely of male labour, 480,000 Chinese poured into the region as farm workers, industrial workers, and domestic servants. But this immigration also proved to be transient. Besides, before the Great War Russia was already aware of the "yellow peril," and a law was issued on June 26, 1910, restricting the employment of foreigners as labourers, which essentially was directed against the Chinese labourer. In 1926, according to the census figures, there were only 77,223 Chinese in the entire territory of what used to be Siberia and is to-day Sibkrai, the Burjat-Mongolian Republic and the Far Eastern provinces, and in the rest of the Soviet Union only 25,000, that is a total of roughly 100,000 Chinese in the whole of Russia. This should not be regarded as proving an increase in the Chinese immigration to the Far Eastern provinces as compared with the pre-War period. There was, on the contrary, a decline as a result of the restrictions on Chinese immigration passed to fight against the competition of yellow labour. Except for this, the Russian coastal provinces would be most suitable for Chinese immigration. But the colonization by the Chinese of Russian territory, which is above all a political problem, will take place only as a result of the colonization of North Manchuria.

The second great objective is that of the Chinese emigration from Chih-li and Shan-tung, i.e. Manchuria and especially North Manchuria. The Chinese settlement of North Manchuria in the course of the last fifteen years is an extraordinary event to which the only parallel in modern history is the colonization by European settlers of North America in the second half of the nineteenth century. In the two northern provinces of Manchuria, Kirin and Heilung-kiang, there was a population of roughly 1,500,000 in 1890, of 9,000,000 in 1919, and more than 13,000,000 in 1928; that is, a ten times increase in forty years.

In the period between the end of the sixteenth and the beginning of the seventeenth century, in the Ming dynasty period, Manchuria was for the most part absolutely independent of China. In the south-east were the Manchus, in the west the Mongols, and in the north the Tunguses. By the end of the sixteenth century the Manchu tribes conquered the Tunguses and the Mongols, and finally the Chinese Empire itself. During the period of the Manchu dynasty Ch'-ing (1644–1912), China and Mongolo-Manchuria were united under the same rule. But even at the beginning of the Ch'ing epoch, i.e. about the middle of the seventeenth century, there was quite a large Chinese population in the south of Manchuria. They supplied a part of the Manchu troops which conquered China. These Chinese soldiers in the Manchu army (Chan-tsun) later received as reward large allotments of land especially in the Mukden province and possibly in the southern part of the Kirin province also. Manchuria itself, however, was fundamentally regarded as the hereditary possession of the Manchu tribes, and, as a result, Chinese immigration to its provinces was kept within very narrow limits. The prohibition against the settlement of Chinese women outside the Great Chinese Wall was another consequence of this view. But even then restrictive measures proved to be difficult to carry out: the great Manchurian landowners, without troubling about the anti-Chinese laws, accepted Chinese tenants and even sold them their land.

At the end of the eighteenth century the Chinese immigration had reached Chan-chun, and by the middle of the nineteenth century the district round the modern Harbin. In 1860 the Chinese were allowed to settle north of Harbin. This was an answer to the Russian advance into the Amur valley. The Peking Government saw that it was necessary simply on political grounds to settle Manchuria, and particularly the Chinese bank of the Amur river. This settlement of Chinese in the neighbourhood of the Russian frontier as a military administrative measure had already begun in the seventeenth and in the eighteenth centuries, and went on into the twentieth century. But this type of settlement is secondary in importance to the voluntary colonization by the North Chinese peasants.

The Chinese immigration to Manchuria during the period before the construction of the Manchurian railway has all the characteristics of the old Chinese migration movements which created the Chinese Empire. The rate at which this settlement process proceeds is a very slow one. Herein lies the difference between the Chinese and the Russian colonization, the waves of the latter encountering the Chinese in North-Eastern Asia on the shores of the Pacific. The Russian colonization of Siberia was emphatically extensive colonization. There is a strong feature of extensivity about the way in which the colonizing of Siberia by the Russians was done. It aimed at the rapid and continuous conquest of new territory. The Russian is always land-hungry, though he does not attach importance to the possession of a particular piece of land. Like the American farmer, he exhausts the land he possesses and leaves it to trek eastwards. This probably is the result of his feeble sense of individual private property.

The Chinese colonizes infinitely more slowly but with assiduity, tenacity, and strong attachment to the piece of land of which he has got possession. To the Chinese settler his piece of land in Manchuria is but a continuation of his old holding in his home country, which for hundreds of generations had been passed from father to son.

The Chinese immigration to Manchuria began not later than the fifteenth century, and in the course of the next three centuries reached scarcely to the Sungari, hardly 1,000 km. from Peking, while in the same period Russian pioneers and settlers had traversed and taken possession of Siberia, a distance of 6,000 to 7,000 km.

As already stated, Chinese immigration to Manchuria was favoured by the Peking Government from the middle of the nineteenth century. In 1878 the territory of the Mongolian princes in Western Manchuria was given up to the colonists. In the same year the ban on the emigration of the Chinese women beyond the Great Wall was raised, so that that year may be regarded as the beginning of legal Chinese immigration to Manchuria. Even earlier the law forbidding the purchase of land by the Chinese had been withdrawn. None the less, at the end of the nineteenth century, i.e. during the period of the construction of the Chinese Eastern Railway, Manchuria was far from having been conquered by the Chinese settlers; vast tracts in the north and in the west were still in the possession of half-nomadic tribes. Considering the traditional slowness of Chinese settlement, even with all the aid of the Peking Government it would have needed centuries, certainly many decades, to give the Chinese settlement of Manchuria the aspect it now presents. A radical, an almost revolutionary change in the situation began with the construction of the Chinese Eastern Railway (1896–1901). Once again we find the old story repeated: French and Belgian capital under Russian administration took possession of Northern Manchuria and attracted there huge masses of seasonal workers from the overpopulated provinces of North China. The capitalist "opening up" of Manchuria needed, on the one hand, modern means of transport and on the other provoked a sharp conflict between Russia and Japan, leading finally to war (1904–5). Yet it was this capitalist enterprise, the construction of the railway and the conflict that resulted from it that were the necessary pre-conditions for a rapid and successful settlement of Manchuria by the Chinese. Li Hung-Chang, the ablest and also the most "modern" Chinese statesman of the nineteenth century, is alleged to have said: "Don't hinder the Russians building railways in Manchuria." For him the Russo-Japanese competition in Manchuria and the rivalry that consequently arose in railway construction was a condition of the Chinese immigration to Manchuria, as indeed it was. As has already been stated, hundreds of thousands of coolies were brought in as a result of the construction of the Chinese Eastern Railway. During the Russo-Japanese War many more hundreds of thousands of Chinese workers were employed behind the lines on either side in the construction of roads and military railways, and in transport. The partitioning of Manchuria into a northern or Russian and a southern or Japanese sphere of influence meant increased activity in railway construction and so many more Chinese workers were needed, especially in the Japanese sphere. It was the building of railways that first made possible that extraordinarily rapid colonization of Manchuria, the rate of which is so different from the Chinese migration of the classic type.[27]

The rapid colonization of Manchuria, particularly North Manchuria, took place in the course of the last fifteen years, i.e. after the World War, and especially when the civil war in China entered an acute phase. The main sources of this immigration are the two northern provinces of China, Chih-li and Shan-tung. In addition to the general reasons for Chinese emigration already stated—over-population, extreme division of land, and the small possibility of migration to the towns as a result of the feeble development of industry—there now appear the destruction of the economic life and the devastation of the land as a result of the civil war.

The Chih-li and Shan-tung provinces are the most densely populated districts of China. With a warning to the reader that it is based on Chinese statistics, we give the population figure for the two northern provinces of China and the three Manchurian provinces in the following table:[28]

AREA, POPULATION, AND THE DENSITY OF POPULATION FOR CHIH-LI (HOPEI), SHAN-TUNG, FENG-TIEN, KIRIN, HEILUNG-KIANG

	Territory (in Square Miles)	Population	Population per Square Mile
Chih-li*	115,830	38,905,695	335
Shan-tung*	55,984	34,375,849	614
Feng-tien†	71,508	15,151,630	212
Kirin†	103,379	9,191,980	89
Heilung-kiang† ..	224,944	5,321,370	23

* Chinese Post Office Estimate, 1926.

† Estimate of the Research Office of the South Manchuria Railway Co., December 31, 1930.

Thus we have the two northern provinces of China, with a population of roughly 73,000,000, probably more, and with an area 40,000 sq. km. less than Germany, and the three sparsely settled Manchurian provinces with a population in 1922 of about 22,000,000, and an area roughly equal to France and Germany together. Obviously, when we remember that transport is easy, the climate moderate, and the land very much like that of China, there was a tremendous inducement to migrate. Equally powerful as a factor was the fact that as in North China, the summer is the rainy season. In Manchuria the Chinese colonist does not need to alter his habits. The cultivation of late-ripening plants, the abundant crop of plants rich in nitrogen are what give stability to both the Manchurian and Chinese agriculture.

Up to 1925–26 the colonization of the two Northern Manchurian provinces was done by the peasants of the more densely populated Feng-tien province in Southern Manchuria. Later we have the direct migration from the northern provinces of China proper to Northern Manchuria, which caused the amazingly rapid colonization of Kirin and Heilung-kiang. Between 1922 and 1925 the migration still continued to be to some extent a seasonal migration; about half the coolies returned after the harvest in the late autumn to their Northern Chinese home. This seasonal character is retained in the following years also, but every year there are more and more coolies who choose to settle definitely on the land. There are no reliable statistics of this migration. C. Walter Young[29] gives the following estimate:

Before 1926, about 400,000 annually.
In 1926, about 600,000 annually.
In 1927, about 1,000,000 annually.

These estimates nearly coincide with the figures given by the authorities at the ports and by the railway administrations. According to the latter, the number of Chinese workers who landed during 1922–25 in the ports of Dairen, Ying-kou, and An-tung, or who were transported north by the Peiping–Mukden railway, is roughly 400,000 to 500,000 annually. The following table gives an estimate of the total number of immigrants, of the number who return, and of the number who stay permanently, according to official sources.

IMMIGRATION TO MANCHURIA IN 1923–30[30]

Year	Immigrants	Returning	Remaining in Manchuria
1923	433,689	240,565	193,124
1924	482,470	200,045	282,435
1925	532,770	237,746	295,024
1926	607,352	323,694	183,658
1927	1,178,254	341,959	936,295
1928	938,472	394,247	544,225
1929	1,046,291	621,897	424,394
1930	810,000	560,000	250,000

Both the South Manchurian and the Chinese Eastern Railway offer very favourable terms of transport to Chinese immigrants—a 40 per cent reduction in fare, the free transport of children under 15 and old people over 60. This greatly aids family migration, and it is certain that in the last few years this type of immigrant, which is so suitable for peasant colonization in Northern Manchuria, has been steadily increasing. It is not at all rare to see in Northern Manchuria a family of as many as 200 members working land which is owned by the family as a whole. As a rule, however, agricultural holdings are on a smaller scale. Tenant families are mostly of 5 to 6 persons, and families owning their own land of 8 to 12 persons. The tenant-farming is much more widespread in Northern Manchuria than in Northern China. In Northern Manchuria the land set aside for settlement which is supposed to be ownerless is sold by the State to private persons, mostly of the well-to-do class—officials, officers, and merchants. These owners are not farmers at all, but people who as a rule do not take up farming; actually they are real estate speculators. They often form companies for the purchase of land, and occasionally they buy properties of from 20,000 to 25,000 hectares and more for re-sale. The Government sells on condition that the purchaser will work the land within five years. But only a fraction of the purchasers cultivate the land themselves; most of the land is rented to colonists. The owners offer the tenants very favourable conditions and seek to attract them by offering to supply buildings, tools, and livestock. Naturally, this form of tenancy involves a good deal of hardship to the tenant. Usually in the first years half the produce and sometimes more goes to the landlord. The indebtedness of the tenant and his complete dependence on the landowner, who is also his creditor, seriously hampers him. This form of land occupation, however, gives the poorest classes of immigrants a chance to get on the land, those classes who arrive without capital or equipment of any kind. Provided the harvest is good and he works hard, the immigrant may succeed within ten to fifteen years in buying his lease from the landlord and so become the owner of his holding. A considerable number of the immigrants, however, continue to be tenants, or, if circumstances are unfavourable, sink to the level of hired labourers.

From 1922 to 1930 the population of Manchuria, excluding the south-western province of Jehol, rose from 22 to about 30 million, i.e. by about 8 million or by 36 per cent. This was, of course, not just the result of the flow of immigrants, but was also the result of a birth-rate which must have been very high. Manchuria has a great future as a land for colonization; colonization is just at its beginnings, and if the scale of migration from the North Chinese provinces is maintained, as is probable, will enormously develop. The total area in the two northern provinces of Manchuria which can be considered suitable for colonization, including Barga, is about 862,000 sq. km., that is an area 57 per cent larger than France and 27 per cent larger than that of the whole Japanese Empire. Japan proper is less than half the size of Northern Manchuria, which is almost four times larger than Korea.

A well-known Russian expert, Jashnov, who has been a member of the department for scientific investigation of the Chinese Eastern Railway in Harbin, estimated in 1927 that the total area in Northern Manchuria then available for settlement was 187,000 sq. km., i.e. 21·9 per cent of the whole territory. The most important areas for the agricultural development in Manchuria in the future are Barga (central part), the district of Tsitsikar, and above all the fertile lower valleys of the Sungari and Ussuri, which is mainly rich black earth. According to Jashnov's estimates, Northern Manchuria alone could maintain a population of 30 million, i.e. double the present population. But this figure is a theoretical minimum which leaves out of account the natural increase of the population. Naturally, the rate at which colonization proceeds in the future will be mainly determined by the conditions prevailing in Manchuria and in the Chinese provinces whence the migrants come. Nor ought we to forget that the industrial development of Manchuria and its railway construction are just in their beginnings, and that both will offer many possibilities of attracting immigrants. It need not be added that for the development of a country like Manchuria, the state of world trade is of supreme importance, and especially the development of grain prices. Manchuria is already an important exporting country; if the harvest is good it has an export surplus of grain of 4,000,000 tons. The Chinese Eastern Railway transported 113,000 tons of grain in 1903, 747,000 tons in 1911, 983,000 tons in 1920, and 2,852,000 tons in 1926, which means a twenty-five-fold increase within a quarter of a century. There is no reason whatever why the population of Manchuria should not reach that of the Chinese northern provinces, Chih-li and Shan-tung, which supply the bulk of the immigrants, i.e. roughly 75 million, and be able to export three times as much grain as it does to-day. If that is achieved, Manchuria, from the economic as well as from the political point of view, will be the decisive factor in the Northern Pacific.[31]

While Chinese colonization in its historic forms—the millennial internal migration, then the colonization of the Pacific islands, and then, and especially, the modern continental colonization of Manchuria—is of enormous importance for the history, economics, and politics of Eastern Asia, the Japanese colonization, after the completion of the colonization of the Japanese islands, has not played anything like so great a part in determining the character of the Western Pacific. The influence of Japan in the Pacific is not founded on the physiological vitality of a race which sends out its numerous children all over the world and so spreads its culture, and finally its economic and political influence. Japanese expansion is in no way a demographic phenomenon. That, however, does not mean that the Japanese migration in the Pacific may be disregarded.

It is obvious at once that in Japan proper there is a large excess of births. This excess in the five-year period 1927–31, according to official figures, is one of 847,000. The birth-rate in Japan has shown in the fifty years, 1870 to 1920, that is to say in the period when the birth-rate in Europe was falling steadily, an amazing tendency to increase, a tendency which, however we may be dubious of the accuracy of pre-War Japanese official statistics, must be regarded as an established fact.

BIRTH-RATE FIGURES FOR JAPAN PROPER, 1871–1933[32]

(*Per* 1,000)

Year	Number of Births	Excess of Births	Year	Number of Births	Excess of Births
1871–80	25·1	7·2	1921–25	34·6	12·8
1881–90	27·1	7·2	1926–30	33·5	14·2
1891–1900	29·8	8·9	1929	32·7	12·8
1901–10	32·4	11·7	1930	32·4	14·3
1911–16	33·5	13·4	1931	32·2	13·2
1920	36·2	—	1932	32·9	15·2
1921	35·1	—	1933*	31·6	13·8

* Provisional or approximate figures.

Japan proper undoubtedly is one of the most densely populated countries in the world. In 1931 there were 177·4 persons to the sq. km., while the respective figures for Germany and France were 138 and 76. Moreover, Japan is also one of the most densely populated countries in Asia.

DENSITY OF POPULATION OF ASIATIC COUNTRIES[33]

	Persons per sq. km.
Japan (1931)	177
British India (1932)	77
Korea (1932)	95
Dutch East Indies (1932)	33
Manchuria (including Jehol)	30

We shall discuss the population problem of Japan and what it involves in its political and economic aspects in another connection. Here it is sufficient to state that in the last twenty years there has undoubtedly been a distinct demographic pressure in Japan. The population of Japan proper, the so-called "legal population," was only 43,800,000 in 1898, but in 1931 it was 67,900,000, i.e. a 24,100,000 or 54 per cent increase in thirty-three years. Between 1913 and 1931—i.e. in eighteen years—the population increased 26 per cent—53,400,000 in 1913, 67,900,000 in 1931. We may cite Germany in comparison, whose population in its dynamic period of development, i.e. between 1880 and 1930, increased by 50 per cent. But that was the period when German capitalism was at its height, when the young German Empire was making every possible effort to catch up and outstrip its English cousins. Between 1895 and 1913, that is in the eighteen years before the World War, the increase in its population was 28 per cent. But no other country which is not a country receiving immigrants can show anything like the increase in population of Japan in the last thirty-three, and, still more, in the last eighteen years.

This increase of population has remained in the country. Some shrewd observers believe that as early as 1930 the Japanese birth-rate lost its upward tendency, and that, equally, the excess of births shows a tendency to become static, if not actually to decline. Teyiro Uyeda,[34] a Japanese demographic expert, declares that it is only since the second decade of this century that the rapid increase in the Japanese birth-rate in the last decade of the nineteenth and the first decade of the twentieth century has begun to be felt in the labour market. The pressure on that market has been increasingly felt during that period, and is still felt to-day when something like 10,000,000 new recruits come annually into the labour market. This situation will continue until 1950. From that year onwards a considerable easing of the conditions on the labour market can be expected. It can be equally expected that by that time the structure of the Japanese population, as far as age is concerned, will also become normal. To-day, as a result of the high birth-rate during the last twenty years, the youngest section of the population in Japan is numerically abnormally large.

NUMBER OF CHILDREN OF 0–14 YEARS OLD IN VARIOUS COUNTRIES AS PERCENTAGE OF THE TOTAL POPULATION[35]

Germany (1930)	23·5
England and Wales (1931)	25·8
Australia (1932)	28·3
Italy (1931)	29·7
Japan proper (1930)	36·7
U.S.S.R. (including Asiatic provinces, 1926) ..	37·2

This great pressure of population has, however, not been able to produce a corresponding emigration on an adequate scale or, to state the problem better, has not been great enough to overcome the internal and external obstacles which prevent the Japanese emigrating. Colonization within Greater Japan has, however, been decidedly successful in the last twenty years. The great northern island, Hokkaido, which was first occupied about the middle of the eighteenth century (1767), and which has an area of 89,000 sq. km., that is, roughly, the area of Portugal, has still a population of only 2,800,000. But the population of this island, which is rich in raw materials, has practically doubled in the last twenty years, and according to the census of 1930 there were thirty-two persons to the square kilometre, while there were only nineteen to the square kilometre twenty years earlier. The population of Sakhalin (Karafuto) is roughly 300,000, but there are relatively few Japanese among them. It is not possible either to state in what proportion the population of Hokkaido is Japanese or aboriginal Ainu. The Kurile islands, a fishing centre of great importance, need hardly be taken into account as a colonial domain. On the other hand, the Southern Pacific islands belonging to Japan, Tai-wan (Formosa) with 4,600,000 inhabitants, the Ryû-kyû islands, as well as the former German colonies in the Southern Pacific, offer a much more suitable field for colonization by Japanese immigrants. The density of population in Ryû-kyû reaches a remarkably high figure of 264 persons to the square kilometre, and a very large proportion of these are immigrant Japanese rice growers. Japanese industry has transformed Formosa, too, into a flourishing tropical colony—camphor (a monopoly), sugar-cane, tea, rice, sago, and also coal, valuable timber and oil. In the former German colonies Japanese settlers form only one-third of a population of 70,000, the majority of which is Malayo-Polynesian. Here we see the strength of the tendency innate in the Japanese to go to the Southern Pacific, a tendency best explained by the origin of the Japanese race and its prehistoric migrations. But there is a barrier in the way of the Japanese advance southward, just as there is to the advance to the Eastern Pacific.

In the course of the last twenty to twenty-five years Japanese internal colonization has moved towards the continent of Asia. In Korea (Chosen) there is a population of 21,000,000, of whom about 500,000 are Japanese. Only about one-tenth of these are settlers on the land, the rest being officials, merchants, employees, and manufacturers. In Manchuria (including the Kwan-tung peninsula and the territory leased to the South Manchuria Railway) there is a population of from 31,000,000 to 34,000,000, of whom five-sixths are purely Chinese by culture and about 600,000 Japanese. Half of these are probably soldiers; the rest are officials, merchants, and railway employees. There are just under 10,000 miners and about 3,000 farmers.[36]

Even the official Japanese statistics do not include as "Japanese" settlers those Koreans who have migrated to Manchuria from Korea—mostly rice growers. These Korean immigrants, who are for the most part to be found in the districts of Chien-tao and Hun-chun in the province of Kirin, who are extremely important for the development of the rice cultivation, are not to be regarded as indicating a nationalist Japanese advance; on the contrary, they represent the desire of the Koreans to escape the oppressive rule of the Japanese administration.

It can be hardly doubted that from the cultural-political point of view Manchuria will sooner or later be submerged by the flow of immigrants from China into a cultural and political ocean. The plans drawn up in Japan for a great colonization scheme in Manchuria—a figure of 5,000,000

Japanese settlers during the next ten years is mentioned—can hardly be said to be practical because the Japanese settler cannot meet the competition of the Chinese. While in the Southern Pacific the Japanese agricultural settler is well able to compete with the native Malay and the Australo-Asiatic population, the Sino-Manchu-Russian mainland can hardly be regarded as likely to see any large-scale colonization by Japanese. The Japanese does not go to the mainland of Asia as a settler to cultivate the soil, but as an official, engineer, soldier, and business man, to be a ruler.[37]

The Japanese who live outside Japan proper but within the frontier of Greater Japan or in its direct sphere of occupation, were estimated in 1931 at 1 to 1½ million thus distributed:

Korea, about	500,000
Manchuria (including Kwan-tung and the territory leased to the South Manchuria Railway, as well as troops there stationed)	600,000[38]
The isles under mandate	25,000
Tai-wan, Ryû-kyû, Karafuto, etc... ..	300,000
Total about	1,500,000

Outside Greater Japan and Manchuria there lived, according to official figures, 522,492 Japanese, i.e. 0·8 per cent of the population of Japan proper, and less than 0·6 per cent of the population of Greater Japan. About 70 per cent of these were distributed between three regions: 104,000 in the United States, 144,300 in the Hawaiian islands, and 119,700 in Brazil, while of the remainder 53,000 are in China, 20,000 in the Philippines and Guam, 20,000 in Canada, and 20,000 in Peru. Apart from these seven countries, no single country in the world has more than 7,000 Japanese residing in it. On October 1, 1931, there were only 3,696 Japanese in the whole of Europe.

If we examine the development in the last thirty years and include Manchuria and the islands under Japanese mandate as centres of emigration, we see (1) a great increase in emigration and (2) a change in the proportion of Japanese among the inhabitants of the countries concerned.[39]

DISTRIBUTION OF JAPANESE IN VARIOUS COUNTRIES[40]

Country	1904		1920		1931	
		Per cent		Per cent		Per cent
United States (excluding overseas territories) ..	48,354	34·9	125,476	23·2	103,996	13·3
Hawaii	65,008	46·9	108,109	20·0	144,295	19·8
Philippines (including Guam)	2,652	1·9	9,337	1·7	19,695	2·5
Canada	3,838	2·8	17,668	3·3	20,156	2·6
Brazil	5	—	33,456	6·2	119,740	15·3
Peru	1,486	1·1	5,910	1·1	20,650	2·6
Manchuria (including Kwantung)	1,151	0·8	150,465	27·8	232,753	29·7
China (including Hong-Kong) ..	7,399	5·3	54,544	10·0	55,433	7·1
Mandated Pacific Islands.. ..	—	—	2,303	0·4	22,663	2·9
Others	8,698	6·3	34,516	6·3	38,517	4·9
Total ..	138,591	100·0	541,784	100·0	777,898	100·0

Thus in the course of roughly thirty years, 1904–31, the number of Japanese living outside Japan has increased six-fold. That to some extent is proof that there has been some important reason for emigration. But just as clearly is it evident that the direction of emigration has changed. Thirty years ago emigration went eastward, across the Pacific to the Hawaiian islands, midway between Asia and America, and to the Western States of the United States. Four-fifths of the total number of Japanese living outside Japan lived in these two countries. As late as 1920 43 per cent of Japanese living outside Japan lived in Hawaii and the United States. In 1931 scarcely did one-third, while the proportion living in Manchuria and Brazil had greatly increased. The movement of Japanese migrants to the Eastern Pacific had been blocked by legislative restrictions in the countries to which it was directed, especially the United States. It was compelled, therefore, to take another direction, and even to discover new outlets (Brazil).[41] In the eleven years 1921–31, Japanese migration made no real progress; in that period 170,534 Japanese left Japan, but in the same period 157,706 emigrants returned, so that the emigration figure for the period is 12,828. That means that the entire increase in the number of Japanese living outside Japan within 1920–31 (compare table above), which was 43 per cent (the increase in the number of inhabitants of Japan proper during that time was 17·5 per cent), is due either to excess of births or to the increase in the Japanese garrisons in Manchuria. Leaving Manchuria entirely out of our calculations, we see that in the eleven years, 1921–31, the number of Japanese living outside Japan increased 31 per cent, an increase mainly due to excess of births. Thus the Japanese abroad showed a birth-rate which indicates that they had well adapted themselves to their new environment. This contradicts the widespread idea that the Japanese are not suited to foreign colonization. That view in this crude form is clearly false. There are certain districts which are definitely unsuitable for settlement by Japanese peasants for definite climatic and economic reasons. In these districts Japanese colonization takes the form of a ruling class immigration. Thus in Manchuria and Korea the Japanese immigrant is as a rule an army officer, official, or business man. In other parts of the world and under different climatic and economic conditions the Japanese immigrant can be very successful as a farmer or plantation labourer.

§ 5. THE ADVANCE OF THE WHITE RACES

So far we have been describing how the shores of the Pacific were peopled by the yellow races, Chinese and Japanese. Of no less a significance for that process was the colonizing movement of the white race, Russians and Anglo-Saxons. Had it not been for this white colonization, the whole problem of the Pacific to-day would be very different, for the whole nature of the problem is determined by the collision of the white and of the yellow race.

From New England on the one hand and from Moscow on the other, there have issued in the last two centuries great waves of colonization in opposite directions; from Moscow eastwards across the Ural mountains to Siberia and to the Western Pacific; from New England westwards across the Appalachians and the Rockies, across the Mississippi-Missouri valley, to the Eastern Pacific. These two waves of white colonization ultimately meet in the Pacific (see Map 3).

The feature common to both the Russian and the American streams of colonization is that both are extensive. The Russian and the American—prospector, trapper, and settler—are both predatory, seeking passionately to win more and yet more land.

That explains the rapidity with which possession was taken of the vast lands of Siberia and America.

The most important dates in the colonization of Siberia are these:

1551. The first conqueror Yermak passes the Ural mountains.

1616. The Yenissei river is reached—an advance of about 1,500 km. in 65 years.

1633. The Sea of Okhotsk and so the shores of the Western Pacific is reached (the Cossack Ivan Moskurtin).

1640. The Lena river is reached—an advance of about 1,000 km. in twenty-four years.

1648. Semen Deshnev (before Behring) discovers the Behring Straits.

1650. Habaroff's expedition to the Amur district.

1689. Treaty of Nerchinsk with China by which the Russian advance to the Pacific is temporarily checked.

1697. Occupation of the Kamchatka peninsula.

1768–69. The Russian expedition under Commander Krinizin and Lieutenant Levaschev reaches the Aleutian islands and Alaska where are established fur factories and fisheries, also in the Commodore islands.

1848. Russian activity begins again in the Amur valley.
1858. Treaty of Aigun with China by which Russia obtained the region east of the Ussuri and the whole left bank of the Amur.
1860. Foundation of Vladivostok, "the citadel of the East."
1867. Alaska sold to the United States.
1891–1905. Building of the Transsiberian railway.
1904–5. The Russo-Japanese War, beginning of the counter-movement against the Russian advance to the Pacific.
1916. Completion of the Amur railway.

It must be observed that the Russian west to east colonization was not halted at the shores of the Pacific. It is a geopolitical commonplace that a forward movement which is continental in character and is worked out on the continent invariably shows a tendency to push across that continent's sea frontiers. That is seen in Roman history (campaigns in Africa and the struggle against Carthage), in Persian (the invasion of Greece from Asia Minor), in Chinese (the Mongol expeditions against Japan, the advance to the Pacific), in American (the extension of American colonization to Hawaii). The Russian advance did not stop at the shores of the Sea of Okhotsk. The Krinizin-Levaschev expedition comes in the second half of the eighteenth century, but the whole of that century and the first decades of the nineteenth century are full of expeditions by Russian explorers and adventurers not only in the Northern Pacific and the Arctic, but in the Southern Pacific as well. The Kurile island, the Aleutian islands, the north-western coast of America, between $55\frac{1}{2}°$ and 60° N., were discovered by the Russian expedition under Behring (1725–43) and partly by other Russian explorers before him. Especially important for the history of the Southern Pacific were the expeditions of Krusenstern-Lisiansky (1803–7), Kotzebu (1815–16), Bellingshausen (1819–20), and Littke (1826–29), which explored the Paumotu, Marshall, Caroline groups, and discovered many new islands.

Some of the islands in the Aleutian group were discovered by the Behring expedition. In 1784 the Siberian merchant, Grigori Shelekhow, sailed east from Okhotsk and set up a factory on the island of Kodiak; he crossed to Alaska and built forts there at several points; in 1796 at Baranov's instance possession was taken of the bay of Yakutat; in 1798 the famous Russo-American Company was established on the model of the Dutch and the English colonial companies, Baranov becoming the managing director; in 1804 the settlement Novoarchangelsk was founded on Sitka island.[42]

This Baranov (managing director or governor-general), whose activity went on until 1819, was a man cast in the mould of the Spanish, Dutch, and English conquistadores. His contemporaries speak of him as a clever, courageous, enterprising and stern man with a frame of iron and nerves of steel, and uncouth in manner. Thanks to his courage and indomitable will he maintained himself for twenty years as unchallenged ruler of the whole Russo-American coasts. He paid little attention to the instructions of his board, or even to those of the Czar, if they happened to be opposed to his own schemes.[43] Baranov probably dreamed of a great Russian empire in the Pacific region; at any rate, he tried to establish further bases, besides those in Alaska, along the American Pacific coast and in the Pacific islands. It was on his advice that Captain Kuskov established in 1812 a factory on the shores of California, then under Spanish rule, not far from San Francisco, and also a fortified base at Port Ross, which was ceded to Mexico in 1840. Even farther-reaching was the attempt of the Russian adventurer Sheffer, which equally must be ascribed to Baranov's initiative, to secure for Russia the possession of the Hawaiian islands, or at least of some of the islands of the group. This happened in 1815–17, but it was soon brought to an end by the English.[44]

In 1867 the Russo-American Company was dissolved and

Alaska itself was sold to the United States. That was the end of the Russian effort to advance beyond the Siberian shores of the Pacific. These efforts, though they had no lasting results, are of great interest, for they illustrate the inevitable tendency of a great continental nation to pursue an ocean policy.

The Russian population of Siberia, with its area of 11,500,000 sq. km., of which, however, only one-third is suitable for settling, numbered in 1815 about 1,100,000. In 1911 the figure had risen to 8,400,000, and in 1927 to 11,800,000. The increase is for the most part the result of emigration from European Russia. From the beginning of the nineteenth century and up to the outbreak of the Great War, 4,700,000 persons crossed the Ural mountains into Siberia, and the overwhelming majority of them stayed there as peasant colonists. This migration, which, until the abolition of serfdom which prevented the peasant leaving home, was very meagre in extent—on the average 3,000–6,000 annually—increased steadily until at the time when the Transsiberian railway was finished, or after the Russo-Japanese War, it reached its peak. In 1901–10 the yearly average was 226,000; for 1908 the figure is 746,000. During the first years after the World War emigration to Siberia was apparently checked by the civil war, but it is safe to assume that, because of the resulting famine in several regions of European Russia, immigration to Siberia continued, although the emigration was illegal in character, and official figures regarding it are very deficient. From official statistics it may be estimated that more than 400,000 persons went to Siberia and stayed there between 1918 and 1924.[45]

Since 1925 the migration to Siberia has been encouraged by land and it is organized by the Soviet Government as part of the great economic planning. There are no exact figures available—no figures have been given in the Russian Press; possibly secrecy is preserved for strategical reasons. According to the colonization scheme for 1927–36, worked out by Narkomsem (the Board of Agriculture), approved on July 31, 1926, by the W.S.I.K., which is the supreme authority in Russia—

what is now known as "Sibkrai" [46]—is to receive within the next decade 1,800,000 to 2,000,000 immigrants, and the region of the Far East, "Dalkrai," 1,200,000 immigrants from European Russia, producing in this way a total of 3,000,000 to 3,200,000 immigrants.

About 22,000,000 hectares have been set aside for colonization purposes. Agriculture is practicable throughout West Siberia up to the 60° N. lat., and in East Siberia up to 58° N. lat. The whole area to the south of these, that is south of the line Tobolsk–Vitimsk (on the Upper Lena)–Olekminsk–Ustj–Maisk (on the Lower Aldan)–Jamsk (in the northern part of the Kamchatka peninsula), is suitable for settlement. According to the estimates of Narkomsem, 73,000,000 hectares in this territory are perfectly suitable for farm settlement, and could provide for seven to eight million settlers. But of that total only the 22,000,000 hectares already mentioned are immediately available, and considerable improvements are needed to make the rest accessible and profitable.

The immigration to Siberia (Sibkrai and the Far East) under the Soviet Government is extremely important, for to Siberia in the years 1924–29 65 to 75 per cent of the whole migration from European Russia to Russia's colonial districts was directed. But under present conditions the prospects are not too bright, for at most between 200,000 and 300,000 persons (annual average) will go to Siberia within the next ten years. The decisive factor will be the conditions prevailing in European Russia. If the rate at which industrialization is proceeding to-day slackens, then there will be a strong impulse, as a result of unemployment, to emigrate to the colonial territories. On the contrary, new changes in agricultural policy, possibly in the form of increasing the proportion of private farms, will result in the absorption of the surplus of the population and so lessen the necessity for emigration.

The Far Eastern Region (Dalkrai) at present includes the former provinces of Transbaikalia (excluding Aginsk), the Amur Province, the Coastal Province, the district Okhotsk–

Kamchatsk (including the Kamchatka peninsula) and the Russian (northern) part of Sakhalin. This vast territory of 2,800,000 sq. km., i.e. nearly half the size of Europe, excluding European Russia, which extends from the Middle Amur and the Sea of Japan round the Sea of Okhotsk up to the Behring Sea, has a population of two millions, and as the crow flies, with a length of 2,700 km. from Blagoveshtensk to Cape Navarin (on the gulf of Anadyr), i.e. a distance equal to that between Madrid and Riga. It has a population of about 2,000,000 (less than one person to the square kilometre) even if we exclude the extremely sparsely populated Kamchatka district (including the peninsula). The comparison between the density of population here and in the neighbouring Manchurian provinces is extremely unfavourable for Russia.

DENSITY OF POPULATION IN THE RUSSIAN FAR EAST DISTRICT AND IN MANCHURIA (1927)[47]

	Area in 1,000 sq. km.	Population in 1,000	Inhabitants per 1 sq. km.
Russian Far East (without Kamchatka)	1,171·2	1,568·8	1·3
Manchuria (3 provinces) ..	967·3	30,000·0	32·0
North Manchuria (2 provinces: Heilung-kiang and Kirin)	812·2	13,000·0	16·0

The pressure of population from Manchuria towards the Russian Far East is evident. There is certainly considerable difference in climate between the Russian Far East and Northern Manchuria, but it is an established fact that the Chinese settler adapts himself very easily to any sort of climate. There is a difference between the type of agriculture in the two districts, but this difference in itself cannot be explained simply on climatic grounds. It is rather a matter of the fundamental difference in methods of cultivation. Chinese agriculture is intensive; it prefers vegetable to grain growing, while in the

Far East (as elsewhere) Russian agriculture is extensive and concentrates on grain growing. Both races cling to the habits to which centuries have inured them, even in a new country, as is seen above all in the type of crop chosen. While the Russian settler in the Far East devotes three-quarters of his holding to the cultivation of the four classical European crops, wheat, barley, rye, and oats, the Chinese settler in Northern Manchuria cultivates wheat, oats, and barley on a very limited scale, devoting to them hardly 14 per cent of his holding, and no rye at all. One-third of his holding is as a rule reserved for soya bean cultivation, one-fifth for millet, and one-sixth for gaoljan. He also cultivates rice and maize. It would be quite possible to adopt Chinese ideas in cultivation in the Far Eastern provinces of Russia. Here a rotation of crops would give good results and here late harvests would afford a solid basis to the farming industry, quite apart from the fact that the northern frontier of bean cultivation, which is at present the real basis of Manchurian farming, could be carried much farther north, and has actually been carried northward in the last twenty-five years. Other crops have also been carried farther north: rice in Japan and barley in Canada. But in all these fields the Russian settler in the Far East cannot stand up to the competition of the Chinese or Korean peasant. The immigration of Chinese and Koreans to the Far Eastern provinces is already a serious problem. In 1925 Chinese, Japanese, and Koreans constituted already 11·2 per cent of the total population, and more than 25 per cent of all labour in agriculture and industry is Chinese and Korean. The fisheries, one of the most important branches of industry in the Far East, are practically altogether in the hands of Japanese. Especially important is the fact that the Russian Far East, or at least an important part of it, is supplied with grain from North Manchuria, while in the extreme north the Jakutsk Republic obtains grain from Western Siberia.

Russian sources are vague and contain no positive data for an estimate of the capacity of the Russian Far East to provide for new settlers. These vast spaces are so incompletely explored that there is insufficient information as to the climatic conditions in certain parts of these provinces. All that one can say is that there are still large districts in these provinces ready for agricultural colonization.

The proportion of settled to unsettled land in the most thickly settled districts where most transport is available is as follows:

Districts	Total Area in sq. km.	Populated Area in Hectares	Percentage	Density
Transbaikalia	296,432	753,827	2·5	1·8
The Amur Province ..	401,007	719,506	1·8	0·9
The Coastal District ..	592,449	498,107	0·9	1·1

The density of the population in Northern Sakhalin is 0·21 per sq. km., and in Kamchatka 0·03 per sq. km.

According to the plan of the Narkomsem of 1926, to which we have already alluded, approximately 1,200,000 agricultural colonists are to be settled in the Far Eastern region by 1936. Russian experts give much lower figures, between 100,000 and 300,000 colonists annually between 1927 and 1936. These estimates are concerned only with purely agricultural colonization. If the necessary resources were obtainable to open up the Russian Far East to industry and particularly to mining, the possibilities of colonization would take on a very different aspect. Apart altogether from the fishing industry, which is already second to the farming industry, and gold mining, which has been going on now for several decades and which, if there is adequate capital expenditure and organization, is likely to be much more profitable, there are according to Russian accounts very large deposits of best quality coal (Sakhalin and Suchan near Vladivostok). The wealth of the Russian Far East in timber is practically unlimited, and there is a splendid market for it in Japan, which is at present dominated by Canadian timber. On the other hand, the fact that Japan, a land poor in raw materials, is so near is politically a source of danger for the Russian Far East.[48]

There is one point on which no doubt is possible. Had it not been for the strict watch kept on the Amur frontier the Russian Far East would have been already swamped by the waves of Chinese settlers. The extensive method of colonization, which has enabled the Russians in so short a time to gain legal possession of vast regions, completely fails in the economic field, and cannot compete with the strenuous, intensive colonization of the Chinese and Koreans. If there is any weakening of the restrictive measures which to-day make any "legal" immigration absolutely impossible, the Russian Far East is threatened with the fate of all the white settlements in the Pacific—to be submerged by the yellow flood. The Russians were able, as a result of the favourable political situation in the middle of the last century when the Chinese Empire had been terribly weakened by the Tai-ping rebellion and the wars with France and England, to secure the outlet to the Western Pacific (Treaty of Aigun 1858, ratified in Peking 1860). But to-day Soviet Russia lacks the capital and suitable reserves of man-power to make these conquests safe. When the Czarist Empire established itself on the Pacific and on the Amur, Manchuria, and particularly its northern provinces, were hardly populated at all, and Japan was a weak country, so far untouched by European civilization, with a population of 30,000,000. To-day Soviet Russia faces on the one hand the steadily rising waves of the Chinese migration into adjacent Manchuria and, on the other, a Japan amazingly strengthened which has built up an empire on the mainland in the immediate neighbourhood of the Far Eastern provinces of the Union. The Russian Far East, and with it Russia's outlet to the Pacific, are caught in the pincer-like grip of the Chinese-Japanese menace.[49]

The other wave of white colonization is in a much more favourable situation, that which—also in the middle of the last century—won firm hold on the Pacific region from the opposite direction. The colonization, in the proper sense of the term, of the present territory of the United States took place in the nineteenth and twentieth centuries. At the close of the seventeenth century the total white population in all the settlements in the territory which is now the United States, is estimated to have been about 200,000. At the end of the eighteenth century this population figure was just under 4,000,000. Between 1816 and 1925 there poured into the United States a mighty human stream of more than 36,000,000 immigrants, of whom 32,000,000 came from Europe. Neither before nor after has the history of human migration recorded any movement of masses on such a scale as that. This immigration not only created a "second Europe" overseas, but it created the modern Atlantic world, as the chief centre of the world trade and world politics.

The migration of the Europeans across the Atlantic, however, had simultaneously important consequences for the colonization of the eastern shores of the Pacific. For each new wave of European immigrants which crossed the Atlantic produced in the land to which they came a population crisis which drove the earlier immigrants to move westwards until finally the European colonizing of America which began in the middle of the seventeenth century on the western shores of the Atlantic reached in the middle of the nineteenth century, that is two centuries later, the Eastern Pacific. Thus within two hundred years a distance of 4,000 km. has been traversed by the white man—an achievement which, if compared with the slowness of the Chinese colonization, is brilliant in the extreme; it gave to the white race the dominant position in the Pacific. Yet the speed with which the Russians overran the wide area of Siberia was still greater. It was in 1551 that Yermak crossed the Urals, and in 1639 the Russian conquerors had reached the Sea of Okhotsk and so the Western Pacific. A distance of 4,500 km. was covered in eighty-eight years.

But it is not only distance that counts. The colonization

in America was incomparably more thorough. A far greater number of settlers, backed up by the planned construction of continental railways, moved westward across the Mississippi-Missouri valley. In the course of seventy years (1850–1920) there was a tremendous shifting of population from east to west. In 1850 91·4 per cent of the population in the United States lived east of the Mississippi, and 8·6 per cent to the west of it; in 1920 only 70 per cent lived east of the Mississippi and 30 per cent (that is, nearly one-third) to the west of it. Thus "the centre of gravity of the population" (the so-called demographical centre) had, in seventy years (1850–1920), shifted 291 miles westward.

This distribution of the population over the territory of the United States has, according to the census of 1930, changed very little, a proof of the fact that between 1920 and 1930 internal colonization, and so the shift of the demographical centre westward, had ceased. To-day there live in the Pacific States (Washington, Oregon, and California) 8,200,000 or 6·7 per cent (in 1920 5,600,000 or 5·3 per cent); in the mountain States more or less adjacent to the Pacific region (Montana, Idaho, Wyoming, Colorado, New Mexico, Arizona, Utah, and Nevada) live 3,700,000 or 3 per cent (in 1920 3,300,000 or 3·2 per cent). In these eleven States live 11,900,000 or 9·7 per cent (in 1920 8,900,000 or 8·5 per cent).[50]

As is seen, the white race sent out incomparably larger masses of settlers than those which the Russian colonizations brought to the Western Pacific. But the advance of the settlers from east to west has slackened in the last decade because the chief cause of it, the ceaseless waves of immigrants from Europe, is no longer at work, and besides the American population in the Pacific States is too far from the real centre of events in the Pacific to exercise an influence corresponding to its size and energy.

The American advance westward, however, did not stop at the eastern shores of the Pacific. Just as the Russians, after establishing themselves on the shores of the Sea of Okhotsk, seized, in the second half of the eighteenth century, the Aleutian islands and Alaska, and even pressed on as far as California and the Hawaiian islands, the Americans from the middle of the nineteenth century sought to extend their influence over the Pacific. Twenty years after the Russians in 1867 had been finally driven from the American continent, the Americans occupied the Hawaiian islands, half-way between America and Asia. At the close of the nineteenth century the Philippine islands, after a short war with Spain, came into the possession of the United States, and so made the United States an East Asian, or at least a Western Pacific Power. American influence has crossed the ocean, but American colonization has stopped at the western coast of the American continent. Just like all other colonizing nations of Europe, the Dutch, the Portuguese, and the English, the Americans failed to solve the problem of the colonization of the Pacific. In the Hawaiian islands the Japanese form one-third of a population of which 80 per cent are of Malay and yellow stock; the Americans form hardly one-tenth.[51]

The settlement of Australia and New Zealand is the work of a separate stream of white colonization in the Pacific. If one regards the increase in the Australian population within the last sixty years without comparing it with the increase in other colonial regions, it is seen to be a very respectable one. In thirty years (1871–1901) the population of Australia was doubled, while during the next thirty years (1901–31) there was a further increase of 71 per cent. Comparing Australia with, let us say, Germany, as the most "dynamic" of all the European capitalist countries whose increase in population is due almost entirely to the high birth-rate, the increase in the population of Australia may be regarded as typical of a colonial country. This increase took place almost at the same rate as the increase of the greatest field of European colonization, the United States, the population of which also doubled between 1870 and 1900, and increased by 61·8 per cent from 1900 to 1930, that is slightly less than did Australia's.

Percentage Increase of the Population in Some Parts of the Pacific World, 1901–30

Commonwealth of Australia	71·0
New Zealand	87·5
The Pacific States of the United States ..	239·1
Japan	39·0
Manchuria	400·0

In the second half of the nineteenth century (1861–1900) 778,000 and 327,000, for the most part immigrants from the British Isles, came to Australia and New Zealand. The net increase in the first thirty years of the twentieth century (1900–32), i.e. the number of immigrants minus the number of immigrants who re-emigrated, was for Australia 521,000, and for New Zealand 178,000. In the last few years the immigration to the two Southern Pacific Dominions has almost completely ceased, in spite of the plans for large-scale migration of the Governments both of the mother country and the Commonwealth of Australia. An agreement between the two Governments, concluded in April 1925, provided for the settlement in Australia of 450,000 British migrants within the succeeding ten years. Sir Leo Chiozza Money calculated that if circumstances were favourable the number of immigrants could be raised to about 60,000 annually. Actually the total number arriving within the first five years (1926–30) was 116,000, and in the two following years (1931 and 1932) Australia lost 15,000 inhabitants as a result of re-emigration. Just as unhappy has been the development in New Zealand.

Immigration is stagnant and at the same time the birth-rate is falling in the two British Dominions in the Southern Pacific. Australia and New Zealand in the post-War period have become typical examples of countries with a stable population, a type which we know so well in industrialized Europe. The Australian and the New Zealand birth-rates are very similar to that in England and are much below that in a semi-agricultural country as Italy, not to mention Japan.

Immigration is stagnant, and at the same time the birth-rate is rapidly falling, while in countries like Japan and most notably

BIRTHS PER THOUSAND INHABITANTS[52]

	1921–25	1926–30	1929	1930	1931	1932	1933
Australia	23·9	21·0	20·2	19·9	18·2	16·9	16·8
New Zealand ..	22·2	19·7	19·0	18·8	18·4	17·1	16·6
United Kingdom ..	20·4	17·2	16·7	16·8	16·3	15·8	14·9
Japan	34·6	33·5	32·7	32·4	32·2	32·9	31·6
Italy	29·7	26·8	25·6	26·7	24·9	23·8	23·5
Hawaii	39·4	33·6	31·9	29·3	28·4	28·0	26·3
EXCESS OF BIRTHS PER THOUSAND INHABITANTS							
Australia	14·4	11·7	10·7	11·3	9·5	8·3	7·9
New Zealand ..	13·6	11·1	10·2	10·2	10·1	9·1	8·6
Japan	12·8	14·2	12·8	14·3	13·2	15·2	13·8
Hawaii	25·3	21·9	19·5	18·6	18·4	18·3	16·7

the Hawaiian islands, where Chinese and Japanese account for 45 per cent of the population and whites of every nation only for 20 per cent, although the birth-rate is falling, it is still maintained at a relatively very high level. The Southern Pacific Dominions are sharing the fate of all the countries with a European industrial civilization and a high percentage of urban population. As to the latter, urbanization has reached a high level of development in both Dominions.

URBAN POPULATION (TOWNS OF OVER 100,000 INHABITANTS AS PERCENTAGE OF TOTAL POPULATION)[53]

	1910	1920	1930–33
Commonwealth of Australia*	37·5	43·3	47·5 (June 30, 1933 census)
New Zealand†	10·2	30·4	32·2 (April 1, 1931 estimate)
Germany	24·2	25·4	30·2 (June 16, 1933 census)
England and Wales ..	38·8	38·9	39·8 (May 26, 1931 census)
Japan proper	11·2	11·3	17·1 (Oct. 1, 1930 census)

* On June 30, 1933, there were six big towns with more than 100,000 inhabitants: Sydney, Melbourne, Adelaide, Brisbane, Perth, Newcastle.

† Towns with over 100,000 inhabitants: Auckland, Wellington, Christchurch.

There is no doubt that a great future lies before both Australia and New Zealand, but it depends on the colonization and settlement, above all, of the Australian mainland, and more precisely on agricultural settlement. According to an official estimate made in 1931, 9·85 per cent of the total area of the Commonwealth, that is 188,000,000 acres, are under cultivation. About 40 per cent of the total area is nominally owned by the Government or is practically ownerless. Sir John McWhae, the Agent-General for Victoria in 1922, described as the "heart of Australia" a region of 500,000 sq. m., the semi-circle Sydney–Melbourne–Adelaide—an area which is magnificently suited to agricultural settlement. That area is 300,000 sq. m. larger than the area covered by France, Belgium, Germany, Holland, Denmark, and Switzerland put together, and these six countries have a population of roughly 130,000,000. But the most notable thing is that this enormous continent, which seems to have been created for the farmer, within 1911 and 1921, i.e. in ten years, increased its agricultural population only by 163,419 (8·75 per cent). During the same period the population of the big towns: Sydney, Melbourne, Adelaide, Brisbane, Perth, and Hobart (Tasmania), together increased by 643,750 (38 per cent). In the two great cities, Sydney and Melbourne, in 1925 there was a population of about 1,000,000, while in all the rest of Australia there was only about 4,000,000. English immigrants so far have been townfolk, and it was natural that town dwellers should have settled in big towns such as they were accustomed to at home. That is just as natural as it is for the North Chinese peasant to start cultivating the soil whenever he gets to North Manchuria. The immigrant brings to the new country just those habits which he had at home. Chiozza Money is perfectly right when he says that the degree of urbanization of the European and especially of the English has generally been underestimated: "The case may be summed up not unfairly by saying that the Dominions offer difficult virgin land to people who, for the most part, do not know how to manage a suburban garden." To put it another way: what Australia and New Zealand need are real peasants and not townfolk. In all the schemes for large-scale colonization an essential feature is training in farming, and there is no doubt that under favourable circumstances it will in time produce results, but it may be doubted whether there can be results on a large scale and whether it is possible to persuade any really great number of white, that is to say British, people to migrate, and particularly to migrate to cultivate the soil.

The population of Australia, a country of immigration,

POPULATION OF THE COMMONWEALTH OF AUSTRALIA AND OF NEW ZEALAND (EXCLUDING THE MAORIS), 1871–1933[54]

(*In Millions*)

	1871	1881	1891	1901	1911	1921	1933*
Commonwealth of of Australia ..	1·7	2·3	3·2	3·8	4·6	5·5	6·6
New Zealand ..	—	—	—	0·77	1·00	1·20	1·46

* June 30th.

increased within the ten years 1921–30 by 1,064,735, that means by about 18 per cent, whereas the population of a definitely emigration country like Japan increased within the same period by 16 per cent. The increase certainly was a little less, but it must not be forgotten that the Japanese increase is exclusively the result of a high birth-rate. At the present rate of increase the population of the Commonwealth will, about 1950, have a population of 10,000,000 at the most, while Japan proper, if her population continues to increase only by 700,000 annually, i.e. reckoning with a fall in the birth-rate, will have by 1950 a population of 80,000,000, and Greater Japan one of nearly 124,000,000, and the population of the United States, all their overseas possessions included, will be in 1950 between 155,000,000 and 157,000,000.

The population of our planet, from the geopolitical point of view, can be divided up into three oceanic spheres—the Atlantic-Mediterranean, the Pacific, and the Indian. Such a division is in no way arbitrary. It corresponds very much to the historical, economic, and political developments. To the European his world has long ceased to be just the Mediterranean world, as it was at the time of the Roman Empire. Since the beginning of modern history, and especially since the sixteenth and seventeenth centuries, the Mediterranean world has extended in two directions: eastwards and south-eastwards, i.e. in the directions which European trade with the Near East, Arabia, and India took in antiquity. This time, however, it was by sea and not by land that the extension was made.

The eastward trend seems at first the more important and the more productive for increasing the wealth of Europe. Soon, however, this line of expansion taken by the Mediterranean sphere of culture is superseded by another line, the western, Atlantic line. In the course of the nineteenth century the European world, which as late as the tenth century was essentially a Mediterranean world, becomes an Atlantic world. To-day, with the first third of the twentieth century already behind us, we can say that the European world is still essentially an Atlantic world—the world in which both sides of the Atlantic exchange men, ideas, and goods. The countries of Southern Europe and Hither Asia which are on the Mediterranean have also an Atlantic orientation. That orientation has become much more decided since the World War, to such an extent indeed that the West Atlantic Power, the United States, has become the first economic and political Power on our planet.

But we must not schematize overmuch. It is in no way our intention to exaggerate the Atlantic character of the European world, or to minimize the intimate connection that world has with the Indian and Pacific spheres. On the contrary. But to get a correct conception of the place which Europe holds between these two, we must not fail to recognize the essentially Atlantic character of that continent.

On the shores of the Atlantic, of the Mediterranean, and of the Black Sea—the two last can be regarded as mere tributaries of the Atlantic—there live to-day about 900,000,000 people, i.e. about 44 per cent of the total population of the globe.

This "Atlantic World" is numerically stronger than the Indian and the Pacific worlds. The supremacy of this world will appear even greater if we look not only at the size of its population but—to coin a phrase—at the geopolitical importance of its average inhabitant. To the Atlantic world come at least two-thirds of the world exports, probably more. The traffic across the Atlantic is 75 per cent of the whole sea-going traffic. The production of the most important raw materials and finished goods is equally concentrated on the shores of the Atlantic within the Atlantic world. One can assert to-day that the Atlantic Ocean is still the centre of the globe. But it would be a fallacy, and a dangerous fallacy, to underestimate the significance for the world development of our epoch of the two other great worlds.

As far as population and geopolitical importance are concerned, the Pacific world comes next to the Atlantic.

About 723,000,000 people, or about 35·4 per cent of the total population of the world, live on the shores of the Pacific. But the geopolitical importance of the Pacific world's average inhabitant is much less than that of the average inhabitant of the Atlantic world.

Geographically, the Indian world lies between the other two. The Indian Ocean to-day serves as a channel between the Atlantic and the Pacific, the Mediterranean and the Suez canal being the routes connecting it with the Atlantic, and the Malacca Straits as the route to the Pacific.

The Indian Ocean can be regarded as a British ocean. The triangle Capetown (South Africa)–Colombo (Ceylon)–Perth (West Australia) is the frame inside which the internal activity of the Indian Ocean world goes on, a world whose shores are almost entirely under British influence. About 400,000,000 people, i.e. 19·8 per cent of the total population of the world, live here.

DISTRIBUTION OF THE WORLD POPULATION AT THE END OF 1932[55]

	In Millions	Percentage of the Total Population of the Planet
The Atlantic world	900	44·0
The Pacific world	723	35·4
The Indian world	405	19·8
Total	2,028	99·2

From a European point of view, the Atlantic and the Mediterranean worlds have been until now the stage on which the drama of world history has been played. The two other oceanic worlds are generally looked on as simply an appendage to the Atlantic-Mediterranean world. In our days, however, the European must go to school again. World history is not the history of Europe, and world politics are not a European-Atlantic concern. If in the last two hundred years the European West has been the centre of the world, that is to be considered simply as a phase in world history. To-day the axis of world politics goes through the Atlantic Ocean, but there is already visible the beginning of a development which may be the first stage in the shifting of the centre of gravity from the Atlantic-European world.

NOTES TO CHAPTER I

1. "The history of mankind began with a Mediterranean epoch, it continued in the Atlantic period, and now it is entering into the Pacific era."

2. Bruno Dietrich and Hermann Leiter, *Produktion, Verkehr und Handel*, in Andree-Heiderich-Sieger, *Geographie des Welthandels*, Vienna, 1930, vol. 3, p. 383.

3. *Statistisches Jahrbuch für das Deutsche Reich*, Berlin, 1934, p. 110.

4. Compiled from the informations given in the *Statistical Year Books of the League of Nations*, Geneva, 1927, 1928, 1933. The most important and most representative Atlantic and Pacific countries have been chosen. We did not make a comparison with the foreign trade of so representative a country as Holland because in consequence of a complete change in the method of compiling foreign trade statistics, pre-War and post-War Dutch statistics cannot be compared. The post-War foreign trade statistics of France and Germany are equally difficult to compare because of the change of frontier due to the Versailles Treaty. As far as getting a picture of Atlantic trade is concerned they are quite comparable. Ships from every Atlantic country sail to the Pacific, just as ships from every Pacific country sail to the Atlantic. But the foreign trade of the countries bordering on the Atlantic is for the most part done on that ocean, and the same is true of the Pacific countries and that ocean. The position of the United States is rather more complicated, as its coasts are washed by both oceans. Direct information regarding the diversion of the foreign trade of the United States between the two oceans is completely lacking, and so we have to make a rough estimate in the following way:

We have taken the total turnover of the United States (1929) to: (1) Pacific Asia (Eastern Asia, the Philippine islands, and Siam); (2) Oceania (Australia, New Zealand, and the rest of the Pacific islands); and (3) the countries on the western coast of South America, and taken the total of these three as an approximate figure for the Pacific trade of the United States.

PACIFIC FOREIGN TRADE OF THE UNITED STATES, 1929
(IN MILLION DOLLARS)

(1) Pacific Asia	1,251·3
(2) Oceania	278·5
(3) The Western Coast of South America	232·0
	1,761·8

The figures are taken from the *Statistical Abstract of the United States, 1933*, Washington, 1933.

The foreign trade of the United States in the Pacific for 1929 was roughly one-fifth of the total foreign trade of the United States. The figures in the table were raised to the nearest round figure, for at the moment no data are obtainable for certain sections of the United States trade in the Pacific.

For 1913 we have taken the United States foreign trade in the Pacific as one-tenth of the total foreign trade, for it was above all the opening of the Panama canal to trade in 1914, just before the outbreak of the World War, which stimulated the growth of the United States trade with the countries of the Pacific. Figures for traffic through the canal, 6,600,000 net tons in 1918, 29,800,000 in 1929. We have taken 1929 as the year for comparison, for it was the last normal trading, i.e. pre-crisis, year.

5. Compiled from the *Statistical Year Book of the League of Nations for 1927* and *1932–33*.

6. *Ibid.*

7. *Statistisches Jahrbuch für das Deutsche Reich, 1934*, Berlin, 1934.

8. Dietrich and Leiter, *op. cit.*, pp. 408–10. We have compared 1913 and 1928 as both are normal years, and also years of good trade.

9. Gregor Bienstock, *Einführung in die Weltwirtschaft*, Berlin, 1927, pp. 28–31.

10. Grover Clark, *Economic Rivalries in China*, New Haven, 1932, pp. 16–32; M. I. Michailov, *K voprosu o transportnoj probleme v Kitaje* (in Russ) ("Transport Problems in China"), in *Vestnik Mandschuriji* (*Manchuria Monitor*), Nos. 6 and 7, 1932. This is the organ of the Board of the Chinese Eastern Railway, and is published in Harbin.

11. C. Nagakura (of the New York office, South Manchurian Railway, Hsinking Speeding Railroad Building), in the *New York Times*, March 25, 1934.

12. Wilhelm Teubert, *Die Welt im Querschnitt des Verkehrs*, Berlin, 1928, pp. 175, 181; Andree-Heiderich-Sieger, vol. iii, p. 338; Hermann G. James and Percy A. Martin, *The Republics of Latin America*, New York and London, 1923, p. 286.

13. Compiled from various sources, including *Statistisches Jahrbuch für das Deutsche Reich*, Berlin, 1934, p. 100; Andree-Heiderich-Sieger, *op. cit.*, p. 291; Grover Clark, *op. cit.*, pp.18–19.

14. *Die wirtschaftlichen Kräfte der Welt*, published by the Dresdner Bank, Berlin, 1930, p. 166.

15. *Statistisches Jahrbuch für das Deutsche Reich, 1934*, Berlin, 1934, p. 101.

16. The development of aviation in the countries of the Western and Southern Pacific is taken from the special aviation number of the *East Asiatic Review* (*Ostasiatische Rundschau*, Hamburg), Nos. 21–22, October–November 1934.

17. F. E. A. Krause, *Geschichte Ostasiens*, Göttingen, 1925, vol. i, pp. 46, 187.

18. Krause, *op. cit.*, vol. i, pp. 212 sq., 248.

19. Hans Mosolf, *Die chinesische Auswanderung. Ursachen, Wesen und Wirkungen*, Rostock, 1932 (Hamburger Wirtschafts- und Sozialwissenschaftliche Schriften).

20. Quoted by Mosolf, p. 145.

21. Of a population of roughly 4,000,000 (1928), Formosa contained 3,500,000 Chinese and Hakka Chinese and 200,000 Japanese (Mosolf, *l.c.*, p. 345). Hakka (K'o-chia = "aliens") is the name given to the descendants of the families who were transplanted by the Emperor Ch'in Shi-huang-ti from the north to the south, where they still speak their own dialect, which differs from that of the Southern Chinese population (cf. F. E. A. Krause, *l.c.*, vol. i, p. 280).

22. For 1930 (*Statistical Abstract of the United States for 1933*).

23. Mosolf, *l.c.*, pp. 321, 346, 349, 364.

24. De Quatrefages, *Les Polynésiens et leur migration*, Paris, 1860.

25. *Statistical Abstract of the United States for 1933.*

26. Stephen H. Roberts (formerly Lecturer in Modern History, University of Melbourne, Harbison-Higinbotham and Fred Knight Research Student. Author of *History of Australian Land Settlement, 1788–1920*), *Population Problems of the Pacific*, London, 1927.

27. L. I. Ljubimov, *Kitajskaja Emigrazija* (in Russ.) ("The Chinese Emigration"), Harbin, 1932; E. E. Jaschnov, *Kitakjskaja kolonizacija Severnoj Mandschuriji i ee perspektivy* (in Russ.) ("The Colonization of Northern Manchuria by the Chinese, and its Future"); published by the Ekonomicheskoje Büro Kit. Vost. Gel. Dor., i.e. The Economic Office of the East China Railway, Harbin, 1928; M. J. Michailov, *l.c.*

28. *The China Year Book, 1933*, Shanghai, pp. 2, 202.

29. "Chinese Labour Migration to Manchuria," in the *Chinese Economic Journal*, 1927, No. 7.

30. *The China Year Book, 1933*, p. 202.

31. L. I. Ljubimov, *l.c.*; E. E. Jaschnov, *l.c.*

32. Wl. Woytinsky, *Die Welt in Zahlen*, vol. i, Berlin, 1925; *Annuaire Statistique de la Société des Nations*, 1933–34, Geneva, 1934.

33. *Résumé Statistique de l'Empire du Japon*, 47 *année*, Tokio, 1933; *Statistical Year Book of the League of Nations, 1933–34*, Geneva, 1934.

34. Teyiro Uyeda, *Future of the Japanese Population*, 1933 (in Japanese), quoted in *Revue de la situation économique mondiale*, League of Nations, Geneva, 1934, p. 68.

35. *Statistical Year Book of the League of Nations, 1933–34*, Geneva, 1934.

36. This is the official estimate made by the Manchukuo Government at the end of 1932, quoted in the *Revue du Pacifique*, 1934, Nrs. 9–10, p. 497.

37. Karl Haushofer, *Japans Werdegang als Weltmacht und Empire*, Berlin–Leipzig, 1933, pp. 114–18.

38. In Formosa with the total population of 4,000,000 there are only about 200,000 Japanese. Mosolf, *l.c.*, p. 345.

39. *Résumé Statistique de l'Empire du Japon*, Tokio, 1933, p. 22.

40. *The Japan Year Book, 1933*, The Foreign Affairs Association of Japan.

41. The Japanese immigrants residing in Brazil numbered at the end of 1933 roughly 150,000. The dictatorial Government of Getulio Vargas, who came into power after the revolution of October 1930, intends to introduce radical measures to restrict Japanese immigration. In May 1934 a revision of the constitution in this sense was passed by the necessary majority in the Brazilian Parliament. The immigration of those (racial) elements which are regarded as not easily assimilated is to be greatly restricted. The announcement of the proposed restriction provoked deep resentment in Japan, and diplomatic representations were made by the Tokio Government (*Japon: Bulletin d'Informations économiques et financières*, Paris, edited by Balet, Juin 1934, p. 29).

42. L. S. Berg, *Otkrytia ruskyh v Tyhom Okeane* (in Russ.) ("The Russian Discoveries in the Pacific") in the series: "Tychij Okean, Russkije nautschnyje issledowanija" ("The Pacific: Russian Scientific Studies"), Akademia Nauk, Leningrad, 1926.

43. R. Greenhow, *History of Oregon and California*, Boston, 1847, p. 271, quoted by P. Gronski, "Les Russes aux Iles Hawai au début du XIXe Siècle," in the *Monde Slave*, Paris, 1928, No. 10, p. 23.

44. Gronski, *l.c.*, p. 21 sq. As representative of Baranov, the Governor-General of the Russian possessions in North America, Dr. Sheffer, arrived in 1815 in Hawaii apparently simply for trade purposes, and he was therefore very well received by King Kameha-meha I, the "Napoleon of Hawaii," who not long before had united under his rule all the islands of the Hawaiian group. But these friendly relations soon came to an end when the Russians attempted to build a fort in the island of Wagou, in which the capital of Hawaii, Honolulu, is situated. At the instigation of his English adviser, the King decided to evict the Russian. Sheffer then, with the two ships of the Russo-American Company under his command, went to the northern island Attoi (Kaouai), which is quite near, and succeeded in concluding with a local chief, who did not acknowledge the suzerainty of Kameha-meha, a treaty by which the chief placed his "kingdom" under the rule of the Czar of Russia. The Russians then built a fort here. Finally Kameha-meha by threats succeeded in making the Russians leave this island too. Sheffer in 1818 submitted a memorandum to the St. Petersburg Government in which he demonstrated the necessity of creating a strong Russian base in Hawaii. At the same time the Russo-American Company petitioned the Russian Government to the effect that such a base could considerably facilitate the supply of necessities to Alaska. Alexander I's Government, however, rejected these ambitious plans, and the able colonial pioneer,

Baranov, who in other circumstances might have become a Russian Cecil Rhodes, died in 1819 while he was on his way to St. Petersburg to put his schemes before the Imperial Government. His successor, Hagemeister, abandoned completely the idea of founding a Russian colony in Hawaii.

45. J. G. Losovoj, "Voprosy pereselenija i kolonizacii Ssibiry " (in Russ.) ("The Problem of Migration and Colonization in Siberia"), in *Volnaja Ssibirj*, Prague, 1928, Nr. 3, p. 123.

46. The contemporary administrative divisions of Siberia differ considerably from those of the pre-revolutionary period. The old geographical Siberia is now divided into the following administrative units (area and population according to the last census, 1926):

	Area (in millions sq. km.)	Percentage of Total Area	Population (in 1,000)	Percentage of Total Population
Siberia	4·2	29·7	8,686·4	51·1
Ural District (Siberian part)	1·2	8·4	1,619·6	9·5
Kasakstan	1·8	12·6	4,166·9	24·5
Burjat Mongolian Republic	0·4	2·7	484·4	2·9
Jakutsk Republic	3·8	26·6	236·7	1·4
Far Eastern Region (Dalkrai)	2·8	20·0	1,805·8	10·6
Total	14·2	100·0	1,7000·0	100·0

Over 90 per cent of the Siberian population (91·1 per cent roughly) are the Russians (Great Russians, Uranians, and White Russians), while the aboriginal population is at the most 500,000, or about 3 per cent.

Cf. J. Jakuschev, "Rayonisowannaja Sibirj w zyfrach" (in Russ.), ("The Regions of Siberia in Figures"), in *Volnaja Ssibirj*, Prague, 1930, Nr. 8, pp. 47, 53.

47. Jaschnov, *l.c.*, p. 21.

48. J. G. Losovoj, *l.c.*, pp. 133, 136.

49. N. N. Firsov, *Tschtenija po istoriji Sibiri* (in Russ.) ("Lectures on the History of Siberia"), Moscow, 1920, pp. 21–3, 29; I. A. Jakuschev, *Die Zukunft Sibiriens*, Prague, 1928; Maurice Courant, *La Sibérie Colonie Russe jusqu'a la Construction du Transsibérien*, Paris, 1920; *Eastern Siberia*, London, 1920 (No. 55 of the handbooks prepared under the direction of the Historical Section of the Foreign Office: G. W. Prothero, General Editor and formerly Director of the Historical Section).

50. *Statistical Abstract of the United States, 1933*, Washington, 1933.

51. Wl. Woytinsky, *l.c.*, vol. i, p. 129; *Statistisches Jahrbuch für das Deutsche Reich, 1930*, p. 21 , Berlin, 1930.

52. *Statistical Year Book of the League of Nations, 1933–34*, Geneva, 1934.

53. *Statistisches Jahrbuch für das Deutsche Reich, 1934*, Berlin, 1934, Intern. Uebers., pp. 13–15[x].

54. *Official Year Book of the Commonwealth of Australia*, No. 26, 1933; *The New Zealand Official Year Book, 1934*, Wellington, 1934.

55. Calculated on the basis of data supplied by the *Statistical Year Book of the League of Nations, 1933–34*, Geneva, 1934. The figures are raised to the nearest round figure because it is a question here mostly of estimates for December 31, 1932, and because we are concerned mainly with the relative size of the populations belonging to the three ocean worlds. The *Statistical Year Book* estimates the total population of the globe planet on December 31, 1932, at 2,041,600,000. In our tables some 14,000,000 to 15,000,000 are not reckoned in, or less than 1 per cent, which hardly affects the totals at all.

1. Population of the Atlantic-Mediterranean World (in Millions)

Europe (without the U.S.S.R.)	384·0
U.S.S.R. in so far as it belongs to this world ..	150·0
Atlantic and Mediterranean Africa (all countries in Africa bordering on the Atlantic and the Mediterranean)	118·5
Atlantic and Mediterranean Asia (Syria and Lebanon, Palestine and Transjordania, Turkey in Asia, Cyprus)	18·6
Atlantic Northern America (population of continental United States and Alaska minus the population of the three Pacific States and five Mountain States (Idaho, New Mexico, Arizona, Utah, Nevada), Canada (minus its Pacific States) ..	136·6
Atlantic Mexico and Central America	26·0
Atlantic South America (all the countries bordering on the Atlantic)	65·5
	899·2

2. The Population of the Pacific Oceanic World (in Millions)

Pacific Asia (China, Japan, Korea, Formosa, Kwantung, Karafuto, Dutch East Indies, the Philippines, British Malaya, Siam, French Indo-China, the Portuguese colonies, the Russian Far East) ..	670·0
Oceania (Australia, New Zealand, and the adjoining Pacific isles)	10·0
Pacific South America (all countries bordering on the Pacific)	21·8
Pacific North America (the Pacific States of Canada, the Pacific States of the United States, and the five Mountain States—Idaho, New Mexico, Arizona, Utah, and Nevada)	11·0
Pacific Mexico and Central America	10·0
	722·8

3. The Population of the Indian Oceanic World (in Millions)

Indian Asia (British India, Ceylon, with the Maldive islands, Persia)	375·9
Indian Africa and Arabia (Kenya, Mauritius, Tanganyika, Italian Somaliland, Portuguese Mozambique, the Union of South Africa, Madagascar) ..	27·8
Indian Oceania (West and South Australia)	1·0
	404·7

CHAPTER II

RIVALRIES IN THE PACIFIC

THE history of Europe can only be understood when we link it up with the history of Asia. It would be better if we Europeans kept firmly in mind the fact that it is only in the course of the last half-millennium that our continent has become a decisive factor of *world* policy, in the full sense of the former word; for even the most important political achievement of the ancient West, the Roman Empire, was confined to the Mediterranean world and did little more than touch the shores of the Atlantic.

Europe first appears on the stage of world history as a peninsula of Asia. The myth of Europa who flies from the eastern land of Asia and reaches the western land which is called after her, is characteristic of the old conception of the Asiatic origin of European culture. Europe developed in action and reaction in a long conflict with Asia. Eastern cultural and political influences, the wars of conquest in both directions constitute an essential part of the history of Europe.[1] Leaving aside the various migratory movements and clashes between the two continents in pre-history, we need remember only the Greco-Persian wars in the sixth century B.C., the Hellenistic European-Asiatic Empires between the fourth and second centuries B.C., and the great struggle between Rome and Carthage in the third century B.C. We can only conjecture what were the earliest movements in the interior of Asia which are the first known events in the history of the Near East. All later history, however, establishes the fact that the continent of Asia constitutes one single gigantic transmission system whereby movements generated in Central and Eastern Asia affect the extreme limits of the continent. When we consider the Arab wars of conquest (seventh to tenth century), conquest of the Eastern Mongols under Jenghiz Khan (T'uh-mu-chan) in the thirteenth century, of the Western Mongols under

Timor (Timor Lenk, Tamerlan) in the thirteenth to sixteenth century, and finally the wars of the Turks (fifteenth to seventeenth century), we can see plainly the intimate connection between the great migration in Western Asia which arose in Central Eastern Asia.

The Eurasian and transcontinental nature of the Mongol wars may be taken as admitted, for they took place in a relatively short period and left visible results in the shape of the great empires: Qipêâq, Golden Horde, which spread over the area between Lake Balkash to the Volga and even to South Russia (1223–1556); the Mongol Chinese Empire of the Yuan dynasty (1280–1368); and later the Indian Empire of the Great Mogul (1526–1765). Less known is the connection between the Arab and Turkish wars of conquest and the movements inside Central and Eastern Asia.[2]

In the age of the Chinese T'ang dynasty (618–907) there was a very close connection between the Chinese and the Arabian domains. Never before that period was China so intimately connected with the affairs of the Near East. In the first half of the T'ang period China was the great Power of Asia and Chinese westward expansion reached its climax. Now the Chinese westward expansion came into conflict with the victorious expansion eastward of Islam. At that time the western boundary of China reached the Pamirs. Both the Eastern and Western Turks were defeated and subjugated by the Chinese (middle of the seventh century). While these events were taking place in Central Asia there arose in Arabia a great movement of emigration and conquest, which broke forth from that peninsula in every direction. Under the first Khalifs the Sassanid Empire was overthrown by the Arabs, who in this way came into direct contact with the Chinese. Clashes between Chinese troops and the Arabs (the Ta-shih of the Chinese chronicles) begin in the eighth century and end with the decisive defeat of the Chinese in 751 on the Talass river in what is to-day Russian Turkestan. With that defeat the great period (from the foreign political viewpoint) of the T'ang dynasty was over and the decline of China as a Great Power began. She became a battleground for gangs of mercenaries. The Chinese chronicles of this period mention an attack by sea on Canton by the Arabs in 754. This was merely an episode, for Arab expansion in Central Asia apparently was so checked by its encounter with the Chinese that soon afterwards a movement was taken in the opposite direction from east to west. The most significant aspect of that movement is the fact that it was reinforced and carried through by the Turks. In the second half of the ninth century, that is a century after the Chinese defeat on the Talass river, the infiltration of the Turks into the Empire of the Khalifs is quite apparent.[3]

The "Turks," a term by which is meant a mixture of tribes of Mongol, Turkish, and Aryan origin, are in succession to the Huns (Hsiung-un of the Chinese chronicles, second century B.C. to fifth century A.D.), and "Mongols" (Jinghiz Khan to Timur) form the third type of that steppe "imperialism" which plays so tremendous a part in the history of Asia. In the course of the last millennium the Turks thrice emerge as rulers of vast empires with pan-Asiatic ambitions; first, between the middles of the sixth and eighth century, when they ruled a series of territories lying between North China and the eastern frontier of the Byzantine Empire, with its centre in what is to-day Russian Turkestan. This empire was in the eighth century completely dissolved by the Arabs and the Chinese. The nomadic empires possess, however, as does every primitive organism, tremendous power of regeneration. As early as the eleventh and twelfth centuries the Seljuk Empire was founded whose frontier stretched from the Mediterranean to Turkestan. This Asiatic Empire, which already showed a tendency to expand westwards, was defeated by the Crusaders and driven backwards. The nomadic movements from east to west, which may be considered as historic from about the seventh century B.C.—the Cimmerians of the Assyrian inscriptions; the Scythians of Herodotus; and "the Northern horsemen" of

Jeremiah—came to an end only in the fifteenth century (i.e. more than two thousand years later) with the capture of Constantinople in 1458 by the Osmanlis. The later Turkish expedition and the conquests of the Turks in Europe in the sixteenth century (annexation of Hungary in 1541) and in the seventeenth century, are only appendices to these gigantic movements, and have no geopolitical significance of their own. As early as the sixteenth century the great counter-attack by Europe begins, an attack colossal in its nature: the Portuguese appear in the Pacific and the Russians cross the Urals.

The successful offensive of Asia as far as the eastern gates of Europe had, however, a consequence which could not have been foreseen either by the Europeans or by the Asiatics. The Ottoman Turks by their capture of Constantinople, of the whole of the Eastern Mediterranean—between 1512 and 1520 they had conquered Mesopotamia, Syria, Egypt, and Arabia—and of the northern coast of the Black Sea—in 1475 the Krim Tartars recognized the suzerainty of the Sultan—interposed between Europe and Asia (Indo-China) but in very different fashion from their predecessors the Arabs and the Mongols. Here the determining feature is the military character of the Turkish State with its strong tendency to State monopolization and its relatively hostile attitude to private trade. During the period of Arab domination over the Near East the old Central Asian trade routes were carefully tended and traffic on them protected and favoured simply because the Arab States were strongly influenced by the trading bourgeoisie of Asia Minor, and later by the African-Asiatic Jews. The Arabs never had any intention of hindering trade between Europe and Eastern Asia, at the most they sought to interpose as middlemen. Besides, in the first period of Arab domination, up to the tenth century, there was a distinctly greater trade activity between Byzantium, as representative of European culture on the one hand, and India, Turkestan, and China on the other via the northern shores of the Black Sea, through the media of the Khazar Empire, whose greatest period is between the middle second half of the eighth century and the beginning of the tenth century, and of the numerous Jewish factories in South Russia. This route, too, was blocked by the annexation of the Crimea to the Turkish Empire.

The first Mongol domination in the thirteenth century, as is well known, was very favourable to trade between Europe and Eastern Asia, because the pan-Asiatic Empire of Jinghiz Khan made the preservation of the old trade routes one of its primary concerns. The policy of the Mongol rulers was greatly influenced by the bourgeois trading communities of Eastern Turkestan, and those settled at the central point of trans-Asiatic trade routes were intensely interested in the development of relations with the West.

It may even be assumed that the Mongol expeditions to the West had as one aim the opening of new trade routes. After the extension of Ottoman rule the situation radically alters, for, as already stated, the Ottoman State, particularly in the first decade after its foundation, was distinctly indifferent if not actually hostile to European-Asiatic trade. Equally significant, however, is the fact that, although the Ottoman Empire was able to maintain its rule in the Eastern Mediterranean, it was faced with great difficulties in its rear, i.e. in the east of Asia Minor and in Central Asia. One need only remember the victorious wars waged by the Great Han Timur against the Ottoman Sultan Bayezid in the first years of the fifteenth century, and to the conquests of the Persian shah, Abbas the Great, who wrested from the Turks the important regions in Transcaucasia (1607). Thus, even if they had wished, the Ottomans would not have been able to keep open the trans-Asian trade routes. The young European capitalism and the mercantile States thus had to seek new routes in order to maintain trade connections with India and China. And so there now begins the age of oceanic expeditions to discover a sea route to Eastern Asia.[4]

§ 1. THE ENTRY OF EUROPE

One of the most decisive "episodes" in world history was the discovery of America by the two Genoese: Columbus in 1493–1504 and John Cabot (1498), and by the Spaniard Pinson (1500). Cabot was commissioned by Henry VIII to find a north-west passage to Cathay and Tataria, but instead discovered Newfoundland; Columbus, who had hoped on behalf of the sovereigns of Aragon and Castile to plant the standard of Christendom in China and India, believed, inspired by his countryman Toscanelli, that he would reach these lands by a more southerly route. The Portuguese Cabral landed in Brazil at the same time as the Spaniard Pinson, while the French Jacques Cartier sought in 1524–40 to occupy the Canadian coast for France. These discoveries are to be regarded as the first steps in the foundations of those great Atlantic colonial empires which were built up from the fourteenth to the eighteenth century and in the creation of an economic and cultured Atlantic world which reaches its full development in the nineteenth century.

From the very first the European Powers had hoped by conquests oversea to strengthen their position in Europe for those perpetual universal wars which are so characteristic of the early period of modern history. Then, however, it was not a matter so much of actual territorial gains as of obtaining gold, silver, spices, jewels, the possession of which meant a really valuable reinforcement of their political and military position. Thus the Spanish hegemony in the sixteenth century was largely based on the unlimited flow of treasure which came to the treasuries of Charles and Philip II from Peru and Mexico. To fight successfully the Spanish and Austrian Habsburgs the French Valois had to endeavour to get their share of the loot of the "Indias" as very characteristically the possessions in America were called. But the same motive for colonial conquest and gain determined the policies of the other Great Powers of the period, Portugal, Holland, and England.

In the sixteenth and even in the seventeenth century the centre of gravity of the colonial activity of the European States is in America and in the Atlantic region. The oldest and most powerful colonial Power, Spain, had—apart from the occupation in 1564 of the Philippine and Caroline islands—built up the whole of its giant colonial empire in the southern part of North America, in South America, and in the American Mediterranean, the Caribbean. Although it was a Spaniard, Balboa, who was the first to discover the Pacific (1513) and even on behalf of his king annexed it, the Pacific actually was quite unimportant to Spanish policy, and the Philippines were always regarded from their American standpoint as "western isles" (Islas de poniente), while by the Portuguese, whose effort was directed to the Pacific, the Philippines were regarded as "eastern islands" (Islas de oriente). To illustrate the importance of historical connections, it is worth noting that in our days the Philippine islands by the American annexation in 1898 have entered again into the sphere of domination of a Great Power advancing from the west.[5]

The same Atlantic-American conception is visible in the colonial policies of France and England at this period; as late as the Treaty of Utrecht (1715), the centre of gravity of the colonial empire of both France and Britain is the Atlantic, while their possessions in the Indian zone are to be regarded merely as outposts and bases.

As to Portugal and Holland, the situation is rather more complicated. Among all the colonizing nations of this period the Portuguese was undoubtedly that most endowed with a practical geopolitical sense. They looked to the same goal as the other seafaring nations, the discovery of the sea route to the Indies and Cathay, but they were clever enough to direct their colonial policy in a masterly way as a whole with a complexity of aims which they sought to realize with remarkable persistence. The origin of the Portuguese colonial advance is the struggle with the Arabs for hegemony in the Eastern Atlantic, which is the direct continuation of the struggle with them of years earlier in the Iberian peninsula. Prince Henry of Portugal, the seafaring prince, had a double plan, a last crusade against the Muslims, but this time not in the Mediterranean as in the eleventh to the thirteenth centuries, but in the Atlantic and the Pacific, and second and simultaneously the foundation of a "Greater Portugal" on the shores of the Atlantic. The Portuguese were the first of the colonizing nations to realize the importance of controlling both coasts of the Atlantic where they are nearest. As early as the fifteenth century the foundation of a coastal empire was laid in West Africa, from the Pillars of Hercules to Tiger Bay, an empire which actually was a chain of factories whose main concern was the slave trade. The idea of using slave labour for the plantations in America originated in Portugal. At the beginning of the sixteenth century the struggle between the Portuguese and Arab slave-traders in West Africa and the Indian Ocean ended with the victory of the former. Later in the 'thirties of that century, there began the systematic colonizing of Brazil by the Portuguese, and that, be it noted, not as a mere area from which to obtain wealth, but much more, as was later the English method, as a land for settlement with the help of slave labour. In spite of the declaration of independence in 1822, Brazil almost to the end of the nineteenth century was under a Portuguese dynasty, so well laid geopolitically had been the foundations of Portugal's Atlantic empire. As a last relic of that empire Portugal still holds the great West African colony Angola. The colonial policy of the Portuguese—in this respect not unlike the English policy in the next period—it may again be stated, did not confine itself to purely Atlantic aims; rather the Atlantic policy served as basis for a policy of expansion in the Indo-Pacific area. The Portuguese even at the time of Henry the Traveller were the best-informed of all the European nations on the geography of Africa, and had a scheme, somewhat fantastic it is true, but inspired fundamentally by sound geopolitical instinct, for a trans-African route, using the Arab caravan tracks and in part the great rivers of the interior. The

Portuguese schemes to reach the Indo-Pacific area via Africa—it was then believed that the Senegal—the "Western Nile"—rose somewhere near the source of the "Eastern Nile" which was believed to pass through Christian Ethiopia—were actually much more realist than the Italian (Genoese), English, and French schemes of a sea route from the West to India.

That the Portuguese at the very beginning of the age of discovery and colonial conquest had the East in view is seen by the fact that in the division of spheres of influence made by Pope Alexander VI between Spaniards and Portuguese (May 4, 1493), all lands discovered east of an imaginary line one hundred Portuguese leagues to the west of Azores and the Cape Verde isles were to fall to Portugal. The Portuguese expeditions of Bartolomeo Dias and Vasco da Gama (end of fifteenth century) were all in the same direction along the western and southern and then along the eastern coast of Africa to India. The circumnavigation of the globe (1519–22) by Magellan, who was a Portuguese in Spanish service, shows the same world aim to connect the Atlantic and the Indo-Pacific regions. Almeida and Albuquerque, at the beginning of the sixteenth century, signally defeated the Arabs in Africa and took from them their fortified factories on the African coast and in India (Goa in 1510; Malacca in 1511). About the same time the Portuguese appeared on the Spice islands, as the Moluccas were then called, and in 1516–1517, under the leadership of Perestrillo, they reached Canton. In 1551 the settlement of Macao was founded to which Portuguese trade activity remained confined.[6]

Dutch colonial policy in many respects developed on the same bases as did that of the Portuguese. It is, however, only much later that it is important. Dutch sea trade developed in very close contact with the Portuguese, at first in co-operation, afterwards in extreme rivalry. The Portuguese so completely devoted their energy to trade with the Far East that the Dutch merchants were allowed to divert the spice trade—then the most profitable of imports—from Lisbon to other European ports. After the union of Spain and Portugal in 1580 the port of Lisbon was closed to the Dutch, and they were compelled to engage in a stubborn fight with their former partners and find a way of their own to the Spice islands. The Dutch merchants simply followed on the tracks of the Portuguese. Their main aim at this period was to secure the sea route to India and to the Spice islands via the Cape of Good Hope, a route at that time controlled by the Portuguese who had conquered it from the Arabs. In 1602 the Dutch East Indian Company was created. Batavia was founded and within a short period became the most important political and economic centre of the Dutch colonial empire (1613).

About the middle of the seventeenth century the Dutch had realized their aim; the Portuguese were driven from Indian waters, and the route via South Africa was under Dutch control. The Treaty of Westphalia in 1648 forbade Spain and Portugal to use the Cape route to the East, and so compelled them to take the longer and more difficult route via Cape Horn. At this period the Dutch possessions included the most valuable harbours along the route to the Far East, e.g. St. Helena and Mauritius; they occupied the Cape of Good Hope and Ceylon in 1656, and established a chain of factories and bases in the Persian Gulf, and in the capital of the Abbassid Empire, Ispahan, along the Malabar and Coromandel coasts, in Bengal, Burma, Malacca, and Formosa, where, in 1624, they built Fort Zeelandia. Geopolitically their furthest advance southeast to the Australasian islands came between 1606 and 1644, when, in voyages to the east of the Sunda islands, they discovered Australia, Tasmania, and New Zealand. This advance, however, had no permanent results, but it indicated plainly the geopolitical connection between the South China Sea and Australasia.

From the geopolitical point of view the Dutch effort to build up a great Atlantic Empire is equally interesting. Here, too, they were in close contact with the Portuguese. They tried to wrest Brazil from Portugal and succeeded in holding the whole northern coast of that country, including Pernambuco, for over thirty years in their possession. Not until in 1654 did the Portuguese succeed in capturing the last Dutch stronghold in Brazil. How completely the Dutch imitated the colonial methods of the Portuguese is seen by the fact that they, without indeed achieving any permanent success, attempted to establish themselves also on the West African coast (Elmina on the Gold Coast) and very successfully broke the Portuguese monopoly of the slave trade. Only in the middle of the seventeenth century did they meet competition here in the shape of the British Royal African Company (1672). The episode of the Dutch colonization of the North American shores of the Atlantic (New Amsterdam, 1622–74), the actual trade monopoly they enjoyed in the West Indies up to the Navigation Act (1651) had no historical results, and as early as the end of the seventeenth century the Dutch colonial power was on the decline.[7]

In the course of the eighteenth and of the first decades of the nineteenth century the transatlantic colonial empires of the European Powers disappeared with the loss of their possessions in America, and England was the only European colonial Power which succeeded in retaining an important part of its American possessions, but the centre of gravity of the British Empire, too, shifted to the east, and as early as the close of the eighteenth century was within the Indo-Pacific region. The old colonial Powers, Spain and Portugal, lost all their American colonies between 1809–24. It is at this point that we first perceive that phenomenon so important for world history which to-day is called "counter-colonization" and which takes form as early as the Declaration of Independence of July 4, 1774. "Counter-Colonization" is action directed against the endeavours beginning with the dawn of the sixteenth century of the European States to conquer possessions and spheres of influence outside Europe.

Closely connected with the struggle of the Latin American colonies for their independence is another significant document of "counter-colonization"—the message of the President of the United States, James Monroe, on December 2, 1823, which was directed not only against any attempt at further colonization of the American continent, but also against any effort on the part of European States to introduce European "systems" to the American continent. The latter warning was directed to the Holy Alliance and France, while the former was addressed particularly to Russia, which, as is known, then possessed Alaska and dreamed of an advance as far south as California and Hawaii (compare Chap. I). A proclamation issued in 1821 by Czar Alexander I stated Russia's claim in the Oregon region which lay within the spheres of influence of England and the United States, a proclamation which was the occasion of Monroe's message. Extremely significant is the fact that the Monroe doctrine was of European origin and that its proclamation was in fact due to the initiative of the liberal English Foreign Secretary George Canning. At that time England as the greatest manufacturing and trading Power was clearly deeply concerned to prevent either France or Russia seizing a part of the American continent, and so close it to English trade. Paradoxical though it may seem, it may be said that when the Monroe doctrine was announced it was in spirit far more attuned to the conceptions of British capitalism now of mature growth than to those of an American capitalism which was still in its infancy. When in the summer of 1823 Canning addressed to the American Ambassador in London, Richard Rush, a proposition for joint diplomatic action to be taken against any intervention by European Powers in America, his purpose was not only "to redress the balance of the Old World by calling in the New" as he much later put it.[8] What England's real policy was, was by maintaining the territorial *status quo* in South America to maintain that state of things which is later known as the "policy of the open door." To the United States, on the other hand, the principal object was the firm establishment of its dominant position in the New World, and actually the promulgation of the Monroe doctrine has never prevented the United States from increasing its territory on the American continent, even by actual war. At any rate, the maintenance of the independence of the Latin American States throughout the first half of the nineteenth century was a gain to England rather than to America. The co-operation of the two Anglo-Saxon nations here, as often later, was a result of varied and very complicated motives. The collaboration of the same partners in the Far East in our day has the same features.[9]

§ 2. FRANCE AND BRITAIN

The French colonial empire in America shared the same fate as the colonial possessions of the two other Latin nations, Spain and Portugal, but the end came later with this difference, that France was driven from America not as a result of a "counter-colonization" movement, but as a result of war with a competing colonial Power. In the four wars between 1688 and 1763 England, besides winning victories in other parts of the world, completely wiped out French colonial possessions in America (Peace Treaties of Utrecht 1715 and Paris 1763). France was left only a few strong points in the Caribbean Sea and Guiana. At the same time, too (1744–61), France's Indian empire was destroyed by Clive. Nevertheless, these disasters did not end France's activity as a colonial Power; the later creation of a great colonial empire in the nineteenth century shows the extraordinary elasticity and adaptability of French policy.

It is worth noting that the French in their colonial policy, just as did in their times the Dutch and Portuguese, but with much greater stubbornness, clung to the aim of linking up their colonial possessions in the Atlantic with those in the Pacific, and securing the control over the sea routes between the two and between each and France itself. First there was the war for the control of the sea route to India and the Indo-Pacific region between England and France in the period of the Napoleonic Wars. Napoleon's unsuccessful attempts to secure

Malta and Egypt are an episode in this struggle (1798–1800). England in the end succeeded in winning this struggle too.

About the middle of the nineteenth century the two shortest routes to the Indo-Pacific region, via the Cape of Good Hope and via the Mediterranean, were under British control. It is striking proof of the persistence of French colonial ambitions and to the strength of old geopolitical reflexes that throughout the nineteenth century France sought to win a firm position in the Indo-Pacific region itself, and also along the routes leading thereto. One need mention only the occupation of numerous points on the West African coast, on the historic route to the Spice islands, in 1830–70, the annexation of the Society islands in the South Pacific in 1847, and the plans of the Second Empire to secure possession of a Suez canal. The conquest of Madagascar (1883–96) is part of the same policy. The advance by the French from the west towards the Sudan in the last years of the nineteenth century constitutes the last echo of a secular struggle which had been waged by France against the British lines of communication between the Atlantic-Mediterranean region and the Indo-Pacific world (Fashoda, 1898). The French Atlantic colonial empire built up in the nineteenth and twentieth centuries is from the geopolitical point of view only remotely connected with the French empire in the Pacific.

The geopolitical structure of the British world empire was virtually completed at the end of Victoria's reign (1901). By that period the centre of gravity of the British Empire was already within the region of the Indian Ocean with a broad insular zone in the South Pacific. The possessions of the Empire in the Atlantic, in spite of their enormous size, take geopolitically second place in importance. Even the acquisition of the mandated territories through the Versailles Treaty has not altered the fact that the British Empire is based on the Indo-Pacific region. Britain's relations to the Pacific region have passed through several phases. Sixty years after the Spaniard Balboa, Francis Drake was the first Englishman to behold from a peak in Darien not far from the Panama canal of to-day the endless wastes of the Pacific which reached to far Cathay (in 1572). Drake was the first to hoist the English flag on the shores of the Pacific (North California in 1579) and establish a direct line of communication between England and the Spice islands. He was also the first to try out one of the three sea routes to the Indo-Pacific world, that via Cape Horn. The further geopolitical advance by the English into the Indo-Pacific region followed, however, in the track of the Portuguese and the Dutch via the Atlantic route (Cape of Good Hope).

Only when the two shortest routes to the Indo-Pacific region were under British control and when the whole Indian peninsula as a result of the victories of Clive, Warren Hastings (1772–86), and Wellesley (1789–1805) and the liquidation of all French possessions had been brought under British rule did a systematic advance into the Pacific proper begin. In these days when the pace of development is so great and our forgetfulness of the past so ready we must remember that British domination over India, which is not only the very basis of the British Empire, but is the basis of Britain's present position in the Pacific, was seriously contested as late as a century and a half ago. Napoleon's plans for the reconquest of the French colonial possessions in India and the eradication of English influence were in no way fantastic dreams, if we consider that at that time the position of Egypt was very dubious, that in India there were large bodies of native troops under French officers, and that by the possession of Mauritius (which came into English hands only in 1810) France had a magnificent naval base, while England was in no way what she was at the end of the Napoleonic Wars, the supreme Power in India. It was the victory of Trafalgar (October 21, 1805) which freed England finally from the danger of invasion, and India as well as Britain.

British policy in the Pacific in the course of the nineteenth and twentieth centuries contains many elements whose interactions made its development extremely complicated. These elements are: England's position—at any rate until Japan becomes a Great Power and Russia is firmly established on the shores of the Pacific—as the strongest Asiatic Power; England's relations with other Powers with possessions in the Pacific; the general political situation in Europe, and finally British trade interests. It is little wonder that England's policy in the Pacific as a result appears full of contradictions.

When during the Napoleonic Wars, England in 1802 and in 1808 occupied the Portuguese colony Macao, it seemed as though China would have the same fate as India. France had already advanced territorial claims in 1787 in Annam, which was under Chinese rule. Still earlier, in 1670, a Greek, Constantine Phaulcon, contrived to persuade the King of Siam to place himself under the protection of Louis XIV. This extraordinary episode was brought to an end in 1685 by a popular rising as a result of which the French were driven from the country.[10] It is in connection with this that we realize the true significance of the proposal made in 1807 by Lord Hastings to conquer China with an army of 20,000 men.[11] Although this tendency to direct territorial conquest soon gave place to other tendencies, it continued to be latent and appears later on in the somewhat milder form of the "spheres of influence" policy.

The two wars which were waged by England against China about the middle of the nineteenth century (Opium War in 1840–42, Lorcha War in 1857–60) were undertaken for trade reasons and ended (except for Hong-Kong and Kowloon) without any territorial gains being made. Both wars, however, and especially the Lorcha War, which was waged in alliance with France, have many features in common with the wars of conquest waged in India by Clive and Warren Hastings.

Men like Captain Elliot, and still more Major Gordon, were just of the type to realize Hastings's plans. But the general trend of English policy at that time, a policy illustrated by the names of Bright and Cobden, by the trade policy of Robert

Peel (in 1842 and in 1845–46), and, later, by that of Gladstone (in 1853 and 1860), was to place a strong check on further territorial expansion. This was the time when Disraeli summed up Britain's Chinese policy in these words (February 1857): "Fifty years ago Hastings offered to conquer China with 20,000 troops. A man so great as Hastings might have been able to accomplish it, but since the days when Clive and Hastings created our Indian Empire the political situation in the East has undergone radical change. Great Powers have become our neighbours in those regions, the Russian Empire and the American Republic, and there has now developed a system of compromise, similar to the balance of power in Europe; unless the greatest care and most serious consideration is taken in dealing with the affairs of China we shall find in all probability that we have not improved our trade but aroused the jealousy of powerful States."[12]

That, however, naturally did not prevent England either from taking part in the opening up of China to foreign trade, or from advancing the frontier of India in the direction of China. Through the first two wars with Burma, in 1823–28 and 1852, Assam was annexed and the whole valley of the Irawadi with the important harbour of Rangoon. Thus India was brought into direct contact on the one side with Siam, and with Southern China on the other. Still earlier, in 1815, Hastings had brought under English influence the mountain State of Nepal, and the Indian frontier had been advanced to the Upper Sutlej. Thereby India became the direct neighbour of Tibet which was under Chinese sovereignty. Between 1850 and 1861 the small district of Sikkim, situated between Nepal and Bhutan, was annexed. Although as a result of these annexations the Indian Empire was in direct continental touch with so weak and apparently disintegrating a State as China then was, further territorial expansion was hindered by the general tendencies already mentioned of British foreign policy. There were also other factors, mainly as a result of Britain's relations with other Powers, which determined this policy.

After the Napoleonic Wars there began a period of political collaboration between England and France based on the hostility existing between the two Western European Powers on the one side and the reactionary Eastern block, Russia, Austria, and Prussia, on the other. The Franco-English alliance against China in the Lorcha War and during the Taiping rebellion was the result of the anti-Russian alliance during the Crimean War. But the aggressive colonial policy of the Second Empire and the Third Republic (Jules Ferry) as well as the rapprochement now beginning between Paris and St. Petersburg, on the whole brought French policy into conflict with England in the Pacific. Napoleon III in the last years of his reign conceived vast plans for the recovery of France's position in the Western Atlantic and for the restoration of the French influence in the Pacific. Almost simultaneously with the French expedition to Mexico (1862–64) a French fleet under Admiral Rose in the autumn of 1866 undertook an expedition to Korea, which ended in a defeat for the French navy. None the less, just as in Mexico, serious action was intended in reliance on the exhaustion of the United States after the Civil War and the will to peace of England where Gladstone was about to form his first Cabinet (1868–78). But in Mexico and in Korea the French challenge was met with the stout opposition of both England and the United States, and the plans had to be given up without more ado.[13]

More successful was the French colonial expansion at the other end of the Pacific region, on the southern borders of China. Here ever since the 'fifties of last century the French, following up their earlier efforts at the end of the seventeenth and in the course of the eighteenth centuries, were systematically seeking to create an Indo-Pacific Empire in the region between Burma, Siam, and the province of Yunnan in Southern China. In 1858 Saigon, situated in the delta of the great Mekong river which crosses the whole of Hither India, was annexed; Cochinchina was seized from Annam, Cambodia from Siam and Tong-King and Annam were both placed (1874–83) under a French protectorate. In 1884 there came the war with China because she refused to surrender her sovereignty over Tong-King and Annam. By the Treaty of Tien-tsin in 1885 China was obliged to recognize the French protectorate over the whole of Indo-China; somewhat later she had to admit special French rights within the Yün-nan province.

The 'eighties of the last century were pre-eminently the era of remarkable activity in the field of colonial policy. The principles of the free trade school gave place in England to the ideology of imperialism. These were the days (1883) when Seeley's *Expansion of England* and Froude's *Oceana* sought to explain to the nation itself the historical significance of the British Empire, when the Imperial Federation League, the chief exponent of the new ideology, was founded (1884), when men like Joseph Chamberlain, Forster, and Rosebery paved the way for the victory of the ideal of the unity and consolidation of the Empire. In 1882 Egypt was occupied; in 1885, after the third war against Burma, what was left of this old kingdom was incorporated into the Indian Empire, and so the latter became the immediate neighbour of the French in Tong-King on the Upper Mekong.

While France was approaching the Chinese Empire from the South Pacific side, Russia, which was already showing a tendency to co-operate with France in Europe against Britain, was making a series of successive advances, the result of which was on the one hand the encirclement of China from the north, and a threat to British India on the other. Even earlier, in 1865–76, Tashkent, Samarkand, and Kokand were incorporated in the Russian Empire, and Fergana, Khiva, and Buchara placed under the Czar's sovereignty. As a result of these acquisitions, Russia reached the borders of Chinese Turkestan from the west, and at the same time advancing from the north she approached Afghanistan, coming into direct contact with that State by the annexation of the oasis of Merv in 1884. Afghanistan at that time was under British protection, and in 1885 as a result of frontier frictions between Russia and Afghanistan there was acute tension between the two world-Powers which almost ended in war. At the same time relations between Britain and France was strained in Upper Burma.[14]

The rivalry in the Pacific between England and France at that time had a dual aspect. On the one hand there was a rivalry of relative local character and a conflict of interests in South China and Further India. On the other hand there was the general problem which Power was to have supreme influence in China. In the latter case the Franco-English rivalry became a definite conflict between the Dual Alliance, France-Russia on the one side and England on the other.

In Further India the bone of contention was the district situated between the Irawadi and the Mekong. Shortly before his fall, Ferry ventured to propose to England that Upper Burma should be proclaimed a neutral territory between the French and English spheres of influence—England's answer was the annexation of the territory in question. At that period an advance by the French from the valley of the Mekong towards the Indian frontier was seriously feared. The bone of contention was Siam, and in 1893 the two Powers nearly went to war over it; there, too, France appeared to be the aggressor.[15] Only several years later did England succeed through a secret treaty with Siam in removing this kingdom from French influence, and so blocking the way to further French advance westwards from the Mekong valley.[16] The same treaty, too, made it impossible for the French without Britain's consent to build a canal through the isthmus of Kra and so shorten the way from the South China Sea to the Indian Ocean by rendering unnecessary the passage via Singapore.

Just as serious was the tension between England and France in the last years of the nineteenth century over South China. Here, however, much more was at stake. For Britain it was a question of nothing less than the creation of a continental connection between her Indian Empire and the Yang-tse valley, which ever since the early 'fifties of the last century had been looked upon by England as her future sphere of influence. According to the so-called McDonald-Stephenson (1864) Scheme, a scheme had been drawn up of a railway connection between Calcutta and Shanghai via Manipur (Upper Burma)–Tun-nan-fu–Chung-king (on the Upper Yang-tse)–Hankow. Technical commissions were twice dispatched (in 1869 and 1874) from Burma to the Yang-tse valley, but the natural obstacles proved to be so serious that the plan, although never wholly abandoned, was postponed to an indefinite period.[17] This transcontinental British line, Calcutta–Shanghai, has not yet lost its attraction and the old tension remains, though latent.

France now sought to upset these geopolitical railway schemes by proposing counter schemes. Even at the close of the 'sixties of last century the French were sending expeditions to explore the valleys of the Song-bo (Black river) and the Song-koi (Red river) in Tong-King, and to report on the possibility of a railway across Yün-nan to the Upper Yang-tse.[18] The Franco-Chinese Treaty of June 20, 1895, opened to the French several trade centres in Yün-nan and some of the other southern provinces and conceded to them certain rights; moreover, in principle the French were to be allowed to prolong their railway lines to Chinese territory. The following years witnessed a Franco-British conflict for railway concessions in South China. France laid claim to predominant influence in the provinces of Yün-nan, Szu-ch'uan, Kuei-chou, Hu-pei, and Hu-nan, that is to say the whole Yang-tse region. At the end of 1896 French participation in the Belgo-Chinese railway plans for the line Peking–Hankow was secured. At about the same time Russia began the construction of the Transsiberian railways (1891). In the treaty concluded by the Russian Finance Minister with the great Chinese statesman, Li-Hung-Chang (May 1896), Russia was given a concession for the construction of a line across Manchuria connecting Irkutsk and Vladivostok, which, apart altogether from the immediate object of considerably shortening the Transsiberian route, greatly strengthened Russia's position in North China. It was clear that the Dual Alliance, France-Russia, was striving to realize the linking up of the two railway systems—the Russians in North China and the French in South China—by the contemplated Belgo-Chinese Peking–Hankow line. The aim of the two Powers is still more clearly seen by the fact that the plan was to be financed by the founding of the Russo-Chinese (later on the Russo-Asiatic) bank which was to take over the railway concessions and by Franco-Belgian capital[19] (see Map 5 on railway concessions).

The realization of such a connection between the Russian and the French railway systems would have seriously threatened Britain's sphere of influence in the Yang-tse valley and weakened her whole position in China. In this way the conflict between Britain and Russia which threw its shadow over the last twenty years of last century became a dominant factor in Far Eastern politics.

§ 3. RUSSIA AND BRITAIN

But it is precisely the play and counter play in the Asiatic policies of the Great Powers at the end of the nineteenth century that show plainly that in politics there are no permanent friendships or enmities. There are no immanent world political conflicts; the political battlefield constantly changes, and not just from century to century, but even from decade to decade alliances and conflicts change completely. If we may speak of secular conflicts, the conflict between the British and the Russian Empires may be described as such. And yet this conflict is entirely local in character. It is an Asiatic conflict, the conflict between a definitely continental entity which received its political form by a steady colonization movement east and south, and a maritime empire which with its bases on the coasts expanded into the continent, an empire based on a system of maritime strongholds.

The Russian Empire has a tendency to develop eastwards. The demographic centre (the centre of population) of the

Russian Empire has shifted in the course of eighty years (1850–1930) from Kaluga, 36° E. long., to Saratow, 46° E. long., i.e. by 10° or 820 km. The speed of this progress is twice as high as the rate at which the centre of population has shifted in America—408 km. between 1850 and 1920. According to the great Russian scientist, D. I. Mendeleieff, the centre of the inhabitable surface of Russia lies in the neighbourhood of Omsk (74° E. long.). It is obvious that the Russian demographical centre is shifting in the direction of Omsk. Before the Great War Russian industry was essentially concentrated within the European part of the Russian Empire. The textile industry was concentrated in the economic region of Moscow; the heavy iron industry in St. Petersburg and the Ukraine, and coal in the Donetz valley. The Ural industrial area and the Polish were peripheral in character and only of secondary importance. The colonization of Siberia, which, properly speaking, began only in the 'eighties of last century, reached its climax in the course of the seven years preceding the outbreak of the Great War. After the War free emigration to Siberia was checked, but the deportations, especially of wealthy peasants from the interior of Russia to the northern provinces and to Siberia, were on a relatively large scale. Much more significant, however, were the results of the methodical industrializing of the country carried through by the Soviet Government on its Five-Year Plan, one of the main features of which was the establishment of important bases of coal production and of the heavy industries in the Ural and Altai districts. It is not unlikely, as is pointed out by the well-known Russian historian, G. W. Vernadsky, that the triangle the Urals–Lower Volga–Altai will become the scene of the intensive development of Russia's economic life.[20, 21]

In Chapter I it was already shown in detail that the migration of the Russians across the continent led to an attempt to extend Russia overseas.[22] The Behring Sea was to become a Russian inland lake, and Russia's land ambitions on the American north-western coast went as far as to 51° lat.[23] About 1825

Russia and the Spaniards concluded a treaty for the demarcation of their respective spheres of influence in California.[24] This, however, was the climax of Russia's oceanic ambitions. The proclamation of the Monroe doctrine was the first proof of the effort on the part of the United States, supported by England, to drive the Russians from the American continent. With the sale of Alaska in 1867 the dream of a Pacific oceanic empire under Russian rule was brought to an end. Seven years earlier, however, Vladivostok, "the citadel of the East," was founded on the shores of the Sea of Japan. But it was clear from the geographical situation of this stronghold that Russia had abandoned her far-reaching oceanic plans: Vladivostok is in no way a starting-point for oceanic conquest; it is the terminus of a continental development and a defence against possible aggression from the sea.

On the abandonment of her oceanic plans and in the period immediately following the occupation of the Amur province and the Coastal region (Peking Treaty of 1860), Russia maintained in the Far East a position of passive defence. This state of affairs persisted until the 'nineties, when it gave place to lively aggression. If we are to understand the Asiatic—and not only the Asiatic—policy of Russia in the nineteenth and twentieth centuries, it is necessary to grip the fact that that policy developed along a great strategical and political line stretching from Constantinople to Vladivostok. From this long line behind which, between the Carpathians and the Great Hingan (in Manchuria), lie the Eurasian-Russian steppes, there is a tendency to advance south to the "warm seas," i.e. to the Mediterranean, the Indian Ocean, and the Pacific.[25, 26]

The sum total of geopolitical energy shown to obtain these ends is very unevenly distributed in the various periods of development. At one time it is concentrated on one sector of the line; at another on a totally different one. Generally and geopolitically speaking, there are in that line three main sectors closely connected one with the other—the Near Eastern sector, including the whole of the Black Sea coasts and the entrance to the Mediterranean; the Central Asian sector (Persia, Afghanistan, Turkestan); and the Far Eastern sector. In the first decades of the nineteenth century the main effort was made on the most westerly sector. The most important geopolitical aim of Russian policy was the domination of the Balkan peninsula and the straits between the Black Sea and the Mediterranean. That aim was revealed at the end of the eighteenth century by the annexation of the northern coasts of the Black Sea. At that time Russian and British interests were in conflict. In 1844 a secret treaty was concluded between London and St. Petersburg for an eventual partition of Turkey.[27] From that day "the question of the straits" was permanently an order of the day for Russian policy. But by the beginning of the nineteenth century and even earlier appeared the other point of Russia's Asian policy, the advance from the central sector of the line, the advance on India which some decades earlier had become a British possession. Catherine II and Paul I both dreamed of the conquest of India. It is worth noting that the Russians were encouraged in that aim by Paris—Napoleon I in a letter dated February 2, 1808, proposed to the Czar that a Franco-Russian army of 50,000 men should be organized to conquer India.[28]

The advance on the western sector was stopped for a time by the Russian defeat in the Crimean War; the Russian effort was therefore transferred to the central sector to Central Asia. About the beginning of the 'sixties the conquest of the Caucasus was completed. About the same time the Russian advance against Turkestan (see Chap. I) began. Just as England had met the Russian advance in the western sector by creating the Turkish-Sardinian-French-English coalition, so now her reply to the Russian advance in Central Asia was the establishment of her suzerainty over Afghanistan and Baluchistan (1876–80).[29] That is just about the time when the last great British imperialist statesman, then still a young M.P., George N. Curzon, warned his countrymen against the "bear that walks like a man," and saw the destinies of the British Empire find fulfilment in Central

Asia: "Turkestan, Afghanistan, Transcaspia are for me only pieces on a chessboard on which the game for world dominion is being played; the fall of Great Britain will not be decided in Europe but on the continent from which our forebears once came and to which their descendants returned as conquerors."[30]

Three years later, in 1895, a frontier agreement was concluded between Russia and Afghanistan which to some extent put a stop to a further Russian advance in Central Asia; at any rate it created a buffer State between India and the Russian Empire, and so lessened the zone of conflict between the two empires. The geopolitical effect of Russian imperialism meantime shifted to the eastern sector of the line which, as we have said, runs from the Carpathians to Manchuria (see Map 6).

Since the early 'nineties of last century the chief interest of Russian policy was concentrated in the Far East. This development was in the first place due to the fact that the Russian effort on the other two sections of the line weakened, or rather had met serious opposition. We have seen that the effort on the Central Asian sector had been checked by the English counter-effort. A similar state of things resulted in the western sector after the Russo-Turkish War and the Berlin Congress (1878). Here, too, Russia's effort to press southwards had met an English counter-effort, and had not been able to make headway against it. Britain once again succeeded in building an anti-Russian coalition which appears ten years after the Berlin Congress as the three-Power alliance called "Eastern Triple Alliance" between Italy, Austria-Hungary, and Britain (1887). Russia realized that in the Balkans she was faced by a combination of forces too strong for her to overcome. Hence the self-abnegation of the Russian statesmen which is seen so plainly in the treaty signed in 1897 between Russia and Austria; while Russia was making her forward effort in the Far East, she must have nothing to fear in her rear in Europe.[31]

It sounds, perhaps, paradoxical, but it is nevertheless true that the advance of the Russian steam roller between 1890 and 1904 in Northern China and in Manchuria was defensive in character. After the Russian ambitions for a vast oceanic empire had been frustrated by the Anglo-Saxons, the question for Russia was whether she could continue to be the possessor of a strip of the Pacific coast, that is to say a Pacific Power. In the world history the failure of a great plan very often means the loss of the position which was its base. The Russian offensive in the fifteen years preceding the outbreak of the Russo-Japanese War aimed at making secure the gigantic colonial and raw-materials area between Lake Baikal, the Amur, and the Kamchatka peninsula which was threatened not only by the continental Mongolian counter-colonization, but, possibly throughout a somewhat remote future, by American colonization. The plans advanced by the Americans in this period for a North Pacific railway connection from Yukon to the Lena river and the Baikal lake by tunnel under the Behring Straits, fantastic as they may seem, do in fact represent a serious attempt on the part of America to "encircle" the Behring Sea—just as the Russians had planned to do from the opposite direction and failed—and possibly the whole of the North Pacific region. The present strategico-economic aims of the United States regarding the Commodore islands, which are to be transformed into a first-class world traffic centre, the concessions granted to Americans in Kamchatka, the recent conflict between the Soviet Union and Canada over Wrangel land, which can become of great importance as a landing station on the North Pacific air lines—all these are aspects of the struggle to "encircle" the Behring Sea.[32, 33]

In spite, however, of its—from the geopolitical point of view—purely defensive character, the Russian advance in Eastern Asia in itself as far as the other great Asiatic Powers seemed definitely offensive and dangerous, quite apart from the fact that geopolitical defensive movements, if successful, generally develop into a great strategical offensive. It is worth noting that in this period Russia saw herself once again opposed by the same Anglo-Saxon front which in the past had frustrated her vast plans in the Pacific. Not only Britain but also the United States felt itself threatened by the expansion of Russian influence in the Far East.

When in 1902–3 Russia refused to withdraw from Manchuria, an Anglo-American–Japanese front came into being for a time and took up a more or less definitely hostile attitude to Russia. American gunboats in the winter of 1901–2 lay in the bay of Niuchwang, which was in Russian possession.[34] But the real inspirer of opposition to Russian ambition was once again England. Somewhat earlier, at the end of 1899, Joseph Chamberlain, then Secretary for the Colonies in the Salisbury Cabinet, in a conversation with Buelow, then German Foreign Minister, summed up the geopolitical conflict between the two Asiatic Great Powers in the following manner. "He (Chamberlain) entertains no illusions whatever on the fact that Russian influence in China is increasing. He sees with uneasiness how the Russians, in contrast to the English, are able to assimilate the Asiatics. He thinks that a time may come when hundreds of thousands of Chinese and Tartars armed with Russian rifles, and drilled and led by Russian officers, would reinforce the Russian army. To oppose such a force England has no army. . . . England is not in the position to occupy more than she has in Asia. A second 'India' on the Yang-tse would be beyond England's strength. England could not, however, accept to be driven out of China and Persia by Russia. It is in England's interests that China, Persia, and Turkey should continue to exist. Whether this would be possible for long is, however, doubtful. These countries are like empty bags which cannot stand without a support."[35]

Here the outlines of the geopolitical tension between these two world-Powers are quite clearly sketched. Against the line of the Russian offensive from Constantinople to Port Arthur is opposed the English defensive line from Alexandretta to the mouth of the Yang-tse via the Hindu-Kush (see Map 6). That Chamberlain's view was not a mere *ad hoc* utterance but the expression of a far-sighted policy based on deep conviction is seen by the fact that Salisbury's successor Balfour, three years later, when it came to a frank exchange of views between the two Powers, used practically the same terms. The geopolitical definition of the British world sphere of influence —Alexandretta–Hindu-Kush–mouth of the Yang-tse, which we have just mentioned—is taken from a statement by Balfour made at the end of 1902.[36]

The tension between Britain and Russia which overshadows world politics from 1894 to 1904 is a typical case of a modern imperialist conflict. But equally t pical for this tension is, however, the steady desire for compromise so as to bring about a balance of interests. This tendency appears most strongly in London. At the beginning of 1898, at a moment when there was a serious crisis in Franco-British relations, Salisbury approached the St. Petersburg Cabinet with an offer for the division of spheres of influence in China within the framework of a comprehensive Asiatic settlement. Salisbury offered Russia in China much more than she could possibly have expected. Russia was to receive as her sphere of influence the valley of the Huang-ho and the territory situated to the north of it, while England was to have the Yang-tse valley.[37] At the same time at the other end of the great geopolitical line Russia was to come nearer the attainment of her old aim: the occupation of the Straits. The Bosphorus and the Dardanelles as well as the ports of Asia Minor, whose rivers flow into the Black Sea, plus the Euphrates valley as far as Bagdad, were to be considered a Russian sphere of influence, with the prospect later of becoming part of the Russian Empire if Turkey finally was partitioned.[38] This offer by Salisbury, which must be taken as a serious one, was directed principally against France, but also against Germany which at this time was very obviously seeking to insinuate herself between the Russian and British spheres of influence in the Near and in the Far East. It is no accident that there is an interval of only two years between the conclusion of the treaty on the construction of the Bagdad railway (December 1899) and the seizure of Kiautschou

(November 1897). There was a possibility of the creation of a German sphere of influence—running from Berlin via Vienna and Constantinople to the Persian Gulf, and even to the Pacific—which would interpose between the two world-Powers. That central position of the German sphere of influence in Eurasia corresponding to Germany's central position in Europe and in harmony with the general line of German policy, was intended to strengthen her world position. Actually, as we know now, it was what most weakened it. Instead of either acting as broker between the two States, or playing them off against each other for her own ends, Germany estranged them both, and finally brought about their alliance against her.

What is important is the fact that Russia felt herself at the time to be so strong in the Far East that she could calmly reject the English offer. In her rivalry with England, Russia based her policy on good relations with China which then needed Russian support against the rapidly expanding Japan (secret treaty between Witte and Li-Hung-Chang, May 1896, which amounted to an alliance).[39] Russian policy found further support in the combination of Great Powers which came into existence immediately after the peace of Shimono-seki and is, though without much reason, styled Far Eastern Triple Alliance. This Triple Alliance, which on Russia's initiative was adhered to by France and Germany while England definitely declined, was directed against the exaggerated claims made by Japan on the Peking Government after the Chinese defeat in 1894–5.[40] In the preliminary peace of Shimono-seki (April 1895) Japan was to be granted, if not absolute, at any rate preponderating influence in South Manchuria, and so would be able to assert a great influence on the weak Government in Peking. This would have meant a complete check to the Russian plans, which aimed at the acquisition of a more or less exclusive control of North China. By playing off the Cabinets of Paris and Berlin against each other, Russia succeeded in securing the co-operation of both in intervention against Japan, an action which manifestly could have no practical value either to France or to Germany. Japan, as is known, had substantially to reduce her claims. But from that time England felt herself isolated in the Far East while the Russian and Japanese spheres of influence came into direct contact.

From 1895 English policy had sought to secure a compromise with Russia, and when this proved unattainable, England began to look for allies against Russia in the Far East and elsewhere. As possible allies only Japan and Germany came into consideration. But Germany was too absorbed in Europe, and as a result of her central position there had to be very circumspect where Russia was concerned. Besides, Germany then felt herself strong enough to make England pay heavily for any assistance given her in the Far East. Tentative approaches by Britain in Berlin in 1898, three months after the offer to Russia of a general Asiatic settlement, were coolly rejected. Britain had no other course except to take Japan as ally.

The tension between Russia and Japan which now occupies the foreground instead of the conflict between Russia and Britain, and which from the beginning of this century was the main factor in Far Eastern politics, is, by its very nature, in contrast to the antagonism between the Russian and British world-Powers, purely local in character. This local character of the Russo-Japanese tension, which still exists to-day, ought not, however, to blind one to the fact that in Japan's counter-offensive against Russia there is visible in a sense the consequence of that oceanic counter-offensive which (vide supra, pp. 78, 113) in the middle of the nineteenth century compelled Russia to abandon her far-reaching plans of transoceanic expansion. Japan may be regarded as an outpost of the two Anglo-Saxon sea-Powers, but is also a factor which has developed tendencies directed against the Asiatic mainland as a result of its own individual will.

§4. THE EXPANSION OF JAPAN—FIRST PHASE

The key to the understanding of the historic destiny of Japan lies in the recognition of its dual position as an isolated oceanic island on the one hand, and an island geopolitically linked up with the mainland on the other. One may see an analogy here with the modern history of England and of her relations with the European continent. In Japan's history, too, there are periods when events on the continent are of overwhelming concern, and again periods of "splendid isolation." According to the great majority of historians, the dominant race in Japan came from the colonization of the Japanese islands in the prehistoric period, which was probably a consequence of the great Transpacific immigrations and wars of conquest. This northward migratory movement brought the ancestors of the modern Japanese into the area dominated by Chinese culture which for centuries maintained its domination over the islanders. In the seventh and eighth centuries of our era in the period of the great T'ang dynasty in China, Japan took the whole of her culture ready-made from China. Korea for a long period was the bridge between the Japanese islands and the Chinese mainland. The development of the relations between the three States, to be more correct the three complexes—neither China nor Japan, nor, and especially, Korea, could for long periods be regarded as unified—constitutes a substantial portion of the history of the North-western Pacific.[41]

It is safe to say that the fundamental tendency of Japanese foreign policy up to the Medji era was a defensive one. That is true of Japan's relations with the continent and with the ocean-area. The island State, the result of a Southern Malayan colonization, was later colonized, ethnographically and culturally from the West, i.e. from the continent. Not only was the form of government (Tai-kwa reforms of A.D. 645) and the religion (in A.D. 621 Buddhism in its Chinese form of Mahayana was proclaimed as the State religion) taken over from the West, but even in the prehistoric period the islands received a stream of immigrants from the continent which added to the Malay nucleus the strong Mongolian element.[42] The overwhelming influence of Chinese culture did not arouse a natural reaction until the eighteenth century, a reaction which stood for a return to the original elements in Japanese life.

The episodic invasions of the continent undertaken by the island kingdom had no enduring result, although from them one can deduce the lines of Japan's continental development later on. In the seventh century the Japanese first invaded in Korea in alliance with the Chinese. This campaign as far as Japan was concerned was defensive in character, but it is an established fact that the southern end of the peninsula for a time was under Japanese rule until they were driven out, partly by a Korean reaction and partly by the Chinese. In the next conflict, when the Mongolian-Chinese Emperor Hubilai in the thirteenth century twice tried to conquer Japan, Korea was again used as a base for strategic operations. The Japanese succeeded in decisively defeating the Chinese by sea, with the result that the geopolitical offensive of the *Mongolian* continent against the island kingdom was once and for all shattered. That continental offensive was resumed six centuries later by the Russians.

The expedition undertaken by the great predecessor of the Tokugawa Shoguns, Toya-tomi Hide-yoshi (1536–98), who was the first Japanese statesman to recognize the broad geopolitical significance of the problem facing the island kingdom and sought to win for Japan absolute dominion in China and Korea, is also only an episode. What Hide-yoshi aimed at was fundamentally not very different from the aim pursued by the Great Han Hubilai, although he was advancing in the opposite direction; not the "pirates of the steppes" but the "pirates of the seas" were to be masters of Eastern Asia. The moment chosen by the Japanese invader was clearly favourable. The Ming dynasty was already in decline, and as always happens in the history of Chinese dynasties, was now showing obvious signs of decay. On her south-western frontier China was feeling the powerful forward effort of Burma and Siam which both were then rising to the rank of Great Powers. Since the beginning of the seventeenth century the pressure of the Manchus from the north-east had become even more dangerous, and forty-six years after the death of Hide-yoshi China fell for the second time under the rule of the "pirates of the steppes" (1644). Yet the island Emperor Hide-yoshi did not succeed in his attempts to conquer China and Korea, while his contemporary, Philip II of Spain, the master of the European continent, failed in his attempt to conquer the island State of England.[43]

It is also well worth noting that at this time the Chinese-Korean fleet was superior to the Japanese. The continental Powers were technically ahead of the insular; the Korean ships were protected against fire by iron plates. In the thirteenth century, during the Mongolian war against Japan, the Japanese fleet had controlled the sea.

In Asia, too, the old rule about the decisive influence of sea power on strategy holds good.

In the medieval and modern history of Japan we have to deal not only with continental tendencies and efforts, but also with attempts to create an oceanic empire. But while Japan's continental action, whether offensive or defensive, is confined to definite periods and so can be easily studied, we find when we try to study her oceanic action that we have to deal with tendencies which can hardly be distinguished as they develop beneath the surface of the political history. Yet to understand these is important, for when the situation was favourable as in the Medji and Sho-iva periods the area of Japan's imperialist activity extended from the Gulf of Tartary in the north to the Carolines in the south.

The oceanic effort follows two directions. On the one hand is the Satsu-ma district, the southern end of the island Kyû-shû, whose dai-myo (feudal princes) used to send out piratical expeditions against China in the fourteenth and fifteenth centuries, which is revealed as the base for an advance southwards in the direction of Formosa. In 1609 there was something like an occupation of the Liu-chiu islands (Ryû-kyû) by the nobles of Satsu-ma; from that time we may speak of a Chinese-Japanese condominium in this group. We hear, too, of further incursions from Satsu-ma to Formosa. At any rate the Satsu-ma lords had fortified strongholds in the big Sunda islands and all over the Malay Archipelago, and withdrew from them only about the beginning of the seventeenth century under the pressure of the invading Portuguese and Dutch. All their conquests produced no enduring results; they point, however, to one of the geopolitical directions of the Japanese attempt at expansion.

The second line of oceanic expansion had as starting-point the southern end of Tse (on the main island Hon-do) and followed a south-easterly direction to the main islands in the Fuji line, Bonin (Munin-to), Vulkan (Tsu-shima), and as far as the Mariannes. Here, too, the old urge was the forerunner of a concrete geopolitical development.[44]

Soon after the great expedition of Hide-yoshi, Japan fell, as far as foreign policy is concerned, into a long slumber (1636–1854), from which she was awakened at last by the guns of the American and English ships. This is certainly one of the most singular cases of complete and deliberate self-isolation of a great nation in a period when in its immediate neighbourhood decisive changes in world politics were taking place.[45] But even before Perry, an attempt was made from another direction to waken the Japanese from their sleep; from the beginning of the nineteenth century the Russians, in the course of their efforts to create an oceanic empire, knocked loudly at the doors of the Island Empire. The expedition of Resanoff in 1804, the seizure of the northern part of Sakhalin in 1806, the armed landing on Japan's northern island, Yeso, in 1807, the expedition under Golowin in 1810—all these assaults from the North Asiatic mainland then occupied by the Russians are simply forerunners of the much more serious attempts of Russia to establish herself directly in the Japanese sphere.[46] The

United States President Fillmore's dispatch of Commodore Matthew G. Perry to Japan (1852–4) was on the one hand an attempt to put a check to the activities of Russia in the Far East at a time when she was hard pressed as a result of events in the West, and on the other to take advantage of England's Crimean difficulties and adopt an independent attitude in the Pacific. Later we shall discuss the far-reaching plans of a section of American politicians at the time of Perry's expedition. In spite of the shock which Japan received from Perry's appearance and from the treaties subsequently forced on her by the United States and other Powers, the natural mistrust of her people took a sound view of the situation and saw the real danger not in the maritime conflict with America and England, but in the relations with Russia, which was now superseding China as the Great Power in North Eastern Asia.

From the 'fifties of the last century to the outbreak of the Russo-Japanese War there was an uninterrupted series of Russian aggressions in the Japanese sphere which are no longer mere episodes, but must be regarded as parts of one definite plan. The Russian admiral Putiatin suggested to Commodore Perry in 1853 jointly to "open up" Japan.[47] At the time of the Crimean War and the Lorcha War we note certain attempts by the Russians to secure a *rapprochement* with the United States; and which led to something like collaboration, although the Americans always maintained a certain reserve.

By a treaty between Russia and Japan concluded in January 1855, the condominium in Sakhalin was confirmed and the frontier through the Kurile islands was demarcated. In 1859 the conqueror of the Amur, Muravieff, appeared with a squadron in the harbour of Yeddo and demanded the surrender of the whole of Sakhalin.[48] In 1861 Captain Birileff seized Tsu-shima on the Straits of Korea, the most important naval base between South Korea and Japan. The Russian claim to control the Sea of Japan and the consequent direct threat to the very existence of the island kingdom was now brutally clear. The Russian offensive was checked, however, not by weak Japan, but by

England, which controlled the seas: an English squadron appeared off Tsu-shima and threatened to stay there as long as the Russians did. That was enough to compel Birileff to withdraw. This episode is characteristic of a period when discussions were alleged to be in progress between England and France, the allies of the Crimean War, on a plan for dividing up Japan. At any rate Birileff claimed that in occupying Tsu-shima his motive was to anticipate the English or the French. The same situation arose again in 1885 when the Russians seized Gensan (Port Lasareff) in the north-east of Korea, whereupon the British replied by the immediate occupation of Port Hamilton on the Straits of Korea.[49] The Russian offensive in the period of the "opening up" of Japan culminated in 1875 in the imposition of a partition treaty whereby the whole of Sakhalin was assigned to Russia and the Kurile islands to Japan. About the same time Russia took advantage of the Satsu-ma rebellion and the proclamation by the rebellious admiral Eno-moto of the Yezo Republic in 1872, to make an attempt on Hakodate.[50] From this time we may date the beginning of the Japanese counter-offensive. Characteristically enough the first phase of the Japanese counter-offensive develops in the two directions laid down by history and geopolitically justified towards the mainland and towards the ocean. The island kingdom, its self-isolation forcibly ended, looked now to the neighbouring continent; in 1873, on Japan's initiative, political and trade relations were re-established with China.[51] Between 1873 and 1875 a powerful party (the Satsu-ma under Saigo Taka-mori) sought to settle accounts with Korea by war. They did not carry their point; the moderate party under Oku-bô decided for peace, a decision which provoked serious internal trouble ending in the Satsu-ma rebellion and the murder of Oku-bô on May 14, 1878. Oku-bô was the victim of extremists in the sphere of foreign policy just as later statesmen who pursued a moderate foreign policy were to fall victims to a similar faction—Oku-ma (1889), Ito (1909), and in our days Inu-kai (1932) and Taka-hashi (1936).[52]

By dispatching a squadron Japan finally succeeded in compelling Korea to open her gates to foreign trade (1875–6); thus the Asiatic island State, twenty years after it had been "opened up" by the Americans, used the same method towards another Asiatic nation. By this action, Japan set out on the path of imperialism, on which she had been compelled to embark by the white nations, for here, as always, she was faced by the alternative: to swallow, or to be swallowed. We may also note that the first State to follow the Japanese to Korea was the United States, which, since the 'sixties, had been endeavouring to "open up" Korea. Thus again the Japanese appear as an outpost of the maritime Powers. The Japanese welcomed American interest in Korea for they hoped to use it to obtain their chief aim, the separation of Korea from China.[53]

Of much greater geopolitical significance was the Japanese maritime expansion in the same period which secured the island State from the side of the ocean and put in its possession, so to speak, the keys of its own home. Between 1876 and 1879 the Japanese ended the condominium with China in the Ryû-kyû group and incorporated it in their empire. These islands constitute a natural prolongation of the Japanese islands; they cut the East China Sea and the mouth of the Yang-tse (Shanghai) off from the ocean, and so have a great strategical value. Directly linked with this annexation was the announcement of Japanese claims to Formosa. Almost simultaneously with the annexation of Ryû-kyû the sea-frontier problem at the other end of the Japanese islands was settled. Sakhalin was ceded to Russia while the Kurile islands became Japanese territory (1875). The main outlines of Japan's oceanic empire in the north-south direction are already clearly visible even at that period of Japan's weakness. In the south-western direction oceanward of the Fùji line, the Bonin and Vulkan groups were occupied (1876–91) and Japan thus came considerably nearer the future German possessions in the South Pacific. In this direction, too, the geopolitical line of Japanese expansion is clearly seen. The oceanic expansion of Japan in the preparatory period—we may describe the period between 1871 (the year when the Sino-Japanese Treaties (ratified 1873) were concluded) and 1890 (when the Russians renewed their advance on the mainland) as a preparatory period in which the necessary bases for the future struggle into the two continental Powers of Eastern Asia, China and Russia were slowly built up—coincides in time with the period when Russia was deeply involved in Central Asia and the Balkans and France after the defeat of 1870–71 was busy consolidating her colonial empire in Africa and Further India. Japan used Britain's opposition to these two Powers to assure her ocean glacis. The Franco-Russian Dual Alliance which was formed at the end of the period (1891), and which was alleged to be formed exclusively against the military alliance of the two Central European empires, had to stand the test primarily against Japan, but also against England when it, most unexpectedly reinforced by Germany, appeared as in the Eastern Triple Alliance at a very tense moment in Far Eastern history (vide supra, p. 131). The driving force in this combination, which in any case was temporary, was of course Russia, but Japan never forgave either Germany or France for being the allies of her most dangerous enemy at that crisis in her history. That France was not disinclined to give her Further Indian Empire an oceanic extension is, besides, sufficiently indicated by the fact that in the course of the Sino-French War (1884–5), the French fleet under Admiral Courbet blockaded Formosa and occupied a part of the island as well as the Pescadore (Pê'ng-hu) group. Only on the conclusion of peace did France, partly owing to the pressure by England, withdraw from these islands which, ten years later, were to be incorporated in the Japanese Empire.[54]

§ 5. THE EXPANSION OF JAPAN—SECOND PHASE

The next phase of expansion, as well as the struggle which was part of it with the two continental Powers, is much better known. One thing must be said as preface; neither in the period between 1890 and 1904 nor later can we say that a military conflict between continental Powers and the island State was an inevitable development. A compromise was just as likely and as possible as an armed conflict. There were equally all sorts of possible alliances. The continental Powers, Russia and China, could indeed combine against Japan, but an alliance of one of them with Japan against the other continental Power was just as possible. What was inevitable was the geopolitical framework in which the historical events took place. Their course within these limits was, however, affected by various and arbitrary factors.

Japan made herself an East Asian Great Power by the two wars of 1894–5 and 1904–5, which were both preventive wars; both were waged against the same adversary, fought on identical strategic principles and with the same purpose. The real adversary in both wars was Russia, although in the first war she was not directly involved, and the real object of both wars was Korea and the control of the Sea of Japan.

Korea in the 'eighties and the 'nineties was not just an object of conflict between China and Japan; she was also the battlefield on which Russia, England, France, and the United States measured each other's strength. In 1884 Korea negotiated with Russia a secret agreement whose purpose was nothing less than the establishment of a Russian protectorate over Korea. It seems that at first Li-Hung-Chang was not disinclined to give his blessing to this agreement in order to play off Russia against Japan.[55] This is the period of the episode of the occupation of Gensan (Port Lazareff). On May 19, 1891, the heir presumptive to the Russian throne, the future Nicholas II, inaugurated the construction of the Ussuri section of the Transsiberian railway dangerously near the Korean frontier. The conclusion of the Franco-Russian Alliance enormously strengthened Russia's position in East Asia. Once the Transsiberian railway was finished, Russian influence in Peking, already very great, would be invincible. Japan therefore decided on a preventive war in order to shatter Russian influence in Peking and Seoul before it was too strong. The campaign in the autumn and winter of 1894–5 was simply a dress rehearsal for 1904–5. In both wars Japan from the outset of hostilities held a well-nigh undisputed control of the Yellow Sea and the Sea of Japan.

The intermezzo of Shimono-seki (April 17–May 18, 1895) with the temporary Triple Alliance which caused it, showed that the influence of the Russian Government in China and Korea was not so easily destroyed. Paradoxically enough, Japan's offensive on the continent resulted for the moment only in an expansion of her oceanic empire by the long desired acquisition of Formosa and the annexation of the Pescadores in the Marshall group (on the extension of the Fuji line: Bonin–Vulkan), while on the mainland itself Japan acquired nothing. In Korea, where Chinese influence was finally destroyed, there came into existence a vague Russo-Japanese condominium; practically, however, the Russian influence there was all-powerful until 1897; even in 1899 Russia sought to bring the South Korean port of Ma-sam-pho under her exclusive influence. In 1896 the secret agreement between St. Petersburg and Peking, the so-called Li-Lobanoff convention, was concluded whereby Northern Manchuria was surrendered to Russian influence and a Russian protectorate was virtually established over the whole of North China. One must not exaggerate, however, the consequences of the Russian advance in East Asia; then, as later, there were two main camps at the St. Petersburg Court. The first represented by Witte, who may also be regarded as the representative of the Franco-Belgian capitalists who had taken so prominent a part in financing the construction first of the Transsiberian and then of the Chinese Eastern Railway, professed a long-term policy and aimed at the "peaceful" penetration of North China and Korea. Far-reaching political aims were to have first a solid economic basis. A close economic and political collaboration with Peking was proposed, the result of which would be the inclusion of North Manchuria and North Korea in the Russian sphere of influence.[56] From this point of view the occupation of Port Arthur and Dalny (March 1898) was a mistake.

The other camp, composed of the military and Court circles, stood for the policy of the "mailed fist" and demanded vigorous action in both directions, towards the Yellow Sea and South Manchuria as well as towards Korea. As late as the end of the nineteenth century, it would still have been possible in the actual phase of development to demarcate Russian and Japanese spheres of influence just as it was later before and after the Great War, and still is to-day. Thus in April 1898, through the influence of far-seeing elements at both Courts, a treaty was concluded whereby Korea was handed over to Japanese influence, while Manchuria was recognized as essentially a Russian sphere. This agreement was, however, only an episode; neither of the contracting parties felt bound by its limitations, and Russia especially never really gave up her claims to domination in North Korea.

The war of 1904–5 was a continuation of the war of 1894–5, but the diplomatic position was much more favourable to Japan, so that its issue appeared literally as the first stage in the development of a Japanese continental empire. Here we must again note that the war of 1904–5 was in no way inevitable; the situation abounded with possibilities of compromise. The chief historical event between the peace treaty of Shimono-seki and the outbreak of the Russo-Japanese War is the conclusion of the Anglo-Japanese Alliance on January 30, 1902, whereby at a stroke the whole world political situation changed to Japan's advantage. This treaty, however, which marks an epoch in the history of Asia and in the history of world politics, was preceded and followed by negotiations from which one thing clearly emerges, that the legend of "encirclement"—in this case the encirclement of Russia—is to be accepted in the case of Asia too *cum grano salis*. In fact, in England as well as in Japan at this very time, powerful influences were at work to bring about an understanding with Russia. As far as Japan is concerned, there is clear evidence of a difference of opinion since the days when she was forcibly "opened up." In Tokio not only was the possibility of an *entente* with Russia used as a means of bringing pressure to bear on London, but actually serious negotiations went on with St. Petersburg for a partition of the respective spheres (Ito's visit to St. Petersburg in the autumn of 1901). It was with heavy hearts that the Japanese statesmen decided for the alliance with Britain as may be gauged from the fact that we have reliable evidence to show that in order to force the alliance through against Ito, who was the champion of an *entente* with Russia, the Prime Minister Katsura and the Foreign Minister Komura threatened to resign in December 1901.[57] This notable episode plainly indicates the great dividing line in Japanese policy and particularly in Japanese foreign policy. For in Japan it is the foreign political problems which shape the life of the nation and it is in that sphere that it is seen how decisively the whole existence of the country depends on the lands that surround it.

The revolution with which the modern history of Japan really begins, and since which it becomes possible to speak of a "Japanese foreign policy," already showed the names in which the foreign political fate of the country would be settled. The two opposing parties there—the Jo-i-to, the "Anti-barbarian" party, and the Kai-koku-to, the "progressive" party which favoured the opening up of Japan—which finally settled the issue by civil war, fought first and foremost on a foreign political issue. For internal reform, which in the end was carried through by the Jo-i-to, was based on the need to be strong foreign politically. In the "preparatory period," when the first stones of the proud empire were being laid, we again find the old battle between the moderates in foreign policy of the Oku-bô type and radicals of the stamp of Saigo Taka-mo-ri (vide supra, p. 138). In the period between the two continental wars, there sprung up between the old feudal clans, Satsu-ma and Cho-shu, a conflict which even to-day affects Japanese foreign policy. The conclusion of the alliance with England was a victory for the Cho-shu party and its venerable leader, the hero of the Sino-Japanese War, Field-Marshal Yama-gata. The Cho-shu clan with its domains near and in closer proximity to Korea and the straits controlled the army. Its victory meant a victory for that view of foreign policy which sought support from the oceanic Powers and the use of the mailed fist, on the continent in the first place, against Russia. This tendency was predominant until the death of Yama-gata (1922). Since the Washington Conference the other tendency, the policy of the Satsu-ma clan, which controls the navy, has gained ground, as we shall show later. But the policy of the Cho-shu and Yama-gata is not dead. After the victory over Russia and the Treaty of Portsmouth (August 1905), which was concluded by the mediation of England and the United States, and which fully recognized Japan's status as a continental East Asiatic Power and an Asian Great Power, successful efforts were made for a *rapprochement* with Russia. Here it was the original exponent of the mailed-fist policy against Russia, Katsura, who took the lead (second Katsura Cabinet 1908–11, third Katsura Cabinet December 1912).

During the years between the Portsmouth Treaty and the outbreak of the Great War a *rapprochement* between Japan and Russia was accomplished, a *rapprochement* which can only be explained by thc alterations in the international political situation. It was on the one hand conditioned by the new attitude England adopted towards the Dual Alliance, a change caused by the Delcassé policy, and on the other was a result of the antagonism between Japan and the United States, which became evident in the decade before the Great War. Between 1906 and 1913 there was real tension between Japan and America as a result of the Californian immigration laws. In the same period we may note a *rapprochement* between China and the United States, and an American attempt to secure influence in continental Asian affairs. In November 1909 the American Secretary of State, Knox, proposed the neutralization of the railway and the whole economic system of Manchuria by placing them under an international commission, a proposal on the lines of the Hay doctrine (vide infra, p. 153) of the "open door." Washington's policy was opposed by China's two territorial neighbours, Japan and Russia, who, having measured their strength in war, now, on the basis of the existing balance of power, quite openly sought the partition of the northern part of the Far East.

The four Russo-Japanese agreements which were concluded in the period between the Portsmouth Treaty and the outbreak of the Russian Revolution, the agreements of 1907, 1910, 1912, and 1916, amount actually to a Russo-Japanese alliance. Especially significant was the agreement of July 4, 1910, which, to the exclusion of any third Power, delimited the Manchurian spheres of influence and provided for the close co-operation of Russia and Japan throughout the whole of the Far East. Secured by this agreement, which was manifestly directed against the American plans in Manchuria, Japan announced the formal annexation of Korea on August 22, 1910, and by the agreements of October 21, 1912, and May 25, 1915, recognized the Russian protectorate over Outer Mongolia.[58] During the Great War a secret treaty was concluded in Petrograd between the two empires, the so-called Sazonoff-Motono convention of June 20, 1916, which was virtually an offensive and defensive alliance; an alliance which was directed frankly against the United States.[59]

The *rapprochement* between Russia and Japan after 1904–5, the final stage of which was an alliance, supplies yet again a proof that there is no such thing as eternal friendship or eternal enmity among the peoples, and that within the given geopolitical and historical framework any sort of combination is possible. The *rapprochement* between the two Asiatic Great Powers was carried through under British auspices and within the framework of that new system of alliances which England was then building up. For London the alliance with Japan was in no sense the last word in her Asian, much less her world policy. We have already told how Tokio had been for a time hesitating between London and St. Petersburg. In London, too, both before and after the conclusion of the alliance with Japan, the possibility of finally bringing Russia into the new system of alliances had never been forgotten. At the same time there began negotiations with France (Cambon, Delcassé) which aimed at nothing less than the transformation of the two Dual Alliances, the Asiatic and the European, into a quadruple alliance directed in the first place against Germany, but whose further aim was the control of the whole Western Pacific, and so a world supremacy.[60] It was only the opposition of the Czarist Empire, over-confident in her strength, which prevented that aim being realized until defeat in Manchuria and off Tsu-shima made her ready to accept the English system of alliances. That the Quadruple Alliance, however, later did not secure supremacy in the world after the destruction of German power was due in the first place to the fact that even during the first phase of the Anglo-Japanese Alliance there appears on the international political stage, and especially on the Pacific section of it, a new world-Power, an apparition which made England reconsider her whole Pacific policy and fit it to this new development. The fate of the Anglo-Japanese Alliance is another proof thereof.

§ 6. THE U.S. AND THE FAR EAST

The evolution of the original alliance, which was concluded by Lansdowne and Hayashi in London on January 30, 1902, reflects the changes in the international political situation which were heralded by the Russian defeat and the appearance of the United States on the stage of the Pacific politics as a world-Power. The evolution of the relations between Britain and Japan must therefore be judged in the light of these changes in world politics.

America's international policy so far as the Pacific was concerned developed first on a tiny stage which was dominated by the Anglo-Russian rivalry. The strength of these two Powers gave American policy a dual character, and it wavered between a frank expansionism and a policy of abstentionism peculiarly American in character, and conditioned by the fact that American imperialism is above all economic imperialism. Monroe's presidential message of 1823 may be taken as a forecast of the later policy in the Pacific in that it was directed against Russia's Pacific ambitions (vide supra, pp. 113, 125). Corresponding to the political conditions then existing, the Monroe doctrine is defensive in character, although that fact was never an obstacle to the imperialist advance of the American Republic. The war with Mexico gave the United States possession of the Far West up to the Pacific (Peace Treaty of Guadelupe Hidalgo in 1848). But even earlier, in anticipation of a future development, President Tyler had given the Monroe doctrine a rather definite interpretation when he warned the European claimants in 1842 off Hawaii. This intervention paralysed the Anglo-French attempt to bring this group of islands under their control (1843 and 1849).[61]

In spite of this display of strength, America at this period felt herself weak as compared with Russia and England. In the 'forties and 'fifties Washington really feared that England would either herself swallow China just as she swallowed India or in co-operation with France and Russia would partition it. That at least is the sense of the reports sent in 1853 to Washington by the American representative, Humphrey Marshall.[62]

If any such action had been planned and the Great Powers had attempted to carry it through, America at that period would not have been able to offer opposition. None the less, while the Crimean War was going on the Bonin islands were annexed and the Ryû-kyû isles occupied by Commodore Perry; Formosa, too, was also to be annexed. All this was evidence of the necessity felt for oceanic expansion by a nation which had just attained the farther coast by territorial expansion on the continent, but because of the situation then obtaining it could have no lasting effect, and soon had to be repudiated. But Perry's expedition may rightly be regarded as an American incursion in force into what was to be Japan's future sphere of empire.

Anglo-American rivalry in the Pacific manifests itself in the violent disputes on the accesses to the Pacific. On the conclusion of the Clayton-Bulwer convention in 1850, England was still in the position to make the future Panama channel a joint undertaking of the two Anglo-Saxon Powers to be carried through on a parity basis as far as defence and control was concerned; half a century later England was compelled to abandon to the Americans not only the commercial but also the military control of the Panama canal (Hay-Pauncefote Agreement, 1900–02). Between the Clayton-Bulwer Agreement and the Hay-Pauncefote Agreement lay the creation of the colonial empire of the United States, and its transformation into an imperialist Power of the first class.

The American advance in the Pacific in the last decade of the nineteenth century was pursued systematically and swiftly, and an island bridge was created across the Pacific Ocean to the mainland of Asia; in 1893 Hawaii came under American control; in 1898 the Philippines and Guam were acquired; at the same time Hawaii was annexed; in 1899 Tutuila in the Samoa group was annexed. When the United States became a strong Pacific Power, England began to regard it as a very important asset in her own international policy and to pursue a policy of collaboration and *rapprochement* between the two Anglo-Saxon Powers. The international political rivalry, the conflict of imperialist interests which no doubt exists between England and America in many fields were not strong enough to prevent the two Powers at certain periods closely co-operating. Here, too, the maxim holds: No eternal friendships, no eternal enmities.

The policy of the United States towards Russia has not been uniform. Here too we find periods of friendship and mutual sympathy and other periods during which conflict of interests causes tension and enmity. These two powerful continental States in whose development and sociological structure may be found many common features, were first brought together by their common opposition to the world power of England. This is already apparent during the American War of Independence (the league of armed neutrality in 1780). Side by side with this mutual attraction, however, there was a strong counter-tendency caused in the first place by the Russian claim to create a colonial empire in the Pacific (compare above, pp. 113, 136). Joint opposition to England brought the two continental States again together during the period of the American Civil War (1861–5) when the Czarist Empire, which had just proclaimed the liberation of the serfs, sympathized with the Northern States while England supported the Southern States. From that time we notice the existence of a certain sympathy with Russia in the Republican party, which represents industry and regards Russia as a possible important export market, while the Democrats, which represent the agricultural community, look on Russian agriculture as a rather dangerous competitor in the world market. The period of Russo-American friendship culminates on the selling of Alaska in 1867 at an absurdly low price to the United States, and this tradition, in spite of radically changed conditions, continues to exercise its influence almost up to the end of the century.

Already at the end of the nineteenth century rivalry developed between the Czarist Empire and the United States, a rivalry determined by the fundamental difference in their respective policies in the Pacific. In this period American imperialism was already taking on a specific economic character and especially so in reference to the East Asiatic sphere. The financial and industrial power of the United States is so strong that, given "fair play," there is no competition it needs to fear. Naturally, American capitalism had no need to fear the competition of so backward an industry and of so primitive a commercial machinery as Russia possessed at that time. But what the Americans insisted on was just that "fair play." After the Spanish-American War, American trade with China increased at a rate which measured by the standards of the time is tremendous; in 1890 the United States' share of the whole import to China was 6 per cent; in 1905 it was already 20 per cent. In the same period the American share in the total import to Japan doubled. The Americans succeeded in well-nigh completely driving Russian oil from the Chinese market. This oil war was won really by the Americans because of their splendid methods of marketing, which made it possible to bring oil lighting and so a piece of "white civilization" to the remotest villages of China. American oil possibly made a greater impression upon the Chinese people than did electrification later, and it constituted the real foundation of American prestige.

To the brilliant American organization the Russians could oppose nothing but a slow, corrupt trade apparatus incapable of adaptation, and so, in spite of their older rights gave way. The same thing happened in the cigarette trade, where not only Russian but Japanese manufacturers and importers were defeated by the American trust, the British-American Tobacco Co.[63]

It can be easily realized that American capitalists could not admit the possibility of this Chinese market being closed to them by Russia. The danger, however, was real because Russian imperialism bore the primitive character of territorial expansion which was prepared to offset the backwardness of Russian industry and the deficiency of its organization for distribution by brutal protective measures. It was therefore not without good grounds that the Americans feared that Russia might completely destroy American commercial influence within the sphere of her imperialism. Americans believed that their territorial acquisitions in the Pacific were quite different in character from the annexations made by the European Powers. From the American standpoint, for instance, the annexation of the Philippines or of Hawaii was merely a means to the single end of protecting American trade interests in China. Every strategical position that America won in the Pacific, in American opinion, served only one end: the protection of China's integrity. American imperialism did not seek to share in a division of spheres of influence in China, because it considered the whole of China as its *own special* sphere of influence and was absolutely convinced that, if there was "fair play," the whole enormous Chinese market with its 450,000,000 people would be open to American industry. This is the latest interpretation of the American doctrine of the "open door" which then was finally formulated.

Towards the close of the century, the American Government more and more realized that the European Powers were seriously thinking of dividing up China. This was the period of the construction of the Transsiberian railway, the secret Li-Lobanoff convention under which Russia was given a *de facto* protectorate over Manchuria, of the Sino-Japanese War, of the agreements between England and Germany (September 1 and 2, 1898), and between England and Russia (April 28, 1899), with regard to spheres of influence in the matter of railway construction, of the occupation of Kiau-chou, Port Arthur, and Wei-hai-wei, and finally of the Boxer rebellion with the resultant international military expedition (1900–1), which gave Russia the chance to occupy Manchuria for an unspecified time. In view of these developments the Washington Cabinet saw itself obliged to formulate its own policy and intervene decisively in Far Eastern affairs. The Republican, William MacKinley, had just succeeded the Democrat Cleveland in the White House (1897), and the triumvirate John Hay (State Secretary), Elihu Root (Minister for War), and Theodore Roosevelt (Under-Secretary for the Navy) were urging a strong imperialist line in trade policy, and above all radical interventionism in international politics. Soon afterwards her possessions in the Caribbean Sea were wrested from Spain, a measure necessary for the strategic defence of the future Panama canal, and the Philippine islands came under American rule; public opinion in the United States began for the first time to take an interest in naval problems. Admiral Alfred T. Mahan in his books preached the necessity of a strong American navy so that the United States might not be at a disadvantage in international politics.[64] But international politics—and that was fully realized in Washington—means for America a Pacific, and above all a Chinese policy. "He who understands China," said John Hay in 1890, "holds the key to international politics for the next five hundred years."

There is no sign here of a theory of political abstinence underlying the "Hay doctrine." Rather this doctrine, like that other doctrine formulated eighty years earlier by President Monroe, springs from the foreign political instinct of an aggressive bourgeoisie, which intends to defend its place in the sun by all the means in its power. Like the Monroe doctrine, the Hay doctrine is a manifesto of "counter-colonization" directed against the colonial ambitions of the Great Powers of Europe and, just like the Monroe doctrine, the Hay doctrine conceals an offensive spirit under a defensive façade.[65]

The Hay doctrine has been many times formulated, but on every occasion stress has been laid on the conception which is the guiding principle over a whole period in the American foreign policy in the Far East, the conception of "fair play," equal opportunities to all nations competing in the Far East. In a circular note addressed to the Powers during the Boxer rising, Hay formulated his doctrine thus: "The principle of equal and impartial trade with all parts of the Chinese Empire." Even more explicit was Secretary of State Elihu Root, Hay's successor in that office, in his exchange of diplomatic notes with the Japanese Ambassador Takahira (November 30, 1908), when he wrote: "The principle of equal opportunity for commerce and industry of all nations in that empire."[66]

There is no need to point out that this doctrine is in crass contradiction to the practice in this period of the Great Powers in their dealings with the Far East. Yet Washington succeeded in discovering a common language with France and England in that area. British imperialism was then in a phase of satiation and internal consolidation. The main outlines of the new East African Empire, from Cairo to Capetown, were already taking shape, and as a result British rule over the Indian Ocean seemed to be on the point of achievement. British imperialism in this phase was less concerned with territorial gains than with commercial advantages. In London, especially after the defeat of the Boers, the third Salisbury Cabinet, one of the most brilliant Governments England has ever possessed, was prepared to go a long way to reach compromises with other Great Powers.[67]

Particularly in the Far East was London desirous of co-operating with America to keep open the "open door" in China. The more far-sighted of the American politicians realized this and also the significance of a change in British policy in favour of America. For there actually was a radical change in British policy which sought to emerge as quietly as possible from the "splendid isolation" of the second half of last century and was seeking allies. In London it was already realized that the centre of gravity from the international point of view was shifting and so everything would depend in what scale one was. Britain pursues the policy of "splendid isolation" and "aloofness" only in periods when international conditions are relatively calm and stable, but in periods of international upheavals and changes Britain looks for suitable allies. On the other hand, the young Atlantic Republic on her entry on the stage of world politics and especially on that of complicated Pacific politics, felt herself rather isolated and abandoned. Although there had been in the past some not very pleasant conflicts with her British kin, for instance the war of 1812–15, the conflict over the Oregon district in the 'forties ("fifty-five or fight"), the frictions over Panama, "misunderstandings" during the Boer War, America at this time, at any rate, felt, and especially when she faced the problems of the Pacific, a feeling almost of solidarity. In a letter addressed to Henry Cabot Lodge, an influential senator, later chairman of the Senate's commission for foreign affairs and a fierce opponent of and victor over Wilson, Hay, her American Ambassador in London, wrote some days before the declaration of war against Spain: "I do not know whether you especially value the friendship and sympathy of this country (i.e. England). I think it important and desirable in the present state of things, as it is the only European country whose sympathies are not openly against us. We will not waste time in discussing whether the origin of this feeling is wholly selfish or not. Its existence is beyond question. . . . If we wanted it, which of course we do not, we could have the practical assistance of the British Navy—on the *do ut des* principle, naturally."[68]

John Hay remained in office under the two Republican presidents, MacKinley and Theodore Roosevelt, for seven years, eventful years for America's Pacific policy; he died at the time when Russo-Japanese peace negotiations were beginning at Portsmouth under the auspices of Theodore Roosevelt. With these negotiations America's Pacific policy entered a new phase. Until 1905 Russia had been considered by Washington to be the chief opponent of the "open-door" policy.

It is even possible to talk with some justification of an Anglo-American–Japanese alliance before the Russo-Japanese War. If the "Far Eastern Triple Alliance" were recreated against Japan, Roosevelt intended to place America on Japan's side so to prevent Russia becoming too powerful.[69] But after Russia's defeat it was the victorious Power that now seemed to be the chief opponent of America's policy of maintaining a peaceful competition between all the nations in China. America, besides, could not understand that "equality" in economic competition was no real "equality" for Japan, which, in spite of her favourable geographical position, had remained much inferior to the "white" States in the possession of raw materials and in capitalist development. But now Japan was taking up the position evacuated by Russia; she was now the most important continental Power in the Far East, and sought to bring into her political and economic sphere of influence wide stretches of the Chinese mainland. Tokio, with London's support, succeeded, not indeed in making Russia's Far Eastern policy follow her own, but to a very real extent in co-ordinating and making parallel the policies of the two Powers. As a result, no doubt against England's wishes and possibly without any conscious effort to that end either by Japan or Russia, a front was formed against the United States.

London, to whom the conclusion of the treaty with Japan in 1902 was a starting-point for the building up of a world system of alliances against Germany, desired to see Russia take its place therein, but particularly the United States. Hence London's inclination to regard the provisions of the alliance treaty of 1902 not as a *taboo*, but to adapt them continually to new international relations and to the new alliances needed by the British Empire. The treaty of January 30, 1902, was directed against Russia, and, on a long view, represented a front against the Dual Alliance (Russia and France). The main object of it was to isolate Russia from France in the case of a war in the Far East. The renewal treaty of August 12, 1905, three weeks before the conclusion of the Peace of Portsmouth, equally maintained a front against Russia (the Indian clause), but the treaty of July 13, 1911, which formally was a renewal of the alliance of 1902, is very different in character. Between 1905 and 1911 there took place a complete change in the relations between England and Russia (St. Petersburg Agreement of August 31, 1907) and in the relations between Russia and Japan (Motono-Isvolsky Agreement of July 30, 1907, and the treaty of July 4, 1910). In the Anglo-Japanese Alliance Treaty of 1911 the clause aimed at Russia disappears, but—what is of much greater significance in this connection—it is expressly stated that the Alliance is not effective against the United States.[70]

Although in Washington, even in the days before the Great War, Japan's rise to be a world-Power was regarded as a factor making for insecurity in Far Eastern politics, Russia, and perhaps even mainly Russia, was considered an obstacle to the free activity of American capital in China and esecially in Manchuria. John Hay's "open door" policy therefore was modified in the sense that "equal right" for trading with China was no longer stressed; instead the right was stressed of American capital in the economic exploitation of China which was now beginning. The proposal (mentioned above, p. 145) advanced by Secretary Knox for a neutralization of the Manchurian railways is described even by American writers as an expression of "Dollar-Diplomacy." It was a matter here of creating an international bank consortium which would take over the administration of existing railway lines and all future construction in Manchuria. Power in the administration would be distributed according to the share of individual national banking groups in the international loan to be issued.

It is hardly necessary to insist upon the fact that if the Knox scheme had been carried through, Russian and Japanese influence would have been entirely driven from Manchuria to the profit of the great capitalist Powers and in the first place, America. It is interesting to note that it was Russia in full agreement with Tokio which took the lead in uncompromisingly rejecting the scheme. No greater success attended another scheme launched by the Morgan firm for the construction of a West Manchurian railway to link up the Gulf of Petchihli with Tsitsikar and Aigun on the Amur river and so, if not kill, at least cripple the South Manchurian (Japanese) railway. Four months after the rejection of the Knox plan, President William Taft declared that the plan of transforming Manchuria into a buffer State between the three Great Powers (Japan, Russia, and China), into a State whose railway system would be placed under the control of representatives of all the nations and which would not be protected by the military forces of any one State, would secure peace for ever in the Far East.[71]

The situation in the Pacific region in the period preceding the outbreak of the World War was a very complex one. It is impossible to talk here, as is possible for Europe, of two blocs or alliances in opposition to each other. Germany was completely isolated in the Far East. This isolation by itself was enough to make obvious the desperate world-political situation of the

Hohenzollern monarchy. The Triple Entente in the Far East was reinforced by Japan with which each of the Entente Powers had concluded a special agreement on the delimitation of mutual spheres of influence in Asia (Anglo-Japanese Alliance Treaty of 1911; Japanese-French Agreement, Kurino-Pichon, of June 10, 1907; Japanese-Russian Agreement in 1910). As for America, all the Entente Powers, including Japan, were bound by the formal recognition of the "open-door" policy. In reality, however, all of them were preparing for a situation in which the partition of China or a great part of it would become practical politics. It was safe to predict that if this situation arose the old rivalries would not only flare up again but would be greatly sharpened. In that case not only would old alliances be renewed, but new combinations would become possible.

§7. THE WORLD WAR AND AFTER

On the outbreak of the Great War the situation in the Pacific changed in so far as the attention of the European Great Powers was diverted from Pacific developments. Their influence in the Pacific fell enormously. That is true not only of Russia and France whose armies and navies were fully occupied in war operations in Europe, but also of England, which was obliged to concentrate her main fleet in the North Sea and European waters generally in order to maintain the blockade and to protect her own and her Allies' trade against German cruisers and submarines. America, which entered the War only in the spring of 1917 (severance of diplomatic relations with Germany February 3rd, declaration of war April 6, 1917), was psychologically and economically fully occupied with the developments in the Atlantic region and had relatively little energy left to pursue an active Pacific policy. The passionate concern with which the whole American people followed events in Europe from the very beginning of hostilities, the tensions which these events created in American public life, afforded sufficient proof that the Americans actually do consider themselves to be essentially an Atlantic nation. The liberal and "pacifist" policy of President Wilson, in contrast to the "imperialist" policy of his three predecessors, McKinley, Roosevelt, and Taft, could not prevent the United States being drawn into the European War, just as a century earlier it had been drawn into the Napoleonic Wars. Wilson intended to preserve American neutrality in order to be able at the end of the War, at the moment when all belligerents was completely exhausted, to appear as the world's supreme mediator. This policy, for reasons the discussion of which is beyond the scope of this work, failed. But it is reasonable to assume that Wilson, when he decided to enter into the War, also had in his mind the thought that by entering the War America would create a counterweight to Japan's effort to attain hegemony in the Far East.[72]

During the Great War Japan attained a position in the Far East practically equivalent to hegemony. As early as 1915, by a brutal disregard of all international treaties, Japan succeeded in establishing a *de facto* protectorate over China. The history of the "Twenty-One Points" has often been told. What is interesting really is not so much the contents of these demands as the political situation which made it possible for such demands to be addressed to a sovereign State and to be accepted by it. The Japanese protectorate over China did not last long, but in the famous claims Japan has set forth a programme regarding China which is much more serious in character than the no less famous "Testament of Tanaka." The Japanese spheres of influence are clearly defined. Fu-chien, Shantung, South Manchuria, and Inner Mongolia. The rest of the claims in the Twenty-One Points is just typical Oriental exaggeration.

In the so-called "Group V" which was abandoned in the course of the negotiations, the idea of a Japanese protectorate over China was quite openly stated. Japan, however, at that time had no hope of being able to achieve the protectorateship. It was only a theme to be touched on at the moment and worked out in the future. As far as those future plans were concerned, the Allies need not be taken into her confidence nor be asked to support them. All that was asked of them was to let Japan have a free hand. In February–March 1917 the Tokio Cabinet got the Cabinets of London, Paris, St. Petersburg, and Rome to endorse the claim to special Japanese rights in Shantung province, and also to admit her claims in the South Pacific, the future Japanese mandates. England had still earlier attempted to throw an obstacle in the way by inducing China, powerless and torn by civil war as she was, to enter the Great War. And it throws a very clear light on the strength of the position which Japan had now won when we learn that Britain, after a protest from Tokio, had to agree to declare that she would do no political negotiating with China without having first reached agreement with Japan.[73]

The Peking Government broke off diplomatic relations with Germany only in March 1917, and declared war on August 14, 1917. This declaration was part of a new situation, for the United States had already joined the Allies. Peking had long hesitated before taking that decisive step, and it was only under pressure from Washington that China did enter the War.[74] It is from this period that there dates the "moral responsibility" which Washington feels towards China and, simultaneously, the right to protect her which Washington claims. But America's entry into the War, which coincided with the breakdown of the military power of Russia, led at the outset to a further strengthening of Japan's position in the Far East. It is safe to say that towards the end of the War and in the first years after it, i.e. between 1917 and 1920, Japan was very near seeing her boldest dreams in China being realized. The American Navy too was involved in military events in the Atlantic, the blockade, and the war against the German submarines. The whole transport capacity of the mercantile marine was needed by the United States to carry the great expeditionary forces under General Pershing to Europe. It was the first war on a large scale in which America had been engaged since the war with Britain a century earlier. It was obvious that the United States would have no energy to spare for the Pacific. After the collapse of Russia's western front, and the evident inclination of certain circles in Russia to make a separate peace with Berlin, there were even doubts of Japan's fidelity to the cause of the Allies. For these reasons, Wilson and his Secretary of State, Robert Lansing, were compelled in the late autumn of 1917 to take a step which later influential circles in America were to declare not merely to be a political blunder, but an act of treachery towards China. On November 3, 1917, a convention was signed by Lansing and Viscount Ishii, who had been sent on a special mission to the United States, in which Washington recognized Japan's "special interests" in China.

To understand the motives of the Washington Government we must remember the dangerous position of the Allies and especially of the United States at that moment. During the War there came into existence between individual members of the Allied front a whole series of conventions for "mutual collaboration," which would have greatly affected inter-Allied relations if the War had ended without definite victory having been won over the Central Powers; we do not know the contents of all of those yet. We do know, however, the text of the secret alliance treaty between Russia and Japan of July 3, 1916 (Sazonoff–Motono), which was obviously directed, not against Germany, but against the United States. When this document referred to the safeguarding of China from the political domination of any third Power whatsoever, no other Power but America could be meant. This 1916 treaty, besides, was nothing but a culminating stage of the political *rapprochement* towards which from 1905 to 1914 the Cabinets of Tokio and St. Petersburg under London's auspices had been striving. The only difference was that in 1916 London's services seemed no longer needed. But it is very possible that the Okuma Government then in power did not lose sight of the possibility of an understanding with Germany, perhaps even of a German-Russian-Japanese Entente, on the conclusion of peace, or even during the Great War itself. Such plans, or at least similar plans, were at any rate being seriously considered in Tokio in 1916–18.[75] To Japan, the war between the European Powers for objects which meant nothing to Japan was simply an opportunity to attain her ends in the Far East. Alliances with the Entente Powers or against them was for Tokio a matter of great concern, but it was neither vital nor fundamental.

That uncertain balance of power that first came into existence during the last decade before the Great War—the period between the Portsmouth Peace and the outbreak of the War—rested on various assumptions. The most significant of these was that China was bound to disintegrate. The Chinese Empire was regarded by the Powers as an object of their "spheres of influence" policy. Under the urge of Britain there was built up within the period 1905–15—and this was the second factor in the balancing of power in the Western Pacific—a fine-meshed net of agreements which more or less openly envisaged the dismemberment of China. The distribution of "spheres of influence" was settled within the framework of the two great Dual Alliances: England-Japan and France-Russia, which, later on, became the Quadruple Entente. It has already been stated that the World Entente against the Central Powers of Europe had two solid bases, the European and the Asiatic, the latter of which was at least as solid as the former. Behind the obvious and visible aims of the Entente, which sought to defeat Germany's offensive in the field of foreign policy, and so sought to shatter the German position in Central Europe, we can detect other, less visible but no less important, aims which amount to preparation for a new distribution of the world. And the most important object of that new distribution was apparently China. The third presumption for the maintenance of the balance of power in the Western Pacific was the isolation of Germany in the Far East and a certain disinterestedness of the United States in Far Eastern affairs such as had been visible since Wilson had come into power. It is in this period that there comes the Washington Government's declaration that it will not support the participation by American banks in the so-called Six-Power consortium to finance railway construction in China (1913).[76] In spite of this disinterestedness, however, London was still working for a sort of tacit *entente* between the two Anglo-Saxon Powers, which would be a background to all other agreements on the partition of China. For London was considering now, not merely the old-fashioned plans for the distribution of spheres of influence, but a new plan for a joint protectorate of the two Anglo-Saxon Powers over the Far East. In such a situation—between the two methods of dominating the Far East and between the Quadruple Entente on the one hand and the United States on the other—lay the strength of Britain's position in the balance of power in the Western Pacific.

The development of the position in the Western Pacific in the post-War period may be divided into several clearly distinct phases. The most outstanding feature of the first phase, i.e. up to the Washington Conference in 1922, is the fact that Russia and, even more so China, almost entirely disappear as active factors in politics. During this phase China was completely paralysed by internal strife; the Peking Government was practically powerless; the South under Sun-Yat-Sen and T'ang Shao-i to all intents and purposes did not recognize it; in the North, Japan wielded unlimited influence, while the military governors (tu-chun) were the real masters of their respective provinces. In 1918–20, the Anfu Club ruled in Peking, and it was completely under Japanese influence.[77]

Russia, too, in this phase, seemed destined to break up. The civil war in European and Asiatic Russia prevented any foreign political activity, and the war against Poland (1920–21) completely diverted the attention of the Moscow politicians from events in East Asia. It seemed, particularly in the first post-War years, that Russia's Far Eastern territories would, like China, become an object of imperialist policy. England and France were not disinclined to satisfy Japan's appetite for territorial gains—and at that time Japan seemed to have reached the summit of her power at the cost of Russia in the Far East—

and in this way provide an outlet for Japanese energy which later might well become a menace to the interests of the Allied Powers in the Pacific. Tokio used this favourable moment to occupy the Russian coast province, the Amur region, and the northern part of Sakhalin. For Japan the occupation had a double significance. From the economic point of view Japan was seeking to secure for herself the rich deposits of coal, and especially of mineral oil, which Russia had in the Far East, and also to monopolize the fishing industry. On the other hand, the territory occupied was a prolongation and the terminus of the strategical line Hankow–Shantung–Harbin, which was then regarded by the Japanese General Staff as Japan's first line of defence on the mainland. From the naval standpoint the occupation meant complete mastery over the Sea of Japan, which would become a Japanese lake, and also control over the Tatar Sound which connects the Sea of Japan with the Sea of Okhotsk. At the same time, plans were considered for the occupation of the Kamchatka peninsula, a seizure which would have meant Russia's complete expulsion from the Pacific.

The plans of the Japanese imperialists, however, went much farther. The whole of Northern Manchuria, with the Chinese Eastern Railway, which was jointly owned by Russia and China, was occupied by Japanese troops, and Japanese detachments even entered Trans-Baikalia. The tu-chun Chang Tso-lin, who was a creature of the Japanese and militarily and financially dependent on them, was set up in power in Mukden. The valleys and mouths of the four greatest rivers in the Far East, the Amur, the Ussuri, the Sungari, and the Nonni, were now in the hands of the Japanese, who now proceeded to try to bring into their empire or, at any rate, into their sphere of influence the whole of Manchuria and the whole of Mongolia. A Manchuro-Mongolian corridor would completely separate Russia from China. In order to get control of Mongolia the Japanese tried to make the Government of Mongolia accept a loan of 15,000,000 yen, redeemable in fifteen years, secured by mortgage upon the Mongolian forests and mines. At a conference of

North China's tu-chuns in April 1921 the Japanese puppet, Chang Tso-lin, was appointed "Commissar of Mongolia." These were the days of the adventures of General Baron Ungern von Sternberg, who had dreams of his own of a great Mongolian empire stretching from Manchuria to Tibet, but actually was a tool of Japanese policy. What Japan was at this time aiming at was the creation of a gigantic sphere of influence from the Sea of Okhotsk and the Sea of Japan on the one side, to Lake Baikal on the other, which would include the whole of North-eastern China, Mongolia, and the Russian Far East. That was, so to say, the maximum programme. Its realization at that time was seen to be impossible. It was postponed, but it has never been cancelled. We may take the minimum programme at this period to be the annexation of the Russian part of Sakhalin with its rich oil deposits, the seizure of all hunting grounds, fisheries, woodlands, and mineral deposits in the Amur province, in the coast district and Kamchatka, the dismantling of the Vladivostok fortress, and its transformation into a free port under Japanese control. Claims of similar nature were at any rate often advanced by the Japanese in the diplomatic negotiations of the period.[78]

The intervention in Siberia made such claims on Japan in the foreign political sense that Tokio's iron grip on China relaxed. If Germany had won the World War, nothing probably could have saved China from falling under Japanese rule. The disintegration of both Russia and China reached, at the end of 1919, its climax. From that year, however, there began, slowly at first and then ever more quickly, a process of consolidation in the two continental States, a process which was accompanied simultaneously by their *rapprochement*. The Russian civil war ended in Europe in November 1920, in Siberia it had ended in the spring. A year and a half later the last champion of the white restoration, Ungern-Sternberg, was executed in Nowo-Nicolajevsk.[79] In the autumn of 1920 the Anfu club was overthrown in Peking and therewith a first blow given to Japanese influence in Northern China. At the end of the civil war and the war against Poland (March 1921) the so-called NEP era began in Russia, which led to an economic revival and so to a general strengthening of the Soviet State. In April 1920 Dr. Sun-Yat-Sen was elected President of China by the Parliament in Canton, and began to reorganize the whole political life of the nation. In January 1924 the revolutionary popular party, the Kuo-Min-Tang, was reformed, put on a new basis, and issued its famous programmatic manifesto to the nation.[80]

Sun-Yat-Sen, who originally had sought to base his plans for the reorganization of China on the aid of the imperialist world-Powers, England, America, and Japan, at the end of his career decided for an alliance with Soviet Russia. In January 1923, in Shanghai, a conference was held between the Russian statesman Adolf A. Yoffe and Dr. Sun. At that time, it seems, Moscow had no intention of Bolshevizing China, but was prepared to co-operate loyally with the Kuo-Min-Tang as the embodiment of the Chinese national revolutionary movement. One and a half years later, on May 31, 1924, China signed her first agreement with a European Power on a footing of complete equality. This European Power was Soviet Russia, and the treaty was signed in the Peking Foreign Office by the Soviet Ambassador, Leo M. Karakhan, and by the Chinese Foreign Minister Wellington Koo. It was signed in privacy and without any diplomatic publicity, for both signatories feared, and not without reason, an intervention on the part of such Powers as had an interest in preventing a *rapprochement* between the two great continental revolutionary States.[81]

But we have been rather anticipating events. The conclusion of the Russo-Chinese Treaty, whereby both signatories recognized each other on a basis of complete equality, took place in an international atmosphere that had completely changed. Japan's third, or—if the invasion by Hide-yoshi of Korea at the end of the sixteenth century is to be taken into account—her fourth great continental offensive had been defeated or rather had encountered obstacles, which were the consequences not only of the new conditions on the continent, but of a new international situation. Japan was not in a position to overcome these difficulties. Just as in 1895, after a victorious war against China, and as in 1905, after a brilliant victory over Russia, Japanese imperialism faced obstacles and antagonists who reduced the fruits of victory to the lowest possible level.[82] The Washington Conference (Nov. 12, 1921–Feb. 6, 1922) compelled Japan to give up her continental positions in relation to Russia and China. As far as Russia was concerned this meant no permanent renunciation, but Japan now realized that here in the future she might have indeed a weakened rival to deal with, but one who was more or less her equal. Japanese aspirations in the Russian Far East had to be deferred until a new world situation could let them be realized.

§ 8. CHINA AND THE POWERS

As to China after the Conference, the position was rather different. Japan was, however, obliged to withdraw her army of occupation from Shantung where it had been for eight years (1914–22). But her special commercial and political rights in Manchuria remained practically intact, and so the predominant position which she had created for herself in North China. Generally, despite the condemnation of the spheres of influence policy in the Nine-Power Agreement (Clause 4) of February 4, 1922, and in a special resolution, this traditional policy was still a practical one even after the Washington Conference. And yet after the Conference the situation in the Pacific region unmistakably enters a new phase. This new phase is characterized by the beginning of the consolidation of the two continental States, China and Russia, and of *rapprochement* and co-operation between them. Another feature of it is the *rapprochement* between England and the United States, and as a result a certain cooling of the relations between London and Tokio. The Anglo-Japanese Alliance, after twenty years of existence, was formally abrogated (Clause 4 in the Four-

Power Agreement of December 13, 1921). As a result, what Japan considered during all that period the most important condition for success in foreign policy, and particularly for the strength of her position on the Asiatic mainland, disappeared. Japan felt herself at once abandoned by England and alienated from America. The two oceanic Powers were obviously uneasy at Japan's rapid rise to be a world-Power. Thus Japan saw herself faced with a new and distinctly unfavourable situation on the continent.[83]

She was now compelled to abandon the "mailed fist" policy and apply both to Russia and to China the "velvet glove" policy. The last War Cabinet, Terauchi's, which had continued the "Twenty-one Demands" policy of Okuma and had itself addressed "Seventeen Demands" to Russia, was succeeded by the liberal parliamentary Cabinet of Taka-shi Hara (see Note 78). The Ambassador in Washington, Shidehara, later to be Foreign Minister in the Waka-tsuki Cabinet (1926), pleaded successfully for a *rapprochement* with China and Russia. The great earthquake in the autumn of 1923, which shattered the whole economic structure of Japan, was another reason for a milder course in foreign policy, and so Karakhan and the Japanese minister in Peking, Yoshi-zava, were able to sign, on January 20, 1925, a convention providing for the withdrawal of the last Japanese troops from Northern Sakhalin, and in which the Japanese as compensation were given very advantageous conditions for the exploitation of the oil resources in that part of the island.

The conditions for a further *rapprochement* between Tokio and Moscow were now present. It may be observed, however, that a renewal of the old alliance between the two countries was held to be impossible by the Russians.[84] There was *per se* nothing against such a development. A Russo-Japanese Alliance in 1925 would have been only the sequel to the agreements of 1910 and of 1916. Both Russia and Japan were at this time isolated, and both felt that they were cavalierly treated by the world-Powers. Germany was then in a similar situation, and she was bound to Russia by the Rapallo Treaty of 1922 and the Berlin Ágreement of April 24, 1926. Thus there was the possibility of a Eurasian block of continental Powers directed against the Anglo-Saxon world-Powers. It never materialized, for Germany was too "Western minded," and was reluctant to break the bridges leading to Paris and, still more, to London. And between Russia and Japan stood the problem of their relations with China, a problem still unsolved. After the signature of the Karakhan-Koo agreement, the *rapprochement* between China and Russia began very quickly to take the form of a close political and military alliance. Moscow's influence with the Kuo-Min-Tang Government rose so high that it is not unjust to consider the young Chinese Republic almost as a dependency of the Soviet State. In August 1923 General Chiang Kai-shek, then chief of the general staff of the Kuo-Min-Tang army, negotiated on behalf of Sun-Yat-Sen in Moscow, with Trotsky and Chicherin, regarding military assistance for China. In September 1923 there arrived in Canton the emissary of the Moscow Government, Michael M. Borodin (Grusenberg), at the head of a commission of party organizers and a military expert (Galen-Blucher).[85] Borodin, an organizer of the first rank, became the soul of the new Kuo-Min-Tang and the real "father of the victory" of the revolutionary South over the Northern tu-chuns. He remained with the revolutionary Government for four years until July 1927, when the victory over the reactionary North was practically complete, and when bourgeois counter-revolutionary or at least moderate elements had won the upper hand, even in the leadership of the Kuo-Min-Tang.

The geopolitical significance of the Borodin-Galen mission, which was considered by many as unimportant, is not to be underestimated. There is too great an inclination to lay stress on the social revolutionary, class-war feature of the alliance between the Russian and Chinese revolution, between the radical publicists of Canton and Moscow. From the standpoint of foreign politics, however, what is of much greater importance is the fact that Moscow made an attempt on a large scale to bring the two great empires into unison and so to unite Eurasia on a new basis. It was an attempt which in its scope was equivalent to the Eurasian plans of those imperialists of the steppes, Jenghis Khan and Timur. If the attempt had succeeded, the fate of Asia, and so most probably the fate of the whole world, would have been decided; the continental Eurasian steppe imperialism would have overcome oceanic imperialism in its two forms, the Anglo-Saxon and the Japanese. The attempt failed not only because Moscow bent the social revolutionary bow too far, but—and especially—because the technical and financial strength of the Soviet State was not adequate for so great a task.

Chiang Kai-shek,[86] who was a disciple of Dr. Sun and a master of revolutionary technique, as is well shown by the skill with which he balanced himself between Left and Right, playing off extremists against each other and so maintaining power himself, realized very soon both the limits and the possibilities of the Russian Alliance, and particularly the danger it constituted to his own supremacy, that is, the supremacy of the revolutionary centre. As early as April 1927 Chiang shook himself free from the shackles of the Left, and so broke the foreign political bond with Moscow. At that juncture, too, the position of the Southern revolutionaries, who, meantime, had succeeded in advancing the centre of gravity of their rule more than 1,000 km. northwards to the valley of the Lower Yang-tse (Nanking), was so strong as regards the reactionary North that the Russian military assistance seemed to be no longer necessary. The Russian strategical offensive southwards was thus for the time liquidated, but the geopolitical impulse to reach the East China Sea (Tung-hai) remains. This impulse, which was one of the inspirations of the Franco-Russian railway plans at the end of the nineteenth century (cross-line linking the North and South China railways), becomes the stronger, the weaker the Russian position becomes in the Northern Pacific, in the Sea of Japan, and in the Sea of Okhotsk.

But the geographical drive could find support in the social structure of South China. The alliance of Moscow with the Kuo-Min-Tang leaders was cancelled, but very soon after the breach the Soviet Government was able to base policy on a grand-scale movement in those very provinces—Chiang-hsi, Hu-pei, An-hui, Chiang-su—where eighty years earlier the T'ai-p'ing rebellion had raged.[87] This Soviet movement in the southern provinces represents a large-scale strategic effort by Russia to outflank, on the one hand, the Japanese imperialists' main line of defence on the continent, Hailar-Dolon-nor-Ning-hsia, and the English sphere of influence in the Yang-tse valley on the other.

The third phase of the post-War development in the Western Pacific begins with the rupture between Moscow and South China in 1927, and closes with the occupation by the Japanese of Manchuria in the autumn of 1931. The consolidation of China and Russia made further progress, but tension between the two continental States continued to exist both in the South and in the North. In South China the soviet movement developed, and though the Nanking Government has never produced documentary evidence of the support given by Moscow to the Southern rebels, the connection between Moscow and the Chinese Communists may be assumed. At any rate, Nanking, having got rid of Communist influences, was able to consolidate its rule within the territory under its authority, a success, however, almost offset by the fact that great armies had to be mobilized to deal with the soviet movement. At the same time Moscow's propagandist and colonizing offensive began to be felt along the whole line of the Russo-Chinese frontier from Kashgar to Nertchinsk. Although Western Europe did not notice what was happening, the great Chinese colonies of East Turkestan[88] (Hsin-chiang) and Outer Mongolia,[89] became really Russian protectorates. On the other hand, the Russo-Chinese conflict over the Chinese Eastern Railway and the advance of the Red Army (summer and autumn, 1929), in North Manchuria, was a mere demonstration. All that happened later up to the end of 1934 between Moscow and Nanking and Moscow and Tokio fundamentally was nothing more than sham fighting and camouflage.

Since the manifesto addressed on July 25, 1919, by Karakhan to the Chinese nation, the Moscow Government had realized that it had nothing to gain in Manchuria and that the Russian "sphere of influence" lay elsewhere. If diplomatic relations between the two continental empires were not resumed until December 1932, the Moscow Government was less to blame than Nanking. For in Nanking after the episode of the Russian Alliance (1923–27) there was a return to the original plan of Sun-Yat-Sen, i.e. to use the conflicts and tension between the Great Powers of the West to exploit their financial and technical resources for the reconstruction of China. The railway construction plans of Sun Fo, son of Sun-Yat-Sen, who was Minister of Communications in the Nanking Government from 1928 to the end of 1931, and at the same time chairman of the National Aviation Corporation, were based on an annual investment of 200,000,000 United States dollars over a period of fifty years. The Nanking Government on the whole fully recognized the fact that unless there was a regular revolution in the sphere of transport generally—and not merely in railway policy only, but in canal, motor traffic, and air policy—there was no hope of improving the economic situation, increasing industrialization, modernizing agriculture, and freeing the country from dependence on the foreigner. The pre-condition of any modernization and of any new construction in the sphere of transport, however, in the opinion of the Nanking Government, required initially investment of foreign capital, without which no economic recovery was possible.

After the break-up of the revolutionary movement and the rejection of Moscow began, relations with the capitalist Powers of the West were resumed, and particularly with the United States. One has only to read the names of the economic advisers and experts who were summoned to Nanking in the course of 1928–29 to realize the direction and tendency of the present foreign policy of the Kuo-Min-Tang. The Finance and Currency Commission, under Professor Kemmerer, who was invited to Nanking in October 1928 and arrived in February 1929, was composed of the best American experts in the fields of finance, banking, and currency, who were in very close relations with the Washington Government and also with Wall Street. Very significant was the appointment of Mr. J. J. Mantell, formerly Vice-President of the Erie Railways, as Railway Adviser of the Nanking Government. Mantell, as it is well known, was intimately connected with Hoover, who himself, thirty years ago, was an engineer in China. At the same time the well-known American journalist, Thomas F. Millard, the author of many books on Far Eastern problems and a passionate advocate of the "open-door" policy, a policy which he interprets as the establishment of an American economic protectorate over China, was appointed political adviser to the Kuo-Min-Tang Government.[90] American finance capital at that time made a serious effort to get the task of reconstructing China into its own hands, and definitely, it would seem, put its money on Nanking.

In this third phase of the development in the Western Pacific after the collapse of Russian influence in China, the main rivalry in Nanking seemed to be that between England and America. As compared with 1920–22, the tension arises from new geographical and political considerations. In the earlier period the main struggle was fought out in the North, and the Anglo-American Entente supported General Wu Pei-fu, the head of the Chih-li party, against Japan's hireling Marshal Chang-Tso-lin, in the hope of driving Japanese influence out of Manchuria and the whole of Northern China. Here we may see an expression of the Anglo-American World Entente, which attained its highest point at the Conference of Washington, in 1921–22. In 1927–29, however, an Anglo-Japanese Entente against Washington seemed to be being prepared. It is extremely difficult to give any accurate picture of the foreign political situation in the Pacific, with a constantly changing equilibrium and a resultant changing of alliances. The situation changes not merely from year to year but from month to month. The "open" diplomacy of the post-War time chose much more complicated and distracted ways than did the pre-War secret diplomacy. This "liberal" and pacifist foreign policy gained nothing in clarity from the fact that out of "reverence" to public opinion it occasionally felt bound to give the man in the street an explanation of its ways, methods, and aims.

Between 1927 and 1929 a new combination seemed in process of formation, with its centre in London. After the failure of the Naval Disarmament Conference at Geneva in 1927, London endeavoured to reach agreement with France on the one hand, and with Japan on the other. These were the days when renewal of the Anglo-French Entente and re-establishment of the old friendship with Tokio were constantly spoken of. In Tokio, in the autumn of 1927, the Tanaka Cabinet came to power with a "positive programme" towards China. This was the last but one parliamentary Cabinet before the outbreak of the Manchurian conflict and the liquidation of the system of party government.[91] Tanaka feared that the rupture of Chiang with the Communists would lead to a much too rapid and successful consolidation of China which would have been dangerous to Japanese interests in Manchuria and all over North-East China. Tanaka and his chief adviser, Count Ushida, later on Foreign Minister, knew exactly how to exploit the tension between England and America. The Anglo-French naval compromise in the summer of 1928 was to a certain extent directed against the United States, and was more or less openly supported by the Tokio Cabinet (Note of September 7, 1928). Here we have already the explanation of the standpoint adopted later by Japan at the 1930 London Naval Conference against "offensive armaments," especially against battle-cruisers, a view which was definitely stated during the preliminary conference in London in the winter of 1934. At the same time Admiral Okada, then Minister for the Navy and later Prime Minister, openly defended the Anglo-French compromise. What happened, in the summer and in the autumn of 1928, was almost like a renewal, not indeed of the alliance of 1902–11, but of close co-operation between London and Tokio, which, in spite of all denials on both sides, might have, under certain circumstances, blossomed into a real *entente*. If there was simultaneously in the Soviet newspapers much about the Anglo-American tension becoming a turning-point in world politics, that may be treated as characteristic exaggeration.[92] "Monism" of that kind is just as false in foreign policy as it is in internal policy or in natural philosophy. Anglo-American rivalry was not the axis of world politics, but it was one of the weightiest factors in that policy. That rivalry could in certain circumstances lead to tension and even to open conflict, but under other circumstances it might prove simply a useful starting-point for close co-operation. There are many instances of such a development in the history of Anglo-American relationship, too many indeed to mention.

American finance capital intended to carry through its policy of an economic protectorate over China, of the "education" of China in modern capitalism, and thereby it intended to create a new and gigantic market for American exports. But American capitalism, by its structure, is not exclusive; the traditional American policy since the proposal made by Secretary Knox (in 1909) takes the line of seeking to create an international consortium for the exploitation of China. Some reservations on this international consortium policy were made by President Wilson in 1913, but at that time Wall Street felt itself still an equal among equals, or even a Benjamin among the great capitalist States.[93] In Washington then there was still apprehension that in an international consortium England and France would get the better of America. After the Great War the situation radically altered; America could now be sure that in any consortium for China she would be the leader, and so she was not only not against but actually favoured a state of affairs in which her competitors, particularly France and England, should share in the business provided they left the leadership to American capital. The conditions for the success of such a policy were the consolidation of China and the stability of that country. Here we see the radical opposition between the American policy on the one hand and the Japanese, and, perhaps, though to a much lower degree, the English on the other. American finance capital needed, if it was to dominate China, political unity and stability in that great country. In Washington the old spheres of influence policy was despised, and no one would have anything to do with it. Still more in order to attain this capitalist domination, the United States was prepared to give up its colonies in the Pacific (Philippines). In American opinion it would have been political infamy if anyone were to think of attributing a *territorial* sphere of influence to America in China. Nothing short of the whole of China was to be America's sphere.

Very different was the Japanese and also to some extent the English standpoint. In spite of the favourable geographical position of Japan, Japanese capitalism was not yet able to compete on equal terms with American capitalism in China. Here it was in the main a question not of competition for export markets for goods but of markets to which capital could be exported. But the Japanese financial houses and the great industrial firms naturally could not compete with Wall Street and with the American trusts. Who was to dominate in the reconstruction of China? Who was to take in hand first the practical solution of the Chinese transport problem, the construction of railways, motor roads and canals, the organization of aviation? It was in the answers given to these questions that the decision would be reached, how, on what lines, and to whose advantage the economic life of China would in future be shaped. The influence on this shaping process was to be allotted proportionally to the financial power of the partner concerned. In that case Japan would be last of all. The American plans were in crude conflict with those territorial aspirations which Japan had for decades been trying to carry out in North China. The conflict in policy between Japan and America over

China may be expressed thus: a progressive highly developed capitalism against a relatively backward and young capitalism. This formula is not exhaustive, but it can be usefully applied as a working hypothesis. Moreover, the situation was complicated by the fact that the young Japanese capitalism had to depend on American aid. The Japanese financial investment in China was for the main part made possible by American loans. American high finance was very willing to employ Japanese bankers and industrial companies as its managers, representatives, intermediaries in China. In return it was ready to abandon a considerable share of business done in China to Japan. But on one condition, that the Japanese renounce their policy of annexation and spheres of influence, or at least modify it.

§ 9. INTERNAL STRUGGLES IN JAPAN

The real problem of Japanese foreign policy depended for solution on the answer to the question whether the ruling class in Japan was able to substitute for the traditional policy of forcible annexations the more refined methods of Anglo-Saxon capitalism. This was the main source of division among the leaders in Japanese politics who were already divided on other serious issues. Seen through European or American eyes Japan seemed to be a solid whole animated by one united will and ready to rise at a sign from its leaders to realize its aims in foreign policy. One must not under-estimate the power of the "authoritarian" State in Japan. It will, if the need arises, be at least as strong as any other imperialist Great Power. But at the moment Japan was rent by internal differences as deeply rooted as those in Europe and America. The whole country was divided; the conflict appeared in many forms. The controversies which arose as a result of capitalist development were overshadowed by those whose origin was to be sought in remote history. All these difficulties exercised a powerful influence on foreign policy. There was the old conflict between the Cho-shu and Satsu-ma clans which had affected both the home and foreign policy ever since the Mei-ji era. Between 1895 and 1922 the virtual dictator of the country had been the head of the Cho-shu clan, Marshal Yamagata Aritomo, a genro ("elder statesman") of the Emperor Mutsu-hito. The outstanding features of the Yamagata era are the impulse towards the mainland, the wars against the two continental Powers, China and Russia, the tendency to drive Russia definitely back from the Pacific (occupation of the Russian territory up to the Trans-Baikal region in 1919–21), peace and co-operation with the Naval Powers (Anglo-Japanese Alliance Treaty on January 30, 1902; the Lansing–Ishii understanding between Japan and the United States of November 6, 1917). The memory of the old statesman was still venerated in Japan; certain elements of his policy were still actively influential, but the modern generation of politicians as a whole was perfectly aware of the fact that the Cho-shu policy had failed against insuperable obstacles and that the obstacles were elsewhere than on the continent of Asia. After the death of Yama-gata, and especially from 1925, the power of the Cho-shu began definitely to decline. Now the decisive influence was exercised by the Satsu-ma clan, to which belonged the two Admirals and Prime Ministers Sai-to and Okada. With the rise of a new generation of officers of middle-class and lower middle-class origin, and with the radical reconstruction of the army, the standing and influence of the old clan generals was seriously undermined, and it was those generals who were the chief supporters of the Cho-shu. In the Navy, which has not been the object of so complete a reorganization, and in which generally the old clan traditions had succeeded in keeping their hold, the old seafaring clan of Satsu-ma had maintained its monopoly. The present head of Satsu-ma, Keeper of the Great Privy Seal, Baron Makino, stands closest to the Emperor, and even the old Sayon-ji is under his influence. These two Satsu-ma men have arrogated to themselves the right as a monopoly of interpreting the will of Tenno, the divine Emperor.

It would be, however, false to regard the present supremacy of the Satsu-ma as something uniform, with clear-cut aims in international politics. Within both clans and among their immediate adherents a variety of cliques are struggling who in turn get the upper hand and follow their own particular, often selfish, aims. Especially violent are the conflicts within the high command of the Army, where the controversy between the old generation of noble generals, headed, it is said, by the old Minseito leader, Ugaki, and the new bourgeois and provincial elements is very obvious. In spite of its common opposition to the old clan generals, however, the younger generation itself is not united.

The old parliamentary parties are in full disintegration. They have fallen completely under the influence of the big trusts. It is usual in political circles to identify the "conservative" party, the Sejyu-kai, with the great Mitsui concern. Mitsui (the raw silk and rice trade), which arose from the old trading aristocracy which was closely bound for centuries with the feudal aristocracy, has old connections with the Army clan, the Cho-shu. They are manufacturers and exporters of the raw silk for which America is the main market—the raw-silk export amounts to 35 per cent to 40 per cent of the total Japanese export and 95 per cent of it goes to America. Mitsui, therefore, desires a foreign policy friendly towards America. This political complex is reinforced by those financial groups who have invested their capital in Korea, Manchuria, and in North-Eastern China. Their policy is an *entente* with the United States as a basis for Japanese expansion on the continent at the cost of Russia.

Mitsu-bishi (heavy industry, engineering, shipbuilding), plus the "liberal" Minseito party, plus the maritime clan of Satsu-ma—that is the other politico-economic complex. Its aim is the control of the Central China market, the Yang-tse valley and the raw materials in that region, and the elimination of any competitor, a policy which inevitably means a sharp conflict with America. The two Cabinets headed by Admirals Sai-to and Okada were exponents of this view.

The conflict between continental and maritime tendencies is one of the oldest in the history of Japan. Since the early Middle Ages the advance into the South Sea (Nan-yo) has been a national aim, for the Japanese are probably themselves a Southern Pacific race emigrated from there to what is now Japan. But historic reasons apart, the fact of the advance of Japanese colonization to the Southern Pacific remains beyond dispute. The Japanese rice farmer, craftsman, and trader easily get acclimatized in Formosa, the Marianne islands, and Hawaii. The Japanese or Chinese coolie is the main agent of that Asiaticizing of the Pacific islands, which is proceeding at so tremendous a pace in spite of all the obstacles put in its way by the "white" Governments. But this island world is already over-populated. Chinese competition is much too strong. Australia and New Zealand are closed to Japanese colonization, and since 1924 immigration to Hawaii has been made impossible. If to-day it is possible to speak of a Nan-yo tendency in politics, that means less the colonization of the Southern Pacific than the safeguarding of Greater Japan on the oceanic side.

The "oceanic" theory of the Satsu-ma adherents to-day does not imply an alliance with Russia against, say, America. Japanese foreign policy to-day can no longer be formulated as a simple alternative—Ito or Yamagata, as it was at the beginning of the century. Tokio certainly does not want a war, either with Russia or with America. If, however, war should be unavoidable the Japanese do not intend to repeat the experience of the last forty years—brilliant successes on the battlefield at cost of enormous sacrifices of life and money and relatively unsatisfactory peace treaties. Here, at any rate, they will not follow in Yamagata's footsteps. Does Washington understand these views of the Japanese ruling classes?

Equally complex is the situation as regards England and America. Here the differences in policy regarding China are quantitative rather than qualitative. At any rate the rivals are qualitatively equal. England's policy is not so straight-forward and plain as America's. Memories of the traditional "spheres of influence" policy are still alive in London and among the business community in Shanghai. In the first place, English opinion, which is sceptical and trained by long colonial experience, does not believe that the consolidation of China will proceed so rapidly and so easily as certain American circles think. London prefers to keep two alternatives steadily before its eyes: the consolidation of China, or the disintegration of that gigantic State. In the first case, London is prepared to give up the "spheres of influence" policy and to share in the international consortium for the reconstruction of China even under American leadership, for England's long experience in Chinese business makes it in British opinion pretty certain that she will play the chief part in the "reconstruction trust." London does not dismiss, however, the second alternative, i.e. the possibility that reconstruction will not proceed rapidly nor radically enough, and that as a result of new external and internal differences the fate of the young republic may become very uncertain. It would thus be a mistake to assume that England has already made her mind up for either alternative. It would be truer to say that in London a compromise is sought—a middle way between the old and the new methods—by mediating between Washington and Tokio.

The process of consolidation is now showing results, and accordingly American influence in Nanking is rising. Chiang Kai-shek, however, did not succeed in uniting the eighteen provinces of China proper. Actually he controls only four provinces: Chiang-su, Chê-chiang, An-hui, and Chiang-hsi with a population of over a hundred million, although certain districts in An-hui and Chiang-hsi are temporarily controlled by soviets. In the North, through alliance with the son and heir of Chang Tso-lin (who was murdered in June 1928), the young marshal Chang Hsueh-liang, Chiang Kai-shek was able finally, it seems, to get rid of his two antagonists in the North, Generals Feng-Yu-hsiang and Yen-Hsi-shan. By doing so Chiang once again used the old methods of the South and allied himself with the extreme North in order to check those in power in the Huang-ho valley.[94] The predominance of the South was thus apparently secured.

Much more difficult and less favourable in its issue to Nanking was the struggle in the South itself, where the hegemony of Chiang Kai-shek was challenged at once by the communists and by the Kuang-hsi party. For a time, it seemed as if Chiang, in alliance with the pro-American, moderate and civilian elements under T. V. Soong, K'ung Hsiang-hsi,[95] and Sun-fo, all graduates of American universities, would surmount political difficulties. It may be noted that even at this time, when Chiang was at the apparent height of his power, it would have been wrong to ascribe to him too sanguine hopes for a unification of China under himself. Chiang is a realistic politician, and as such belongs to that type of Chinese statesman whom one may call "Little Chinese." What matters to him above everything else is the creation of a solid nucleus of provinces south of the Great Wall, which can be kept in complete order and obedience by the military forces of the central Government. Inside this nucleus any rival Government, and even any opposition, has to be thoroughly crushed. Round this nucleus a Great China may be created, but that is a task not of years but of decades. Meantime, the right policy is to manœuvre and to check the different antagonists by playing them off against each other. That, incidentally, was the method used by the Chinese Empire for millennia.

At this delicate stage came the events of September 1931, which mark the beginning of the fourth phase of the post-War development in the Western Pacific.[96] The occupation of Manchuria by Japanese troops seemed at first to have been the joint achievement of the army of occupation and the Japanese General Staff in Tokio. The Hamaguchi–Shidehara Cabinet, which took office on the fall of the Tanaka Government in 1929, and was supported by the "liberal" parties, Minseito and Kensei-kai, was obviously against this adventure, for General Shidehara and the Satsu-ma clan were against the "positive policy" of Tanaka. But it would be wrong to infer that there was any real antagonism between the military and the civilian foreign policy. Tokio was compelled to intervene in Manchuria not as a preventive measure against a Russian advance—there was no chance at that time of a Russian advance in this direction and the Russian advance in 1929 was purely defensive in character—but to hinder the progress of the consolidation of China and above all to prevent Manchuria being brought into the sphere of influence of Nanking. The occupation of Manchuria was not directed against Russia, but against the alliance Chiang Kai-shek–Chang Hsueh-liang; actually, however, it is in the long run directed against American influence in China. If one likes one can see in the Japanese occupation a sort of defensive action, the sort of defensive action taken by a weak imperialism with territorial ambitions against the financial hegemony of an overwhelmingly stronger opponent. The Japanese refused to submit to the Washington "dictation"; they want to avoid having to enter the Anglo-Saxon consortium for exploiting China as the junior partner. This apprehension on Japan's part at co-operation with American finance capital is probably due to a sort of inferiority complex, to the fear of being exploited by a stronger partner.

By the occupation of Manchuria, Japan, at least for a time, decided to adopt the "spheres of influence" policy. But Japan, as a result of the strengthening of her position in North China, was now able to claim for herself a larger part of the profits of the future international consortium. It is, however, evident that the progress of the Chinese consolidation was seriously retarded by the Japanese advance and that the forces of disintegration on her borders became stronger. As a result the future of the economic life of China became doubtful and the risk of investments proportionately greater. New York and London were still prepared to grant loans to the Nanking Government, but any comprehensive plan for a "great reconstruction" of China had to be postponed. This was the first result of the Japanese occupation of Manchuria; in fact, the first success for Japanese policy. While the old opposition between North and

South and between Nanking and Canton flared up again, while the plans for reconstruction were modified and the American advisers became less assertive, the Japanese influence with the Nanking Government grew. Paradoxical as it may seem, it is in accordance with the Asiatic (and perhaps not only the Asiatic) mentality that after the defeats suffered by the Nanking Government at Japan's hands in Manchuria and in Shanghai in 1931–32, Japan's stock rose in Nanking. The Communist menace and the rebellion in the North could be liquidated only with Japanese assistance. When in the autumn, 1933, the versatile "Christian general" Fêng again risked a rebellion against Nanking he was defeated by the Chinese Government troops, working in close co-operation with the Japanese army of occupation. It was only this co-operation with Japan in North China which enabled the Nanking Government to concentrate all its military forces against the soviet movement, and to achieve a decisive victory over it (December 1934).

Versatile as every Asiatic policy is, Nanking's diplomacy took into account two possibilities: the possibility of Japan being finally driven back by the Western maritime Powers, just as had happened time and again in the course of the last forty years to every initial Japanese success—in 1895, after the victorious war against China; in 1905, after the victories over Russia; in 1922, when after still greater successes the Japanese were compelled to withdraw from the Russian Far East, to give up their alliance with Great Britain and to accept the inferiority of their high-seas fleet as compared with those of England and America—and the other possibility that Japan would finally be victorious, and having secured herself on the oceanic side would establish her empire in the north-east of the Chinese continent. In the first eventuality Japan knows that she cannot count on Chinese friendship; in the second, Chiang Kai-shek, a "Little Chinese," will agree to the temporary loss of the whole of the north-east, Inner Mongolia included, and make the alliance with Japan the basis of his foreign policy. From the standpoint of East Asiatic and Western Pacific politics, the key to the whole problem of the Far East is in the answer to the question: Will Japan be allowed to establish herself on the Asiatic continent or not?

§ 10. THE PROBLEM TO-DAY

Those who are wont to think in absolute terms are fond of talking of an immanent enmity between America and Japan, or a similarly immanent friendship between England and Japan. But as has been often pointed out here, there are no such things in world politics as immanent friendships and immanent enmities. That Washington was not prepared without further ado to accept the fact of Japanese aggression in Manchuria was made quite clear by the Note of Secretary Stimson of January 7, 1932. The point of view stated in that Note, later to be known as the "Stimson Doctrine," was a further development of the "Hay Doctrine." America was not prepared to accept so-called *faits accomplis* if they were inimical to her interests. But between the "Stimson Doctrine" and armed intervention on behalf of American interests in the Far East there is a great gulf fixed, and it is very doubtful if it will ever be bridged—particularly by the Roosevelt administration. But it must be admitted that to-day America feels herself tied to the Pacific rather than to the Atlantic. Or, to put it more clearly, America regards the situation in the Atlantic-European region as more or less stable. Changes on the European continent might be very important for America too, but in American opinion they would be insufficient to upset the balance. Americans in their overwhelming majority are resolved in no case to let themselves again be entangled in European complications. Whether that American view is a far-sighted one, and it will be possible for America to hold entirely aloof from events in Europe should the situation become serious there, is another question. But as far as the shaping of contemporary American policy is concerned, this definite opinion is decisive. On the other hand, America realizes perfectly that the situation in the Pacific is extremely unsettled, and that there changes of the most radical kind are likely to take place which may determine the fate of American foreign trade and, in the long run, the whole future of American economic prosperity. Washington and New York are not prepared to give up 400,000,000 Chinese prospective buyers of American products. American capitalism needs this great market, and needs, too, the other markets in the Western Pacific, and not least the Japanese market, for the development of American industry and as a field for placing the enormous capital surplus accumulated in America. There, in the Western Pacific, is the true field for American economic expansion.

But the Anglo-Saxon, when facing a political problem, is not inclined to be guided by abstract principles like the Frenchman, or by irrational passion like the German; he is guided by practical experience. To a certain extent that is true of the foreign policy of the Washington Government, although there the principle of empiricism is not so visible as it is in Downing Street. In foreign policy the Americans have invented "doctrines" like those of James Monroe, John Hay, or Henry Stimson, or the "Fourteen Points" of Woodrow Wilson. Here they paid tribute to the passionate rationalism which presided over the childhood of the American Republic. But since those distant days a good deal of opportunist water has gone into the rationalist wine. In Washington a fierce conflict on foreign policy is going on between rationalism, doctrinarism, and provincial conservatism on the one side, and opportunism, empiricism, and universalism on the other. American foreign policy is not only a compromise between the views of the White House and those of the Senate's Commission on Foreign Affairs, but above and beyond that it is a compromise between these two very ancient elements in American politics. It would be hardly a mistake to assume that in dealing with the Far-Eastern problem, too, a compromise will finally be reached between "doctrine" and experience.[97] This compromise will be found somewhere between the old policy of "spheres of influence" and the modern policy of an international exploitation or "opening-up" of China. Japan is to-day so strong militarily, and even economically, that she is not only able to claim a larger part in the international consortium, but to demand recognition of her "special interests" in North-East China. On the other hand, Japan knows very well that the opening-up of Manchuria and of any other territory which may be attributed to Japan is impossible without financial support from Wall Street.

An Americo-Japanese entente in the Western Pacific depends simply on whether both partners will be able to reach an agreement at the right moment. For the time being Tokio seems to be still at the bluffing stage—adopting that typically Asiatic method which is now traditional of exaggerating the initial price, for the suggestions made by the former ambassador in Washington, Debuchi, for the division of the Pacific world between Japan and the United States—the West to Japan and the East to America—or the formulation of an "Asiatic Monroe Doctrine," which time and time again peeps out in the utterances of Japanese diplomats, are no practical basis for a compromise. Nor should Japan's claim for naval parity with the Anglo-Saxon Powers be taken any more seriously. British diplomacy once again showed its sound judgment when during the last naval talks in London it did not in the least let itself be bluffed by this claim. In spite of the blunt refusal of the Japanese, Tokio will still be ready for further negotiations on the basis of the recognition by England and the United States of Manchukuo, which is what is meant by the recognition of Japan's "special interests" in North-East China. If Tokio really wants, it can have a recognition of the "Asiatic Monroe Doctrine," but only for the relatively small area of North-East China. A great American loan for the "reconstruction" of Manchuria under Japanese auspices would be forthcoming without more ado and the removal of those clauses in the 1924 Immigration Act which wound Japanese susceptibilities would certainly make easier the relation between the two partners to this enterprise. Japan must, however, renounce for ever—or whatever period looks like eternity to contemporaries—her dream of an economic and military protectorate over China as a whole and all the paraphernalia of Pan-Asiaticism and come of her own accord to join the Anglo-Saxon front in the Western Pacific. A compromise between Russia and Japan is a necessary sequel to the understanding between Washington and Tokio, a sequel without which the value of the latter to either party would be greatly depreciated, if it did not even become valueless altogether. Any excessive expansion of Japanese rule at Russia's expense would destroy the balance of power in the Western Pacific just as a Russian advance in Manchuria would do.

A Russo-Japanese understanding is possible, simply because of the fact that the object upon which compromise is to be reached is so enormous in size. The areas concerned cover a surface equal to Europe, without the European part of Soviet Russia, and their mineral and other wealth is almost unlimited. In the course of the last thirty years five different agreements have been concluded between Russia and Japan regarding the division of "spheres of influence" in China—in 1907, 1910, 1911, 1916, and finally in 1925. Some of these agreements have been little short of alliance treaties, as a rule directed against the United States, against any interference by that Power in Asiatic affairs. Now that Russia has renounced any claim to influence in Manchuria and then by the sale of the Chinese Eastern Railway solemnly proclaimed her disinterestedness, the possibility of a Russo-Japanese entente has become stronger than ever.[98]

Such an entente, however, can hardly be directed in any way against the United States, for both Japan and Russia need the support of American finance capital, although neither State—particularly Russia—as a result of the great progress in industrialization, is in any way compelled to accept such support unconditionally. But to make possible expansion in the Far East, the exploitation of natural resources still undeveloped there, development of transport of every modern description in

Manchuria, Mongolia, and East Turkestan, Moscow and Tokio both look to Wall Street for aid. It is certainly possible to envisage an entente between Tokio and Moscow without Washington, or even against it, but the results of such an entente as a paying economic proposition would be very meagre. Politically, too, an entente of this nature would have real meaning only if it were joined by the other maritime world-Power, i.e. England. But that presupposes a serious conflict between the two Anglo-Saxon Powers, and if there were one, the world situation would be so radically altered that it is idle to speculate on possible constructions.

A Russo-Japanese entente could be very reasonably based on the territorial *status quo*, or better on the present spheres of influence which they control, i.e. Manchuria and Inner Mongolia to Japan and Outer Mongolia and East Turkestan (Hsin-chiang) to Russia. But an almost insurmountable difficulty against such a basis is the future of the Russian Far East in the widest sense of the term, i.e. the future not of Vladivostok, the Amur province, the Coast province, and North Sakhalin, but of the coasts of the Sea of Okhotsk, Kamchatka, the Kamchatka peninsula, and the Commodore islands. That the transformation of the Sea of Japan into a Japanese inland lake is an essential feature of the Japanese imperialist programme, and that the existence of a heavily armed fortress at Vladivostok is regarded as a definite menace to the security of Japan proper and of the Japanese Empire as a whole is well known. On the other hand, after the surrender of the Chinese Eastern Railway and of the sphere of influence in North Manchuria, the position, from this point of view of communications and of strategy, of Vladivostok, the Amur Province, and the Coast district has become difficult if not untenable. In the case of war with Japan, these districts can hardly be held. Moscow knows this perfectly well, and so the Russians would probably be not reluctant to discuss the fate of the Russian Far East in its narrow sense in certain circumstances and in exchange for solid political and economic compensations.

More difficult is the problem of North Sakhalin. The whole island, geopolitically considered, is in the area of the Sea of Japan, and closes that sea on the north. On the other hand, however, North Sakhalin with Tatar Sound and the harbour of Kastrie is the entrance to the Sea of Okhotsk and to the Russian Far East in the wider sense of the term. Moreover, the oil wealth of North Sakhalin is so considerable that control over it would give an absolute supremacy to the navy of the controller in the Northern and Western Pacific. If North Sakhalin were in Japan's possession, her military and economic position in the Sea of Okhotsk would be so strong that the Japanese would then control all the three accesses to that sea: in the east the Kuriles, in the south the La Pérouse Straits, and in the west Tatar Sound, and Russia's exclusion from the Pacific would be only a matter of time. That would mean not only heavy economic loss to Russia—the natural wealth of Kamchatka, especially in mineral oil, fishing, and in hunting-grounds, is very great—but at the same time it would enormously strengthen Japan, a strengthening which from the point of view of the two Anglo-Saxon Powers who seek to maintain the balance of power in the Western Pacific would be very dangerous. Here once again we see the limits of the possible compromise.

To-day, just as in the past, any Russo-Japanese compromise would be attained at the cost of China. It is deplorable from the moral point of view no doubt, but we live in a period in which moral considerations are in no way a factor in politics. The sceptic may say absolute morality never has decisive significance in politics. But if we study history we may console ourselves with the knowledge that Great China, too—especially as far as her outer provinces are concerned—was not a peaceful creation. But be that as it may; the Great Chinese Empire is now in such a situation that even the greatest Chinese patriot may doubt whether the retention of all the parts of that gigantic State is possible or even desirable. But we should not make the other error, of underestimating the colossal significance of China as a factor in Far Eastern politics to-day. It is usual in dealing with the modern developments in the Western Pacific to put Japan in the centre of the stage. That is so far justified by the fact that Japan throughout the last forty years, since the Sino-Japanese War, actually has been the Western Pacific, and has supplied the dynamism in the Far East. But, on the other hand, Japanese dynamism is effective only—and not only since March 1854, when the last but one Shô-gun in Ka-na-gawa was forced by the guns of the American squadron to allow Japan to enter into world politics—in the steady action and reaction of continental and oceanic influences. This is still true to-day. Above all, what must never be forgotten is the extraordinary significance which affairs on the Chinese mainland have always had for the objective as well as for the success of Japanese foreign policy.

After a century-long period of complete impotence, which steadily increasing reached its climax in the course of the last decades, China once again appears as a factor of first-rate importance in Pacific politics. In the sphere of the former Chinese Empire there have been visible during the last ten years two divergent processes which have in their interplay determined China's millennia-old history: the building up of a solid State nucleus in the old cultural centre, in the valleys of the historic rivers Yang-tse and Huang-ho, and the disintegration of the regions on the periphery, accompanied by the loss of these regions to foreign States. The Nanking Government possesses a certain amount of useful doctrinairism, a doctrinairism imported straight from American universities, but really it bases its foreign policy on the old empiricism of the Chinese Chancelleries. It has been already stated that Chiang Kai-shek is a "Little China man." Remembering what has just been said we may expect that to mean that the eventual Russo-Japanese compromise at the cost of China will not find him unprepared. "Let Russia and Japan divide between themselves temporarily—temporarily!—our outer provinces" is the probable verdict of Nanking, "provided that they let us build up our State nucleus and do not hamper us during the period we need for the achievement of economic reconstruction. In the next hundred years, or five hundred years, we shall see who is the real master in the Far East." This is the Chinese interpretation of the English "wait and see" policy on a gigantic scale. And China can wait.

Russo-Japanese compromises and alliances before and during the Great War were, as has been already stated, effected under London's auspices. Only the Peking Convention of 1925, between Karakhan and Yoshi-zawa, was concluded without London, perhaps against London and against the two Anglo-Saxon Powers then in alliance. The decisive problem for the shaping not only of Far Eastern policy but of world policy, is whether the future agreements between Tokio and Moscow and between Tokio and Washington will be concluded with or without Britain's participation. In the pre-War period London used to be the main promoter and the main guarantor of the balance of power in the Western Pacific. English statesmen from Salisbury to Grey, in extremely difficult and complicated circumstances, had succeeded in creating an elaborate system of conventions which gave the Triple Entente a solid foundation in Asia and strengthened it by adding Japan. Above all, London succeeded in keeping under its own control all developments within the triangle Tokio–Petersburg–Washington. The main problem faced by English diplomacy to-day is to bring into existence, taking into account the changes imposed by circumstances, a new balance of power in the Western Pacific which depends on British support for it.

What really matters in these years of decision between the world-Powers is not naval parity, which, incidentally, is rather a theoretical conception which in practice naval experts have learned to circumvent. Parity on a world scale would be a noble achievement, but what sea Power, or what plausible or even possible combination of grand fleets, could really challenge British supremacy in the Indian Ocean or in the North Sea? Or what fleet could challenge the Japanese Navy inside its "sea trenches" between the La Pérouse Straits to the Ballingtang channel? Or what fleet could tackle the united fleets of the United States in the Eastern Pacific or in the Caribbean? No, what is at stake here is something much more substantial than naval parity—it is the balance of power in the Western Pacific.

Before the Great War London was able to maintain that balance of power by a system of alliances and friendships. The main rôle in this system was played by the alliance with Japan, which acted as a counter-weight to Russia and to Germany. After the War, England, facing an entirely new situation, sought to find a new axis for her Far Eastern policy. True to her tradition she tried the experiment of an Anglo-Saxon condominium, but failed to create a balance of power in the Western Pacific; rather she alienated Japan, which showed an inclination to agreement with Russia. American influence was supreme in China, but there was serious tension between Washington and Tokio. Next *rapprochement* with Japan was tried, and this caused tension between London and Washington. After the Naval Conference in London in 1930, British policy in the Western Pacific entered its third stage. The aim now was a triple entente on the basis of naval arrangements. It was, however, soon apparent that the naval "disarmament," which was nothing more than controlled "rearmament"—which had this advantage, that it put the national rearmament plans within a framework of an international system of armament, as land "disarmament" then was—could not bring about a balance of power, and that on the contrary the latter is a necessary condition for achieving disarmament. So it is extremely important that to-day London should occupy the position of a mediator and guarantor between Washington and Tokio on the one hand and between Tokio and Moscow on the other.

For England, however, the balance of power in the Western Pacific is only part of a whole; what she seeks is the balance of power in Asia. Consequently no settlement in the Western Pacific can be allowed to be achieved without decisive British participation. For any settlement without England is likely to degenerate into an agreement against England. The greatest eventual danger to England, however, lies in the shaping of her relations in the future with the Soviet Union. Just as in the 'eighties of last century, a situation may arise in which Russia, hampered and harassed on the extreme west and on the extreme east of that tremendous line stretching from Odessa to Vladivostok, would transfer her geopolitical offensive to Central Asia. That is the more probable as Russia's economic centre of gravity is now moving in the same direction, towards the region between the Urals, Turkestan, and the Altai mountains (vide p. 124).

The obstacle to Russia in the West is the strengthening of Germany and the revival of the German "Drang nach Osten." Here Russia is obviously on the defensive. Equally serious obstacles are met on the extreme eastern frontier of the Soviet Union as a result of the continental advance of the island empire of Japan. Even the eventual agreement between Japan and Russia will mean to some extent the exclusion of Russia from the Pacific. This eventual Russo-Japanese *entente*, driving Russia back from the Pacific, would direct her expansionist impulse towards Central Asia. Here, however, in East Turkestan, Tibet, Afghanistan, and Persia, the Russian line of advance comes into contact with that of Great Britain. Once Russian influence gained ground in Chinese Eastern Turkestan between the Kwen-lung and the Tien-shan mountains, the English position in Tibet would be endangered. But Russian control of Chinese East Turkestan—this old centre of Asiatic empire dominating the communications between China and Central Asia on the one hand, and Tibet and Sungaria on the other—would mean a considerable strengthening of the Russian position throughout Central Asia and Asia Minor. The old Russo-English conflicts and tensions would in this way flare up again along the whole long line between the Persian Gulf and the Pamirs.[99]

London, then, is highly concerned with seeing that the eventual Russo-Japanese entente entails no sharpening or reviving of Russo-English tension. The position of the British Empire in the Southern Pacific as far as Japan is concerned would be certainly not made easier by a sharpening of Russo-English tension within the Indian Ocean area. It is, of course, an exaggeration to take into account to-day the possibility of an acute Anglo-Japanese conflict in the Southern Pacific. All the strategical preparations which are now being made by the British Empire in the Southern Pacific and on the sea routes giving access to the Indian Ocean are, at least for the time being, without political significance.[100]

I have tried here to trace the lines on which a geopolitical compromise between the Powers who decide the destinies of the Western Pacific may be based. These possible bases of compromise are necessarily at the same time causes of tensions and possible conflicts; to sketch the definite outlines of possible conflicts cannot be the subject of a geopolitical investigation. Prophecies of the kind usually are misleading because, besides the main factors at work, there are secondary and even chance elements which cannot be foreseen and which none the less decisively affect the historic issue. What, however, is both necessary and possible is to indicate those limits beyond which conflicts will be unavoidable. Russia can accept, at the worst, to be excluded from the Sea of Japan, but she will never without heavy fighting loose her hold on the Sea of Okhotsk, or let the source of her Siberian rivers in Northern Mongolia be removed from her sphere of influence. In either event Siberia itself would be endangered.

Nothing short of a heavy defeat in war can induce Japan to give up her supremacy inside her "sea trenches" between the La Pérouse Straits and the Ballingtang channel; the same is true of her positions in Manchuria.

The Government of Nanking, prepared as it is to make every kind of compromise on the provinces on the periphery of Great China, will fight to the death for the Chinese state-nucleus on the lower Yang-tse.

England and the United States, in our time at least, will never let themselves be driven from their position of supremacy in China's economy and China's trade; and Britain will not without war permit the handing over to Russian influence of the Indian glacis, Tibet, Afghanistan, and Persia.

Europe first experienced the great offensive of Asiatic "steppe imperialism," which advanced westwards in mighty waves. The Arab and Ottoman conquests were the offspring of this movement. Then in modern times came the counter-offensive of Europe eastwards into Asia, with Africa and America as intermediate stages. Counter-colonization was a European invention: the European peninsula defended itself against its mother Asia. Two great movements on land, the Russian and the American, one of which colonized the Eurasian, the other the American continent, both starting from the Atlantic region, collided in the Pacific. Both movements tend to go on expanding across the Pacific. From the oceanic side—across the Atlantic and Indian oceans—great colonizing movements burst into the Pacific area, after having completely subdued the Indian ocean region. China and Japan were awakened and drawn into the sphere of world politics. Then came the great counter-colonization movement by the peoples of Asia against Europe.

Two cultures come into collision in the Pacific, two cultures intermingled in the course of millennia to their mutual enrichment. Europe had taken the beginnings of her civilization from Asia Minor and for many centuries was open to Asiatic influences. Then things are reversed, for Asia accepts European culture. This European culture, however, is at a declining stage in its development. There is little doubt that the adaptation by Asiatics of European culture is not a final process. The Chinese culture is too old and too stubborn to give way to European culture. The other possibility, the orientalization of European-American culture, is also unlikely.[101] Perhaps we are nearing an epoch when both cultures will coalesce and merge to their mutual benefit.

NOTES TO CHAPTER II

1. "... qu'il n'est, pour ainsi dire, pas un moment de notre histoire occidentale où l'on puisse sans dommage faire abstraction de l'histoire de l'Asie," L. Halphen, "La Place de l'Asie dans l'Histoire du Monde," *Revue historique*, vol. cxlii, p. 13.

2. For the history of Asia I have used F. E. A. Krause, *Geschichte Ostasiens*, Göttingen, 1925, two vols.; René Grousset, *Histoire de l'Asie*, Paris, 1922; E. H. Parker, *A Thousand Years of the Tartars*, London, 1875.

3. A. and E. Kulischer, *Kriegs-und Wanderzüge. Weltgeschichte als Volkerbewegung*, Berlin and Leipzig, 1932, p. 65 sq.; E. Chavannes, *Documents sur les Tou-kioue (Turcs) occidentaux*, St. Petersburg, 1903, p. 264 sq.

4. On the history of the "Steppe-imperialism," besides the works above quoted, also N. P. Toll, *Skify i gunny*, Praga, 1928 (Russ., "Scythians and Huns"); G. W. Vernadsky, *Opyt istoriji Evrasiji*, Berlin, 1934 (Russ., "Essay on the History of Eurasia").

5. K. Haushofer, *Geopolitik des Pacifischen Ozeans*, Berlin, 1924, p. 429.

6. "At that time (i.e. in the second half of the sixteenth century) all that was worth claiming along the ocean sea-board of Africa from Morocco to the Red Sea was, in name at least, theirs; and wherever a European State had asserted political or trading powers along the southern coasts of Asia from Aden to the Moluccas, that State was Portugal. Her eastern capital, religious, commercial, and political, was fixed at Goa on the Malabar coast, and there she maintained a strong fleet" (W. H. Woodward, *A Short History of the Expansion of the British Empire*, 1500–1902, Cambridge, 1907).

7. For the history of colonial policies I have used Paul Leroy-Beaulieu, *De la Colonisation chez les Peuples modernes*, Paris, 1891 (4e ed.); H. E. Egerton, *The Origin and Growth of the English Colonies and of Their System of Government*, Oxford, 1903; W. H. Woodward, and L. C. A. Knowles, *The Economic Development of the British Overseas Empire*, London, 1928.

8. "I called the New World into existence to redress the balance of the Old" (cf. Harold Temperley, *The Foreign Policy of Canning, 1822–1827*, London, 1925).

9. Cf. Albert Bushnell Hart, *The Monroe Doctrine: An Interpretation*, Boston, 1916; Hermann G. James and Percy A. Martin, *The Republics of Latin America*, New York, London, 1923, p. 449 sq.

10. F. E. A. Krause, *l.c.*, vol. ii, pp. 319 and 465; Prince Varanaidya, "Le Statut International du Siam" in *Académie Diplomatique Internationale*, January–March, 1933, p. 55.

11. T. Dennet, *Americans in Eastern Asia*, New York, 1922, p. 298.

12. T. Dennet, *l.c.*, p. 298.

13. James and Martin, *l.c.*, pp. 341–2; F. E. A. Krause, *l.c.*, vol. ii, pp. 249–50.

In the circles most closely connected with Napoleon III it appears that there was a good deal of talk of schemes to create a great Catholic empire in the New World which would check the expansion southward of the United States and give France rich reserves of raw materials and a valuable export market.

14. Herbert Zühlke, *Die Rolle des Fernen Ostens in den politischen Beziehungen der Mächte, 1895–1905*, Berlin, 1929, pp. 31–2.—The new Trans-Caspian regions which had been incorporated into Russia were secured by the construction of the Trans-Caspian Railway (1885–88). Cf. Vernadsky, *l.c.*, p. 149.

15. Zühlke, *l.c.*, p. 32.

16. *British Documents on the Origin of the War, 1898–1914*, London, 1927, vol. ii, p. 270.

17. H. B. Morse, *The International Relations of the Chinese Empire*, London, New York, 1918, vol. ii, p. 286; cf. also Chapter I of this book, p. 27.

18. Morse, *l.c.*, vol. ii, p. 343.

19. Zühlke, *l.c.*, pp. 66–7; S. J. Witte, *Wospominanija*, 1848–94 (Russ.: "My Memoirs"), Berlin, 1923, pp. 391–5.

20, 21. G. Vernadsky, "The Expansion of Russia," in *Transactions of the Connecticut Academy of Arts and Sciences*, vol. xxxi, 1933, p. 425.

To estimate correctly Russia's position as a world-Power it is necessary to remember that Russia is an old iron country. There is in Europe a general tendency to forget that the industrializing and Europeanizing of Russia has been going on for three hundred years. The iron-works in Tula were established in 1632 in the reign of the first Czar of the Romanoff dynasty. At the end of the seventeenth century there was already a definite class of technical experts and of skilled workers, although it was a small one. The policy of Peter the Great, which aimed at making Russia a Great Power, was on the one hand based on the industrial development already achieved, and on the other hand it was just that policy which compelled Peter to seek to make Russia independent of Europe in the matter of armaments. At the end of his reign 14,000 tons of raw iron were produced annually in the State works alone, while at the same period England's total production was 18,000 tons. These were the days when Englishmen thought that it was hopeless for the native iron industry to struggle against Swedish and Russian competition. During the reign of Peter's daughter, Elizabeth, Russia's production of raw iron rose to 100,000 tons annually, while in England no increase in production was achieved. This growth of Russia's iron industry was based on the exploitation of the Ural deposits, where there was gigantic wood resources in the near neighbourhood of the deposits. It was, in fact, this circumstance of the proximity of wood fuel to the iron deposits that conditioned and secured Russia's position as a Great Power. It was not until the end of the eighteenth century that England's raw-iron production caught up with Russia's. English coal beat Russia's charcoal, and Russia's iron industry, which was based on serf-labour, fell behind England's after the marvellous development of capitalist industry in the latter country during the first decades of the nineteenth century. Russia's defeat in the Crimea and the collapse of her position as a Great Power was essentially the result of the change in the position of the two Powers as regards their iron industries. Cf. G. W. Vernadsky, *Opyt istoriji Evrasiji*, Berlin, 1934, p. 134.

22. Cf. Chapter I, pp. 77–79.

23. James and Martin, *l.c.*, p. 450.

24. Haushofer, *l.c.*, p. 136.

25, 26. P. N. Savicky, *O Zadatschach kotschewnikowedenija*, Prague, 1928, p. 88. (Russ.: "On the Problems of the Study of Nomads.")

27. G. W. Vernadsky, p. 140.

28. This letter of Napoleon I is alleged to still exist in the archives of the Russian Foreign Ministry. Napoleon declared emphatically that England would be subjugated, and Alexander I was to obtain as reward Stockholm (Louis Fischer, *The Soviets in World Affairs*, London, New York, 1930, vol. i, p. 418).

29. Woodward, p. 329.

30. Curzon, *Persia and the Persian Question*, London, 1892.

31. Cf. Heinrich Friedjung, *Das Zeitalter des Imperialismus, 1884–1914*, Berlin, 1919, vol. i, pp. 100–1, 162–3.

32, 33. Haushofer, *l.c.*, pp. 138–40.

34. Dennet, *l.c.*, p. 125 sq.

35. *Die grosse Politik der europäischen Kabinette, 1871–1914*, vol. xv, p. 416.

36. *Die grosse Politik*, vol. xvii, p. 557.

37. Zühlke, *l.c.*, pp. 104–8.

38. *British Documents on the Origin of the War, 1898–1914*, vol. i, p. 5 sq.

39. J. V. A. MacMurray, *Treaties and Agreements With and Concerning China 1894–1919*, New York, 1921, vol. i, p. 84 sq.

40. Friedjung, *l.c.*, vol. i, p. 149.

41. Krause, *l.c.*, vol. i, p. 269.

42. Karl Rathgen, *Die Entstehung des modernen Japans*, Dresden, 1896, p. 18.

43. The armada of Philip II was destroyed in 1583; the Chinese general, Li Yu-sung, defeated the Japanese at sea in 1597. As a result the latter were driven out of Korea.

44. Karl Haushofer, *Japans Werdegang als Weltmacht und Empire*, Berlin and Leipzig, 1933, pp. 20–6.

45. Virtually at the same time Korea entered on a period of self-isolation. It lasted from 1600 to 1868. As during that period Japan abandoned all attempts at an active foreign policy, China had no occasion to interfere in Korean affairs. Unlike Japan, which conserved the national resources during the period of self-isolation in order to use them later for an extraordinary expansion, Korean vitality was so sapped that when she re-entered world politics it was only as the helpless object of other States' policies. Cf. W. E. Griffiths, *Corea, the Hermit Nation*, London, 1882.

46. M. Pavlowitsch (M. P. Weltmann), *Sowjetskaja Rossija i imperialistitscheskaja Japonija* (Russ.: "Soviet Russia and Imperialist Japan"), Moscow, 1923, p. 10.

47. Dennet, *l.c.*, p. 275.

48. Zühlke, *l.c.*, p. 18.

49. Dennet, *l.c.*, pp. 418–19.

50. Haushofer, *Japans Werdegang*, p. 13.

51. The Treaty between China and Japan, which was ratified on April 3, 1873, is often described as an "Asiatic Alliance," although it was simply a convention of the usual type on reciprocal diplomatic representation, consular Courts, the mutual surrender of criminals, and so on (Krause, vol. ii, chapter i, p. 242). "It is worth while noting that in the course of the negotiations the Europeans for a moment feared lest the Japanese and the Chinese might make an alliance against them—a spectre which again appeared in the 'nineties." (Fühlke, p. 27).

52. Haushofer, *l.c.*, p. 31.

53. Curzon, *The Problems of the Far East*, London, 1894, pp. 215, 223 sq.

54. Krause, *l.c.*, vol. ii, p. 84; Morse, *l.c.*, vol. ii, p. 363.

55. The negotiations of the secret treaty were conducted in 1887 by the German expert adviser, P. G. von Moellendorf, who had been formerly adviser to Li-Hung-Chang (cf. Curzon, *Problems*, London, 1894, p. 24).

56. Zühlke, *l.c.*, p. 91. Cf. *The Secret Memoirs of Count Tadasu Hayashi*, edited by A. M. Pooley, London, 1915, p. 93.

57. Hayashi, Memoirs, p. 161.

58. Krause, *l.c.*, vol. ii, pp. 275–7; Milioukov, *La Politique Extérieure des Soviets*, Paris, 1934, pp. 242–3.

59. The Sazonoff–Motono agreement is reproduced in Thomas F. Millard's *Conflict of Policies in Asia*, London, 1924, pp. 488–9; cf. Millard, *Democracy and the Eastern Question*, London, 1919, p. 67.

60. Zühlke, *l.c.*, pp. 256–7, 267.

61. K. Haushofer, *Geopolitik*, p. 116; Dennet, *l.c.*, p. 177.

The first treaty between the United States and China was concluded on July 3, 1844, at Wang Hiya, near Macao. The negotiations were conducted for the United States by Caleb Cushing, who is the first of those American diplomats in the Far East who, relying less on the powerful position of their own country than on the precarious situation of China, achieved a great measure of success, and so appeared as friends of China. Cf. Louis Martin Sears, *A History of American Foreign Relations*, London, 1928, p. 232. "We should never have advanced a foot nor gained one concession but for the guns of the English; and we have invariably waited until they spent all the needful blood and treasure and then crawled in behind them and demanded (under what is called the 'most-favoured-nation clause' in the treaties) our share of privilege." (A. H. Hayes, "China and the United States," in the *Atlantic Monthly*, vol. lix, pp. 587–8.)

62. Dennet, *l.c.*, p. 216; cf. Sears, *l.c.*, pp. 296–7.

63. M. Pavlovitsch (M. Weltmann), *Sovetskaja Rossija i kapitalistitscheskaja Amerika* (Russ.: "Soviet Russia and Capitalist America"), Moscow, Petrograd, 1922, pp. 19–23.

64. A. T. Mahan, *Influence of Sea-Power Upon History*, 1890; *Influence of Sea-Power Upon the French Revolution and Empire*, 1893; and *The Interest of America in Sea-Power, Present and Future*, Boston, 1898.

65. The first Note of Secretary of State John Hay proclaiming the "open-door" policy regarding China was sent to the American Ambassador in Berlin on the occasion of the seizure by Germany of Kiau-chou on September 6, 1899. This note is reproduced in Millard, *Democracy and the Eastern Question*, pp. 361–3.

66. The Notes exchanged between Root and Takahira are printed in Millard, *l.c.*, pp. 270–2.

67. Cf. Whates, *The Third Salisbury Administration*, London, 1900.

68. W. R. Thayer, *The Life of John Hay*, Boston and New York, 1915, vol. ii, p. 165. Cf. on the development of policy from John Hay to Theodore Roosevelt, Sears, *l.c.*, pp. 433 sq., 455 sq.

69. Tyler Dennet, *Roosevelt and the Russo-Japanese War*, Garden City, New York, 1925, p. 2.

70. The texts of the three treaties of alliance between England and Japan are printed in J. V. A. MacMurray, *Treaties and Agreements With and Concerning China*, New York, 1921; cf. Sears, *l.c.*, pp. 498–9. A very striking analysis of the development of the Anglo-Japanese Alliance from the Soviet standpoint is made in "The Anglo-Japanese Alliance," by "Ajax," in the review *Nowy Wostok*, 1929, pp. 74–102.

71. Pavlovitsch, *l.c.*, p. 32.

72. Frank Fox, *The Mastery of the Pacific: Can the British Empire and the United States Agree?* London, 1928, p. 49. Cf. Sears, *l.c.*, p. 521 sq.

73. The Twenty-one Demands of January 18, 1915, the incomplete communication by the Chinese Government to the Allied Powers, the second edition of the "Twenty-one demands" on April 26, 1915, the Chinese Note in reply, and the Japanese ultimatum of May 7, 1915, the exchange of Notes between Peking and Tokio during the period, and finally the relevant conventions between China and Japan by which the former accepted the demands in milder form are repro-

duced in Millard, *Democracy*, pp. 373–420. Cf. Krause, *l.c.*, vol. ii, pp. 283–5.

74. The exchange of Notes between Washington and Tokio of February 4–9, 1917, will be found in Millard, *Conflict, l.c.*, pp. 450–1.

75. On the preliminaries to the Lansing–Ishii Convention cf. William E. Dodd, *Woodrow Wilson and His Work*, New York, 1920, p. 243 sq.—Lansing attempted afterwards to deprecate the significance of the convention of November 3, 1917, and especially the practical meaning of the phrase "special interests." He maintained that he and Ishii attached to it very different meanings. Cf. *Stenographic Report of the Testimony of Hon. Robert Lansing before the Foreign Relations Committee of the United States Senate, August 11th, 1919*, printed in Millard, *Conflict*, pp. 164–71. The full text of the Russo-Japanese secret treaty of July 3, 1916, will be found in Millard, *Democracy*, pp. 65–6. In 1916 Germany had twice offered the Japanese Government a separate peace between Germany on the one hand and Russia and Japan on the other. The proposal naturally was merely part of the great diplomatic offensive to break the Entente front, which was then being eagerly pursued by Berlin (cable from the Russian Foreign Minister, Sazonoff, to the Ambassadors in London, Paris, and Tokio on May 11, 1916; cit. by Millard, *Democracy*, p. 65). After the Bolshevik revolution Japan was obliged to modify her plans. It is very possible, however, that faced with this new situation Japan still contemplated the possibility of a *rapprochement* with Germany on the conclusion of a general peace. In any case, Japan's attitude toward Germany was a matter of serious comment in the British and American Press. Cf. Millard, *Democracy*, pp. 68–74.

76. Sears, *l.c.*, pp. 512–13. Cf. Wong Ching-wai (Chairman of the Governing Committee of the People's Government of China), *China and the Nations. Being the Draft of the Report on International Problems Prepared for the International Problems Committee of the People's Conference of Delegates in Peking in April 1925*, London, 1927, p. 76.

77. In the Anfu Club (so called from the initials of the provinces of An-hui and Fuchien—from which the most important members of the club came) the leading part was played by the Prime Minister, Tuan Ch'i-jui, who from June 1916, after the death of Yuan-Shi-kai, until May 1917, and then after the monarchist rising from July 1917 until the fall of the Anfu party in the autumn of 1920, held wellnigh dictatorial power in Peking.Cf. Krause, *l.c.*, vol. ii, p. 288 sq.

78. On the general international situation and on the relations of the Entente Powers with Soviet Russia, see Fischer, *l.c.*, vol. i, pp. 92 sq., 96. For the intervention by Japan, cf. Fischer, *l.c.*, vol. i, pp. 101 sq., 135; M. Pavlovitch, *Sovietskaja Rossija i Imperialistitscheskaja Japonija, l.c.*, pp. 44 sq., 61 sq., 67. Pavlovitsch's book contains: (1) the agreement of June 8, 1921, for joint military operations against the Bolshevik troops between the commanders of the Russian White Armies in the Far East and the commander of the Japanese expeditionary

forces. This agreement provided for the protection by the Japanese of the port and fortress of Vladivostok and for the Japanese control of the Chinese Eastern and Ussuri railways. By the same agreement special economic privileges regarding the mineral deposits, fisheries, and forests throughout the Russian Far East were assured to Japan; (2) the so-called "seventeen demands" presented by the Japanese delegation in August 1921 at the conference at Dairen to the Government of the Far Eastern buffer State called the "Far Eastern Republic." In these the Japanese demanded that the Government of the buffer State, which as that Government was completely dependent on the Moscow Government, meant the Soviet Union, should express its readiness to place the Russian Far East under a virtual Japanese protectorate. Cf. also W. L. Wilensky (Sibirjakow), *Japonija* (Russ.: "Japan"), Moscow, 1923, p. 76. On Japan's intervention in Mongolia and the adventure of Baron Ungern-Sternberg, cf. Iwan Jakovlevitch Korostovetz, *Von Cinggis Khan zur Sowjetrepublik. Eine kurze Geschichte der Mongolei unter besonderer Berucksichtigung der neuesten Zeit*, Berlin, 1926, p. 310.

79. General Baron Ungern von Sternberg was by race half a Russian from the Baltic provinces and half a Magyar. He was alleged to be a descendant of Jenghis Khan. His wife was a Manchurian princess, and he was himself a Buddhist. After seizing Urga in February 1921, he entered into an alliance with the Buddhist clergy and intended to avail himself of his ties with the Lamas to carry through his plan for the creation of the Great Mongolian State. Ungern-Sternberg is clearly a reincarnation of "steppe imperialism." Cf. Fischer, vol. ii, chapter i, p. 535.

80. T'Ang Leang-Li, *The Foundation of Modern China*, London, 1928, p. 156.

81. Fischer, *l.c.*, vol. ii, p. 546.

82. Hence the tendency on the part of the Japanese diplomats and statesmen to put forward excessive claims which after long haggling would be considerably modified. To quote one instance from not too remote a past: Even before the beginning of the negotiations at Shimono-seki in 1895 the Prime Minister, Ito, and the Foreign Secretary, Mu-tsu, had been informed that the three European Powers were likely to intervene, and that it would be quite impossible to achieve the "lease" of Port Arthur and the Liaotung peninsula. None the less, not only did the Japanese put forward this claim, but actually in the preliminary facts forced through a clause to that effect. Besides, their opponents, then represented on that occasion by the shrewdest Chinese politician of the nineteenth century, Li-Hung-Chang, were also aware of the impending step by the three Powers, and so cheerfully signed the preliminary peace, being perfectly sure that the treaty would prove to have no significance whatever. In the same cynical way Li ceded to Japan Formosa and the Pescadores, representing this as a great sacrifice; actually he literally talked the

Japanese into taking these islands, which were of no value whatever to China (*Hayashi Memoirs, l.c.*, pp. 53–5, 73–4). Great reserve ought to be shown whenever there comes news that wars are threatening in the Far East because of the "unyielding" attitude of the possible opponents. Unyieldingness usually contains a very big proportion of readiness to compromise. When an Asiatic diplomatist says "No," he very often means "Yes." Maurice Lachin, who was in the Far East from the autumn of 1933 to the spring of 1934, says: "Close relations for four months with the Gaimusho (the Tokio Foreign Office) enabled me to realize that the more alarmist the dispatches from Tokio are, the less is the likelihood that the situation will become critical in the near future" (Lachin, *Japan 1934*, Paris, 1934, p. 117).

83. On the Washington Conference, cf. Sears, *l.c.*, pp. 569–74; George H. Blakeslee, *The Recent Foreign Policy of the United States*, New York and Cincinnati, 1925, pp. 191–237.

84. Fischer, *l.c.*, vol. ii, p. 559.

85. "Americans once asked Sun-Yat-Sen what was Borodin's real name. 'His name is Lafayette,' was the reply. 'You did not help us,' the doctor continued, 'but Russia was the first country to aid us in the national struggle ' " (Fischer, *l.c.*, vol. ii, p. 633). General Galen (Blucher) formerly commanded a Red Army in the Ukraine. In 1923, with fifteen other Russian Staff officers, he was sent on a mission to Canton. Galen and his officers played a decisive part in the working out of the plan of campaign against the North. T. C. Woo, *The Kuomintang and the Future of the Chinese Revolution*, London, George Allen & Unwin, 1928, p. 120 sq.—Borodin, who was called by the Chinese Bao Ti-sing, until the end of his activity in China, exercised unlimited authority over the revolutionary masses of South China although the controversies inside the Kuo-Min-Tang became still sharper while he was there. But he was honoured, as the emissary of the Russian Revolution. Dr. Hu-shih, Professor of Philosophy in Peiping University and a recognized leader of the Chinese cultural renaissance, who has no Bolshevik tendencies, testified as late as the beginning of 1927, i.e. just before the end of Borodin's career in China, that Borodin, while visiting Hankow, had been acclaimed as leader by enormous crowds. Speaking at a luncheon of the Foreign Policy Association, which is one of the most important American societies for the study of foreign politics, Hu-shih asserted that from a Chinese standpoint Russian influence on the Chinese revolutionary movement had been thoroughly healthy. While Japan, as far as organization is concerned, went to school in Germany, China sought her education in Russia. (*Forward or Backward in China? Discussed by Dr. Hu-Shih, Mr. Grover Clark, and Dr. Stanley K. Hornbeck. A Stenographic Report of the 96th New York Luncheon Discussion, February 26, 1927, of the Foreign Policy Association*, New York City, pp. 33–4.) This reference to a connection between Japan and Germany on the one hand and China and Russia on the other is worth noting.

86. Chiang Kai-shek (original name Chiang-Chung-ching) was born in 1886 in the Chu-chiang province. He received his military training in the Japanese General Staff College in Tokio. In 1911 he became private secretary to Sun-Yat-Sen. In 1923, as Chief of the General Staff of Sun-Yat-Sen's army, he was sent to Soviet Russia to study the military system there. Upon the death of Sun-Yat-Sen he commanded in chief in the campaign against the Northern "militarists." In April 1927 he organized a counter-revolutionary coup against the left wing of the Kuo-Min-Tang (*China Year Book, 1933*, edited by H. G. W. Woldhead, Shanghai). Since 1928, with brief intervals of resignation, Chiang Kai-shek has continued in office, and is, in fact, the real ruler in Nanking. He is undoubtedly the most outstanding statesman in contemporary China, but his power is generally over-estimated abroad. Chiang has to "manœuvre" continually inside his own Cabinet, and also among the different military rulers. His foreign policy consists to a great extent in playing the Great Powers off against each other.

87. On the Soviet movement in China, which does not appear as a mass movement until 1927, there is only sporadic and uncritical information in the British and American Press. Nor can one have confidence either in the information from official quarters in Nanking or in the information in the Russian Press. But what is certain is that at times this movement has achieved widespread success, and has deeply influenced the peasant masses. We are dealing here with an agrarian revolution on the Russian model, that is a revolution of the poor peasant not only against the great landowners but also against the rich peasant (Kulaks: tu-hao). As a rule no attempt was made in South China to "collectivize" landed property. Land was not collectivized in the districts dominated by the Soviet movement. The seized land was redistributed first according to the number of mouths to feed, and then according to the man-power available. In South China the Red Army has always been a great throng of partisans but has a strong tendency to centralization, although there is no unity of command in it in any proper sense of that term. The character of the army is always changing, just as the whole Soviet movement is a movement of change and flux. In the autumn, 1930, Nanking put the Red Army at 70,000 strong, of whom only half were armed. In the spring of 1931 the Nanking War Minister estimated it as 300,000 strong, but with only 120,000 rifles. According to Russian sources, the Red Army after its reorganization in 1933 comprised seven corps—sixteen infantry divisions (cf. *Soviety v Kitaje. Sbornik materjalow i dokumentow. Nantschno-issledowatelskij institut po Kitaju pri Kommunistichečkoj Akademiji* (Russ.: "Soviets in China," Moscow, 1934). Chiang Kai-shek had in four years (December 1930–November 1934) to fight six campaigns against the Soviet armies, until he seemed to have got to some extent the upper hand over the movement. It is open to doubt, however, whether the movement can be suppressed by

military measures only. How extremely important is the agrarian revolution, which is the result of the Soviet movement in South China in the opinion of the moderate elements in China, is seen in the views expressed by Professor Hu-Shih, a thinker who is widely known even outside China, a politician of very moderate views—as far as is known he is not even a member of the Kuo-Min-Tang. In an article written in 1932 he asserts that not only should the agrarian revolution carried through by the Communists in the districts under their control (i.e. the expropriation of the great landowners and the cession of their land to the tenant farmers) not be revised, but that rather it should be reccgnized. In his opinion the peasantry in the provinces under the control of the Soviets have economically benefited (cf. *Ostasiatische Rundschau*, 1932, 21, p. 429).

88. Eastern Turkestan was incorporated in China in 1882 under the name Hsin-chiang. It constitutes the nineteenth province of the Chinese Empire. This province, the area of which equals that of France and Germany put together, has a population of 2,000,000 to 2,500,000. For millennia it was a battle-ground for all Asiatic conquerors and a route for their armies. About the middle of the eighteenth century the Peking Government took possession of East Turkestan, but actually never really controlled it. The Mohammedan population consisting of Sarts, Kirghizes, Tatars, and Tungans has never willingly accepted the predominance of the small ruling Chinese class. In the middle of the nineteenth century a great Mohammedan rebellion over the whole of the Sungari and Kashgar districts swept away the Chinese rule (Yakub Beg until 1877). During the rising the Russians occupied Kuldja (1871–81). Somewhat later the Chinese, after a long military campaign from Kan-su province across the desert, reconquered East Turkestan and made it their nineteenth province. Since 1912, and especially since the Great War, Hsin-Kiang has been at once the arena and the prize of warring foreign influences. The population is very mixed; the Tungans, who are Chinese Mohammedans from the Kan-su province whence they immigrated long ago, are the most important section. An important part is also played by *emigrés* from Russia. It seems that East Turkestan is becoming an object of Russian colonial policy, although reliable information on the point is not available. After the completion of the Turkestan-Siberian railway in April 1930 it was pretty clear that as a result of this enterprise East Turkestan would sooner or later be economically united to Russia. According to the *Far Eastern Review* (April 1930), the aim of the Turkestan-Siberian railway ("Turksib") was to make East Turkestan first an economic and then later actually a political part of the Soviet Union. There are only 600 km. between Urumchi (the capital of East Turkestan) and the nearest point of the Soviet Russian frontier, while the caravan route to the Pacific is 3,000 km. long (cf. *The China Year Book, 1933*, pp. 215–19). The very well-informed correspondent at

Harbin of the *emigré* Russian newspaper, *Poslednija Novosti* (published in Paris and edited by Paul Milioukov), asserts that between 1924 and 1928 and later the Russian Government won a decisive influence in East Turkestan (*P.N.*, April 28, 1934). This influence extends to the military and civil agents of the Peking Government as well as the Mohammedan population. Bolshevik influence became ever more apparent in the civil war which has been raging there without respite since 1931. It is therefore very probable that when the day comes when there will be a "general purge" in Asia, East Turkestan will be the object of Russia's annexationist policy. Hsin-chiang is very rich in mineral deposits. In the Western Althyn Tagh (Kerja district) 500,000 ounces of gold have on an average been mined each year. The resources of the country in copper, mineral oil, coal, and antimony are believed to be very extensive. (Cf. Otto Mossdorf, "China's entfremdete Aussenländer," in *Ostasiatische Rundschau*, 1932, Nos. 3 and 4, pp. 51–2, 77–8.)

89. The connection between Outer Mongolia and China had been practically severed even before the Great War after the fall of the Manchu dynasty. This huge area, three times as large as East Turkestan, and with a population of between 1,000,000 and 2,000,000, fell during the Great War, and still more after the victory of the Bolsheviks over their antagonists in Siberia, under Russian influence. The political status of Outer Mongolia in international law is not clear. On the one hand, in the Russo-Chinese Treaty of May 31, 1924, Chinese sovereignty is recognized; on the other, the Government in Urga, now Ulan Bathor (town of the red hero), claims complete independence. Actually the Moscow Government controls the policy, and especially the foreign policy, of Outer Mongolia, and so has secured a strategic position of the first rank. In 1924, upon the death of the last living Buddha (Jebtsun Damba Khotokhto) the Mongolian People's Republic was proclaimed; the dictatorship actually is in the hands of the Mongolian People's Party, which is affiliated to the Communist Internationale in Moscow. Cf. Otto Mossdorf, *l.c.*, pp. 50–1; Owen Lattimore, "Mongolia," in *The China Year Book, 1933*, p. 199.

The infiltration of the Russian influence into Outer Mongolia is facilitated by the Buriat Republic created by the Moscow Government in Trans-Baikalia in close contact with its Buriat kin in Mongolia. How ill-defined are the frontiers between the long stretch of Russian Siberia and the Turko-Mongol districts which are still formally under Chinese sovereignty may be seen by the fact that the district of Uriang-hai at the sources of the Yenisei between the great mountain lake Kossogol and the Sajan range was easily detached and incorporated (1921) in the Soviet Union as the Tanno-Tuva Republic, and in the attempt to create the Mongol Republic of Barga with Hailar as capital in North-west Manchuria during the Russo-Chinese conflict in 1929. Wilhelm Filchner, *Sturm über Asien* (Berlin, 1924), is interesting for the geopolitics of Central Asia, and particularly for the conflict between Russia and England in the first years of the century.

90. Soon after the armistice of 1918 T. F. Millard strongly urged that the United States must take an active and leading part in the reconstruction of China. Cf. e.g. his *Democracy and the Eastern Question*, especially chapter xiv.

91. Baron Giichi Tanaka (1863–1929), the best-known representative of Japan's forward policy on the continent of Asia in the post-War period, was trained in the school of the Cho-shu-genro, Yama-gata Aritomo, who actually guided Japan's foreign policy throughout the period 1895–1922. Like other Cho-shu people, Tanaka had originally served in the active army. In September 1918 he was appointed War Minister in the Hara Cabinet, and then later held the same office in the Taka-hashi Cabinet (1921) and in the Yama-moto Cabinet (1923). In 1925 he became leader of the Seiyukai party, and in April 1927 he formed his first Cabinet. The name Tanaka is in Far Eastern politics inseparably connected with the memorandum which he is alleged to have submitted to the Emperor directly on taking office on July 25, 1927. In the memorandum he asserts the inevitability of a war against Russia for Manchuria and Mongolia. This document, in which a comprehensive programme of territorial expansion on the Asiatic continent and of the strategic and military plans for its accomplishment were set forth with complete frankness, was considered internationally as the expression of the foreign political tendencies of influential military circles, although its authenticity was never admitted in Japan. The document (Memorandum on the positive policy to be pursued in Manchuria presented to the Emperor of Japan by Baron Tanaka, Prime Minister, on July 25, 1927) was, as far as I am aware, first published in the independent Chinese paper, *China Critic*, published in Shanghai in its issue of September 24, 1931.

92. Cf. "Ajax," *l.c.* (quoted in note 70), *Nowy Wostok*, 1929, No. 25, p. 85.

93. When Philander C. Knox was at the head of the State department during Taft's presidency, the participation of the American banks in the Six-Power Consortium for flotation of a loan for China was not only authorized, but actually Wall Street was urged to participate by the Washington Government. Participation was frowned upon when the Wilson administration took office. When asked by leading New York bankers as to the views of the Washington Government on American participation in the loan to China, President Wilson said: "The Government of the United States is earnestly desirous of aiding the great Chinese people. . . . It certainly wishes to participate . . . in opening up to the Chinese themselves and to the world the almost untouched and perhaps unrivalled resources of China. . . . But . . . our interests are those of the open door—the door of friendship and mutual advantage. This is the only door by

which we care to enter" (Edgar E. Robinson and Victor J. West, *The Foreign Policy of Woodrow Wilson, 1913–17*, New York, 1918, p. 182).

94. Thus in the twelfth century there was an alliance between the Sung dynasty in South China and the Northern Tungusic Kingdom of Chin against the Middle Kingdom Liao, and later in the middle of the thirteenth century the last but one Sung emperor, Li-tsung, concluded an alliance with the Northern invaders, the Mongols (under Khan Ugetei), against the State of Chin.

95. T. V. Soong (genuine name Sung Tsu-wen), born in 1891 and a graduate of Harvard, is the creator of China's modern financial system. When in 1925 he took over the Ministry of Finance in the Canton Government, the yearly revenue of the Government was 4,000,000 silver dollars; after he had been Minister for two years it had risen to 120,000,000 dollars. Soong is the representative of the American tendency within the Kuo-Min-Tang; he has close connections with Wall Street, where he spent two years as a voluntary worker in a bank. He is to people everywhere one of the best-known figures of the new China. Of great reforms he carried through we need only mention the suppression of the internal tolls (Li-Kin). As chief delegate of China to the London Economic Conference of 1933, Soong said that the chief task of the National Government was the raising of the standard of life of the people. If that was done China would become one of the greatest world markets and contribute greatly to the solution of the world crisis. In Nanking they talk of the "Soong dynasty," for his three sisters married K'ung Hsiang-hsi, Sun-Yat-Sen, and Chiang Kai-shek. K'ung Hsiang-hsi, born in 1881 and known as H. H. Kung, who in virtue of his direct descent from Confucius in the seventy-fifth generation has a ducal title is, like Soong, a graduate of an American university (Yale). From 1928 to 1930 he was Minister of Industry, and from the autumn of 1932 until the spring of 1933 was a special economic plenipotentiary in the United States and Europe. Kung, too, may be regarded as a connecting link between Chinese economy and international—particular American—financial circles.

96. The Sino-Japanese conflict brought about by the occupation of Manchuria in the spring of 1931, the recognition by Japan of the independent State of Manchu-kuo (protocol of Chang-chun, September 15, 1932), as well as all the diplomatic negotiations concerning these, are fully dealt with in *The China Year Book, 1933*, pp. 598–655. Here, too, can be found a summary of the Lytton report (*Report of the Commission of Inquiry into the Sino-Japanese Dispute*, Peiping, September 4, 1932). A statement of the Chinese official viewpoint will be found in the memorandum, *Le conflit Sino-Japonais Memoranda du Gouvernement Chinois, présentés à la Commission d'Etude de la Société des Nations*, Nanking et Peiping, April–August, 1932. For the American view, see *The United States in World Affairs: An Account of American Foreign Relations, 1931*, by Walter Lippman in collaboration with William O. Scroggs (Publication of the Council on

Foreign Relations), New York and London, 1932, pp. 246–72; and for the Japanese view, K. K. Kawakami (Washington Correspondent of the *Tokio Hochi Shimbun*), *Manchou-kuo Child of Conflict*, New York, 1933.

97. The standpoint of the Washington Government is stated in the note on the occasion of the Manchurian conflict, sent by Secretary of State Stimson, on January 7, 1932. "And that it does not intend to recognize any situation, treaty, or agreement which may be brought about by means contrary to the covenant and obligations of the Pact of Paris of August 27, 1928, to which treaty both China and Japan, as well as the United States, are parties."

The United States succeeded in Geneva in obtaining the adherence of other great Powers to this Stimson doctrine. These undertook not to recognize Manchu-kuo, and Japan withdrew from the League of Nations. It seems, however, that as time goes on Washington is adopting a less radical standpoint towards the Manchurian tangle. Edwin L. James, in the *New York Times* (January 27, 1935), observes resignedly "Washington now denies any intention of disavowing the Stimson doctrine. But there is a difference between an active policy in support of a doctrine and a disinclination publicly to disavow it. If and when the Japanese develop further their expansion into Eastern Asia, we will do one of the two things—something or nothing." Influential circles in the Senate are undoubtedly strongly reluctant to a naval race of armaments, for it is feared that such a race would only strengthen the position of the militarist clique in Tokio. Senator Borah not long ago used the words "sheer madness," and observed that "naval armaments races always have led to war." Cf. Raymond Leslie Buell in the *New York Times*, December 23, 1934.

98. That there is a strong tendency in Moscow towards reaching an understanding with Japan is indicated not only by the offers repeatedly made to Tokio of a non-aggression pact, but also by the reports of conflicting opinions within the Soviet Government on Far Eastern policy. The former first secretary to the Soviet Embassy in Paris, Bessedovski, who fled from the Soviet service in the autumn of 1929, published in the French Press revelations on Soviet diplomacy. According to Bessedovski, Chicherin (the Bolshevik Foreign Minister) in 1926 based his policy on the belief in a quarrel between the Cho-shu and Satsu-ma clans. In a conversation with Bessedovski when the latter was about to leave for Tokio as Counsellor of Embassy, Chicherin observed that while the Cho-shu (the Army clan) was hostile to Soviet Russia, the Navy clan, Satsu-ma, was more far-sighted because in their view the future inevitable clash between Japan and America was the main consideration. Hence, he said, the Satsu-ma clan was more conciliatory towards Moscow and sought agreement with it, an end to which the Prime Minister, Wakatsuki, and his Foreign Secretary, Baron Shide-hara, were also striving to attain. But Russia had to remember the influence of the Cho-shu clan. The circles closely

connected with Stalin entertained at that time the queerest hopes of the possibility of concluding with Japan a pact of non-aggression on the basis of non-intervention in Chinese affairs. Such a pact would have been thė best basis for the sovietization of China; Litwinow and the then Ambassador in Tokio, Kopp, thought such a policy was mere delusion. In 1928 Stalin in a conversation with Bessedovski gave him to understand that he was ready to surrender the Chinese Eastern Railway to Japan; in Stalin's opinion the tension between America and Japan would thereby be increased (v. *Ostasiatische Rundschau*, 1929, No. 22, p. 629 sq). Later, too, Moscow was still inclined to maintain a friendly attitude to Japan. It was ready to show Tokio that the interests of Japan coincided more with those of Russia than with those of England and America. At the same time, Moscow did not fail to point out that Russia could always find allies against Japan. Thus the official and influential Moscow journalist, Karl Radek, in April 1932, wrote: "The ruling classes of Japan ought to consider very carefully Japan's position to-day, and the policies they pursue. The position of Japan is much more difficult than that of Germany before the World War. Japan either will be isolated and at a decisive moment crushed, or she will be, in spite of her present military strength, a mere object in a conflict between England and America. In a great war, what is really decisive is economic resources, and those of Japan are not too large. If Japan chooses to co-operate in unity with the peoples of the Asiatic mainland aiding them and getting from them what she needs, she has a great future. If Russia is challenged, she will be justified in seeking temporary allies among those capitalist Powers who in the present stage of development threatens neither her boundaries and her interests."—K. Radek, *Portrety i pamflety* (Russ.), vol. ii, Moscow, 1934, pp. 303–5.

99. We may note that a worsening, but not too serious a one, of the relations between England and Russia in Central Asia would not cause much displeasure in certain European quarters. In connection with rumours about a pending Russo-Japanese Entente, the *Journal de Genève* (August 25, 1934), for instance, wrote as follows: "Tokio would have its hands free in the north of the Far East, while the Soviets would receive *carte blanche* in Central Asia, Chinese Turkestan, Afghanistan, Persia, even India. The British, indeed, would pay all the expenses of the transactions. The various clauses of the Russo-Japanese trade agreement concluded later (in the autumn of 1934) were discussed at length in the French Press, and it was especially noted that Japan was to buy petroleum and raw iron (40,000 tons within a year) from Russia. Cf. André Duboscq, "D'Extreme Orient en Asie centrale" (in the *Temps* of October 23, 1934), and Jacques Bardoux, "L'Angleterre et l'Asie" (in the *Temps* of January 1, 1935).

100. There is probably a tendency in America to exaggerate the extent to which the British position in the South Pacific is threatened.

But there is no doubt that in London and in the Dominion capitals measures are being taken for the strengthening of the strategic position of the Empire in the outlying district of the Indian oceanic sphere. We may mention the journey of Sir Maurice Hankey to India and the Dominions in the Pacific in the winter of 1934–35. Sir Maurice, who was formerly Secretary to the Committee of Imperial Defence, and since 1919 has been Secretary to the Cabinet, is admittedly the greatest expert in Britain on Imperial defence. During his travels he had the opportunity to discuss the problems of naval strategy with the Governments of Australia, New Zealand, and South Africa. As a result the South African Government placed at the disposal of the Imperial Government the important naval base of Simonstown, in the Cape Province. The Australian Government also agreed to concentrate not on submarines, but on the navy and on aircraft, and to give greater financial support to the fortification of Singapore. Still more important was its resolve to make all the railways in Australia of the same gauge, a factor of immense importance in mobilization (vide the *New York Times*, of January 6, 1935).

101. "Western civilization, sunk in materialism, paralysed, suffered with the crushing burden of capitalist organization, faces catastrophe. It is therefore the task of the East to renew the life of humanity. What is necessary now is to *orientalize* the world."—Ikuta Choko, who translated the works of Nietzsche into Japanese.

CHAPTER III

WAR AND STRATEGY

ANYONE who seeks to prophesy the possible course of a future war has to keep this fact firmly in mind, that an accurate forecast, even a very general one, is next to impossible, because it is beyond one's power to foresee the technical and political factors whereby the progress of the war will necessarily be conditioned. The general staffs, indeed, have to go on constructing plans for military operations without which modern warfare is unthinkable, but the politicians dare not mistake these for prophecy and must consider the future with a caution that is almost cynical in its scepticism.

Strategy constitutes an essential element in foreign policy, and that not only in the sense made famous by Clausewitz, who regarded war as the continuation of political action carried out with distinctly different media, but simply because the hopes and plans of the general staff, who have to weigh the chances of victory and the consequences of defeat, decisively influence action in the field of foreign policy. No one can claim to be an expert in foreign policy who has not to a certain extent grasped the principles of strategy and is not in fact himself a strategist. It is only after having ascertained the position as seen by the chief of the general staff that a Foreign Secretary can take his decisions. In 1911 the French Prime Minister, Joseph Caillaux, faced with the German challenge in what is known as "the Panther leap to Agadir," had to decide what line of policy to take; he asked General Joffre if France in the event of war could positively count on victory. The General gave an evasive reply, and Caillaux thereupon decided on a policy of understanding with Berlin.[1] Here as always plans of campaign in which there is so often an element of fantasy mattered little. What did matter was the necessity to get a view of the strategical situation clear enough to enable a foreign political decision to be taken. Here, then, we are not considering plans of campaign; we seek only to get a clear view of those fundamental strategical considerations which in the Pacific to-day condition the decisions taken by the nations and their Governments.

An attempt was made in the second chapter to explain the political tensions which exist in the Western Pacific and their historical development. In making it we tried to resist the temptation to indulge in prophecy, and to confine ourselves to discovering the possibilities and conditions of future development. Within the pentagon China–Russia–Japan–United States–England, the most acute tensions were found to be that between Russia and Japan on the one hand, and that between Japan and the United States on the other. We saw that this did not mean there were no other tensions. An acute conflict between the United States and England or between England and Russia is perfectly conceivable. Even the most unlikely combination of forces in the Pacific is not impossible. Most people to-day would regard as fantastic a continental alliance between Russia, Japan, and China against the two Anglo-Saxon Powers, or an Anglo-Russian Alliance against the United States and Japan, and yet any such combination is not only not impossible *per se*, but for either a good case could be made. In this chapter, however, we dismiss these and confine ourselves to explaining the strategical beliefs which condition contemporary foreign policies, and so we need consider only the most probable variants of a military conflict in the Pacific. The most probable forms which that conflict will take are (1) a conflict between Russia and Japan, (2) a conflict between Japan and the United States, (3) a combination of both. In what follows we will have to consider each separately, though it may be taken for granted that in the present foreign political situation no two-Power conflict is likely to remain such.

§ 1. RUSSIA AND JAPAN—SOME FIGURES

A war between Russia and Japan would from the military point of view be even more continental in character than the two wars already fought by Japan on the Asiatic mainland—the Sino-Japanese War of 1894–95 and the Russo-Japanese War of 1904–5. The two other military expeditions to the continent in which Japan took part, the international expedition during the Boxer rebellion in 1900–1, and the capture from Germany of her colony Kiau-chou in the autumn of 1914 were very limited in character and cannot be used for purposes of comparison.

In any future war the paramount factor will be one which in the two previous wars was of a secondary importance, and that is the economic factor.

A modern great war—and a future Russo-Japanese war cannot but be on the scale of a great war—is not only a fight between armed forces, but equally, perhaps more so, a contest between the economic mechanisms of the belligerents. It would serve no useful purpose to make here a detailed comparison between the economic structures of Japan or the Soviet Union, and in any case we can gain sufficient knowledge of the comparative strength, from the point of view of war, of both these economic organisms by simple deduction from the main facts of the economic situation.

Both these Powers in the post-War period have passed through a stage of top-speed industrialization, and in both, though not to an equal extent in each, the influence exercised by the State upon the development of economic life has been very great. In Russia, the whole economic machinery, agriculture included, is owned by the State, and centralized management on a uniform plan is exercised by the Government. In Japan, the State, without interfering with private ownership, and without directly controlling the means of production, has acquired fundamental influence over the key-industries, and especially over those industries which will be directly concerned in permitting a war to be carried on, i.e. the heavy industries, engineering, ship-building, and the chemical industries. As a result of State support these industries have flourished; they have had the advantage of heavy subventions and credits, protective tariffs and the like. Besides, State-owned armaments factories form a considerable part of the armament machinery of the country; in peace-time the military arsenals in Osaka, Tokio, and Nagoya employ at a minimum 10,000 hands, and their full capacity, reckoned in terms of man-power, is many times higher.[2]

In Russia and Japan alike, national defence and military preparedness were the chief factors inducing intensive industrialization. For the same reason a large-scale concentration and centralization of the heavy industries was carried through. The tremendous scale upon which this has been achieved in Russia is generally well known, where, too, it was a necessary consequence of the policy of State socialism *plus* State capitalism. It is less well known that by different methods Japan has secured nearly as great a concentration of her armament industry; no less than three-quarters of the whole productive capacity in steel can be in war-time supplied by three factories, of which the biggest is the State-owned factory of Yawata in Northern Kyû-shû.[3]

In the Soviet Union in peace-time the preparation for general economic and political mobilization is entrusted to the "Council for Labour and Defence," which is composed of eight representatives of the Government departments directly involved, and meets under the chairmanship of the President of the Council of Commissaries. This body is responsible for co-ordinating the activities of the various departments (commisariats) from the point of view of national defence. Details of its work are not available.[4] Japan has gone a long way towards the solution of the problem of maintaining the resources of the country in such a state that, when in the event of war they are placed under the direct control of the State, their efficiency will be at the highest level possible. As early as 1926 the

"Council for the Mobilization of the National Reserves," and its agency the "Office for the Mobilization of the National Reserves" were set up. The law defining the limits within which those institutions should function and the regulations thereto were promulgated in 1929. The Council for the Mobilization of the National Reserves is composed of thirty-eight members, including the War Minister, the Minister for the Navy, and the Minister for Commerce and Industry, and their under-secretaries, the Secretary of the Cabinet, the Director of the Social Department of the Home Office, the General Manager of the State-owned iron and steel works in Yawata, the Secretaries of the Mobilization Departments of the War Ministry and the Admiralty, thirteen Members of Parliament, and technical experts. The Office for the Mobilization of the National Reserves is really the executive body which carries out the decisions of the Council. It thus exercises in peace-time a control over the whole of the industry concerned—that is, virtually control over the whole economic life of the country—and naturally enough it devotes especial attention to the militarizing of the population, to militarist propaganda and to the combating of so-called subversive movements. In every Government department in Japan there is a section dealing with questions concerning mobilization, and all these sections are placed under the direct authority of the "Office." Similar sections exist within the administration of all railways and in most private undertakings of national importance. Thus transport, finance, labour, foreign trade, the feeding of the civil population are now all controlled by this Government within the Government. We may note, too, that Japan seems to be ahead of all other countries in her preparations for mobilization and their testing. Thus in 1929 there was a test mobilization lasting a fortnight of all industries, transport included, in the central industrial area—that is the prefectures of Osaka, Kyoto, and Hiogo, with a population of about 18,000,000. The test was very successful.[5]

At this point we may attempt to make a comparison between

the Soviet Union and Japan in respect of those key industries of importance to modern war.

PRODUCTION IN THOUSANDS OF METRIC TONS[6]

	Soviet Union		Japan	
	1934	1935	1934	1935
Coal	93,610	108,900	36,000	37,500
Coke	14,220	16,730	1,316	1,731
Pig Iron	10,428	12,453	1,772	1,930
Steel	9,693	12,520	3,923	4,500
Oil	24,147	25,139	212	268

The advantage held by the Soviet Union in figures is obvious. Its coal and oil not only supply the total demand of home consumption but leave a certain margin for export; in the latter case a very considerable one. Japan's production is much lower. Although her coal production is now just able to meet the home demand, there is very little anthracite in Japan and the coal produced is not fit for coking. As a result her production is of very limited use so far as the iron industry is concerned. Nor is the coal supplied by the Manchurian collieries much better from this point of view. As a result the Japanese iron industry is dependent on coal imported from China on the basis of 1 : 4 to the Japanese home production.

But in war-time another factor has to be considered; the Island of Hokkaido has rich fields of coal perfectly suitable for all industrial purposes. These fields because of their geographical situation are in normal conditions of no commercial value; they constitute, however, an important asset, the existence of which would secure the functioning of Japan's war industries even in the case of a sea blockade.[7]

The mineral oil situation is much less favourable. According to so great an expert in Japanese economics as the American Orchard, only one-third of the whole demand can be covered by home production. This is the most favourable estimate yet made, and it may be explained by the fact that Orchard included in his figures the productive capacity of the Japanese concessions in Russian Sakhalin.[8] Other American estimates state that home supplies, Formosa and Manchuria included, of mineral oil can in peace-time cover hardly more than one-seventh of the demand,[9] and W. Batrak, a contributor to the publications periodically issued by the Russian military authorities, does not believe that Japanese home production can supply more than one-tenth of the demand.[10] Although such differences in estimates make speculation rather uncertain, they enable us to state that for at least one-quarter of her mineral oil consumption Japan depends on foreign sources.

As to the origin of imported mineral oil, a reliable estimate gives 50–60 per cent, as coming from the United States, and above 30 per cent from the Dutch Indies (oil-fields of the "Asiatic Petroleum Co." associated with the "Royal Dutch Shell Company"); the rest is shared between the oil wells in North Sakhalin (Russian part of the island) and those in North Manchuria. Except in the case of an isolated war against Russia, in which the Japanese will certainly maintain their undisputed mastery over the sea, some difficulties in the way of mineral oil supply may arise (especially in a war against the United States).

In the case of an isolated war against Russia, Japan, even if faced with an embargo laid by Washington on the export of mineral oil, not only from the United States, but also from Mexico and Venezuela, can continue to import this product from the Dutch Indies, China (Northern Shen-hsi), and Manchuria. Large quantities of mineral oil have been already stored by the Japanese Government in tanks at Yokosuka and Kure, and in the islands under Japanese mandate. These tanks alone are expected to be able to provide for the country's total needs for a period of six to nine months. Russian experts believe that, even if foreign supplies were completely stopped by an efficient sea blockade, serious difficulty as far as oil is concerned would only begin to be felt in the second year of the war.[11]

In the heavy industries the Soviet Union's position is also far stronger than is Japan's. Russia's heavy industry is solidly based on the home iron ore, while Japan's iron-ore deposits are entirely inadequate. American experts state that on a basis of a yearly consumption of three million tons, Japan's iron-ore deposits would be completely exhausted within twenty-five years.[12] The present annual consumption averages 2,200,000 tons. The main islands of Japan supply 10–12 per cent of this quantity; about 35 per cent comes from Korea, the Kwan-tung peninsula, China, and South Manchuria; and the remaining 50 per cent or so is imported from the Malay States. About 3,500,000 tons of iron ore and 1,500,000 tons of iron scrap are stored in the State-owned steelworks of Yawata.[13] Russian experts incline to believe that, in spite of the weak home basis of the Japanese iron industry and in spite of an efficient sea blockade which would cut off all foreign sources of supply, Japan in this sphere, too, would not begin to find the position serious until the second year of the war.[14]

As far as the bases of armaments—raw iron and raw steel—are concerned, Russian production stands to Japan's at approximately 2·5 : 1 (compare statistics, p. 218). In the event of war the ratio might, as a result of Japanese enterprise, change to Russia's disadvantage; although Russia, too, will undoubtedly be able to increase considerably her production during the war. According to Russian sources, the producing capacity of the Japanese heavy industries in 1935 was 4,500,000 tons of raw steel and 4,000,000 tons of raw iron. In peace-time a considerable portion of the demand in raw iron is covered by regular imports from India and from Manchuria. If war broke out Japan would certainly be able, if necessary, to do without such import.[15]

It is utterly impossible to obtain any reliable information as to the production of the munition industries proper, that is, in the narrow sense of the term, in either State. A study of the output in the engineering industry may give a rough idea, although in this field, too, many items are lacking. There is undoubtedly a large margin in Japan's favour in shipbuilding, a fact frankly recognized by the Soviet technical Press. A very essential factor in the motorizing of the army is the motor industry. Here Russia is much ahead, simply because of the fact that the organization of Russian agriculture on the collective basis opened up a tremendous field for the use of tractors, while the small-estate agriculture of Japan gives little opportunity for large-scale use of such machines and no true comparison is possible.

MOTOR PRODUCTION IN RUSSIA[16]

	1932	Planned for 1933 according to the Second Five Years' Plan	Produced within the Period January to June 1933
Tractors	50,640	80,000	40,000
Lorries	23,845	40,000	22,000
Motor cars	?	?	6,000

This table, which shows a large increase in automobile production within a very short period, may be taken also as illustrating the general growth of industry in Russia.

In Japan the total output of the two biggest factories, Ford in Yokohama and General Motors Co. in Osaka, is 25,000–30,000 cars a year, but both firms actually limit their activity to assembling parts imported from America. According to Russian estimates, the six Japanese arsenals could produce in the event of war 25,000 armoured cars a year. Russian experts sum up Japan's position in this sphere thus: The Japanese home industry is not able to provide more than one-third of the automobiles, armoured cars, and tanks needed in war-time. The remaining two-thirds would have to be imported, while Russia undoubtedly can obtain everything she can possibly need within her own borders.[17]

It may be assumed that the production of the chemical industries in both countries—i.e. the production of explosives and all other chemical stuff likely to be used in a modern war (including anti-gas appliances), will approximately balance.[18]

There is still one raw material to be discussed before the economic comparison is complete, and that is rubber. In the Bonin islands and in Formosa there are about two hundred plantations which now already cover (1932 production, 15,000 tons) 28 per cent of the Japanese peace-time consumption. The Japanese Government has believed it necessary to provide for the further quantities essential by trying to secure for Japan plantation concessions in the Malay States, in the Dutch East Indies, and in South America.[19] Russia possesses plenty of land suitable for plantation, and is believed to have already begun to develop tropical cultures within its borders. German sources state that several large plantations with factories have been lately started which within the next few years will be able to supply Russia's needs.[20]

In general it may be said that the armaments of Japan and of the Soviet Union are of the same standard, or rather that both belong to the same category. Both States have passed in the very near past from a primitive agricultural economy to one based on intensive industrialization. In Russia "technical culture" is much older and more independent than in Japan. Russia is an old iron country (cf. Chapter II, notes 18 and 19), while the basic raw material of the ancient Japanese technique is wood.[21] This radical difference might be of considerable importance in the technical sphere in the course of a war. The history of the Great War is sufficient to prove the extent to which experience gained on the battlefield can revolutionize technique while a war is actually in progress. Here the ingenuity and inventiveness of military technical experts can be decisive,[22] and equally the lack of these qualities or of a technical tradition can contribute to failure. Russia in this respect will probably be far ahead of Japan, which has had to import from abroad not only military machines but military conceptions as well. This is in no way to reflect on Japanese culture as a whole; the development of military technique can never be considered as a just standard of national culture.

In one respect Russia has a clear advantage over Japan in the event of war; her resources of power and raw materials are infinitely greater. This superiority will, however, only tell if Japan is cut off from her overseas sources of raw materials. As far as iron ore, mineral oil, and rubber are concerned, Japan's vital spot is the Southern Pacific. The loss of the South Pacific sources would make it almost impossible for Japan to carry on a long war such as Japan must envisage. Thus Japan is dependent upon the benevolent neutrality of that Power which actually controls trade sea routes and the sources of raw materials in the Southern Pacific. A war against Russia would be a most dangerous adventure for Japan unless she succeeded in securing the benevolent neutrality of the British Empire. The only alternative would be for Japan to have recourse to America which, political obstacles apart, would from the technical point of view mean a very serious complication of the economic situation in war-time, since those new sources lie much farther away. Such a change would imply a new political orientation in the sense of a *rapprochement* between Japan and the United States. We have already shown that such a *rapprochement* is not in itself impossible, but it need not be considered now when we are discussing the general strategical position.

Although there is no doubt that a war in the future will be a "total war" waged "in three dimensions," on land, on sea, and in the air, and will be a war of machinery and raw materials, we still believe that even in the mechanized, motorized warfare of the future, if there is an approximate equality in armament, the ultimate superiority will be with the nation which is better able morally and intellectually to stand the strain which modern war puts on soul and nerves.

No one can deny that in spite of, nay, because of, the achievements of science which have so transformed war, it is always man who carries on a war, no matter how he may be armed and equipped.

Since war has been in the world, what has mattered always has been man and never the machine.[23]

At the present stage of military technique, it is highly probable that in the next war, too, huge masses will prove to be the main factor in it. The present French instructions on the tactical use of large units refer to "the gigantic masses which were set in movement on a conscript system," and of the unbroken fronts which made fire action futile, and declare it to be likely that "similar situations will again occur in the future."[24]

It is foreign to our purpose to draw a comparison between the populations of the two States. But in order to get some idea of the man-power on which each State can draw, we may compare the number of able-bodied men each possesses.

The number of men between 18 and 44 years of age is for Russia about 31,000,000, for Japan about 17,000,000 to 18,000,000. Both figures are for the year 1933. These are not absolute figures, but they are not disconsonant with the fact that Russia's reserves of population are roughly 70–80 per cent greater than Japan's.[25] This comparison, of course, has no bearing on the relative strength which either could bring to bear against the other in the field in the Far East. That is determined principally by technical factors, especially by that of transport. These factors, of which we shall speak presently, make it impossible for either to put in the field an army corresponding to its available population power. But that power is of great significance for the maintenance not only of the army but of the home front. The mechanized army of to-day requires a great labour army at home for the production and repair of war machines and their parts, as well as for the production of raw materials for the armaments industry.

Modern military writers estimate that to keep a machine gun in action needs six workers at home; a tank needs 76, and an aeroplane 125.[26]

In war-time female labour is used on a large scale in the armaments industry. This use of female labour, however, means a withdrawal of labour from those branches of economic activity which are in normal times woman's field of activity, especially domestic duties, a withdrawal which inevitably entails the destruction of the whole social and economic organization of a country.

Therefore, from the point of view of war economy, the reserves of *man*-power are more important than the reserves of *population*-power. Here Russia has a distinct advantage over Japan. Her surplus of reserves is, as we have said, 70–80 per cent greater than Japan's, and it is wrong to assume, as some writers do, that, as the reserves of both are in a sense unlimited for a war on the Asiatic mainland, in that respect they may be regarded as equal.

Much more important, however, than the problem of numbers is the problem of the army, a phrase which to-day is synonymous with the *moral* of the warring nation itself.

It may be said that to-day it is the moral factor which actually determines the result of a war. It is the unanimous opinion of all military experts that one of the chief causes of the Russian defeat in 1904–5 was the low *moral* of the Russian troops. The war was extremely unpopular in Russia; the rank and file had no idea for what they had to fight and to die. "The causes of our failure were varied and complicated," declares one of the Russian commanders in that war, "but the true cause was something fundamental; it was the lack of patriotism, of the sense of duty to one's country."[27] The Japanese soldier, officer and private alike, was, on the contrary, fully conscious that what was at stake was the fate of the fatherland, and so that of themselves and their families. Mothers and wives gladly sent sons and husbands to the war, for the war was the affair of the whole nation. There was even a case of a mother committing suicide for sheer rage or shame that her son had been rejected as unfit.[28]

Thirty years ago, at the time of the Russo-Japanese War,

Japan had not yet passed out of the agricultural stage of her development. Japanese industry was in its beginnings; capitalist development had not yet ruined agricultural economy; home industry and the crafts were still dominant in the economic life of town and country. Social organization was still in the transition stage between feudalism and capitalism, although that stage was marked by the emergence, in a feeble form it is true, of the class struggle, and of a class basis for the social structure. The amount of proletarian labour in the big industries was still very limited, and there was hardly anything worthy the name of a labour movement in the modern technical and political sense. Japan in 1904–5 was an example of a social organism little affected by capitalist development whose ideology was essentially the same throughout. It is here that are to be found the reasons for the high *moral* of the Japanese troops.

On the contrary, in Russia of that period capitalist development and the disintegration of the old order were much more advanced. The Russian proletariat could already be counted in millions, and was concentrated in several big industrial areas. The peasantry was in a state of unrest and revolt, and Russia was ripe for revolution. Actually she entered the war of 1904–5 under revolutionary conditions.

As to the relative strengths of the armies, the decisive factor then was the overwhelming proportion of illiterates in the Russian Army. They were of so low a cultural level that it was extremely difficult to carry through the operations of modern war which require the possession by the individual soldier of intelligence and initiative. On the other hand, the educational level of the Japanese private and especially of the Japanese non-commissioned officer was relatively much higher, and so they could take part intelligently in action.[29]

To-day the "moral situation" has changed greatly to Russia's advantage. The Russian Army of to-day is a much more homogeneous and morally much stronger organism than was the old Czarist army. The "red army of workers and peasants" is a force which is imbued with political conceptions and almost fanaticized. The backbone of this army is the Communist party inside it, which includes about 50 per cent of the rank and file, and approximately 70 per cent of the commissioned officers. Only some 10 per cent are officers of the old army. There are no illiterates in the ranks of Russia's army to-day and, according to the unanimous opinion of observers, even of those unfriendly to Communism, the educational level of the army as among the Russian people generally is infinitely higher than it was fifteen years ago. "The Red Army private is even more different from the Czar's soldier than Napoleon's grenadiers were from the mercenaries of the Bourbons."[30]

One of the results of the great Russian Revolution is undoubtedly a far greater unity throughout the whole social organism. The "classless society," which is the ultimate aim of the Revolution, is, of course, not yet in existence, and will hardly be achieved within a conceivable future, but it is true to say that there is now no longer anything in the nature of a class struggle in the pre-Revolutionary sense. Owing to the authoritarian form of government and the type of education such a regime adopts, there has, in the course of the last fifteen years, come into being a more or less universal ideology, a notable feature of which is an individual patriotism which amounts almost to chauvinism. Although a general mobilization would considerably modify the character of the peace-time army from the political point of view, it cannot be denied that the Russian reservist is very different from his predecessor of thirty years ago. The military education and militarization of the whole population, and especially of youth, has been pushed very far,[31] although counter-factors certainly ought not to be forgotten, such as the existence of many discontented sections of the population and the fact that the Soviet regime is not yet deeply rooted. In the case of a long war these factors would naturally become important. But it would be a serious blunder to assume that in Russia discontent and opposition is more significant than elsewhere. A popular rising against the

Soviet Government is conceivable as the sequel to complete military collapse, but in the case of an isolated war against Japan is, as we shall see later, hardly to be anticipated.[32]

The state of *moral* in the Japanese Army is at least equal to that in the Russian Army, and probably is even better. Soviet journalists talk of the possibility of revolutionary movements in Japan itself, and even in the army in the field, but such possibilities should not be exaggerated.[33] It is, however, true that Japan to-day is not so united and homogeneous as it was in 1904–5. The proletariat employed in the big industries numbers several millions. It is already strongly organized in the trade-union sense. There is a fairly serious tendency to strike.[34] There are also illegal Communist movements on the strength of which there is no accurate information. A certain light, however, is shed by the report, even though it comes from the Soviet Russian sources, that in 1932, 8,000 persons were arrested on charges of Communist activity.[35] There is serious discontent among the peasants expressed in ever more numerous conflicts between the farmer-tenants on the one hand and the landowners on the other.[36] Although it is wrong to exaggerate the significance of all these phenomena, it must be admitted that the social conflict in Japan has since 1904–5 considerably increased in direct ratio to the rapid pace of the social and economic development of the country within the last thirty years. Such social changes may, in the case of an unfavourable turn of events in war-time, prove to be a source of weakness, while the greater social unity of Soviet Russia must be reckoned as one of the main assets of the Moscow Government in the event of war.

The Japanese Army of to-day has undoubtedly fully preserved its old traditions, and also the high *moral* which made victory certain in the war of 1904–5. But the Russian Army of to-day has a *moral* far higher than that of the army of 1904–5, so that if one cannot speak of Russia having an advantage here, one can at least state that what change has taken place is all to Russia's advantage.

§ 2. STRATEGY IN A RUSSO-JAPANESE WAR

Strategy does not, or rather does not entirely, consist in the study of military history. Technical development in warfare and political circumstances so rapidly change that the lessons of history have no decisive significance for strategy. War, too, is one of the most complicated phenomena of life, the course of which is influenced by such different, even totally contradictory, factors that the observer has to ascribe much that he views to "chance."

There is no other human activity, as Clausewitz says, that is so constantly and consistently affected by "chance" as war. But side by side with what may be called "chance" in war, there are the geographical limits within which war is waged and which remain the same no matter how technical, and especially transport, factors may change. Strategy is in a very definite sense determined by the geography of the theatre of war, and so the lessons of the wars fought of old on the same battleground may be useful in the future, although all the political and technical factors have been altered out of recognition.

A war between an insular State like Japan against a neighbour which, like Russia, is a continental State will be greatly influenced by the development of events at sea. In the two wars fought by Japan in the course of the last forty years against the States on the Asiatic continent, sea power proved to be a decisive factor. The supreme significance of the naval operations for the decision on land is well illustrated by the war between Japan and China.[37] The war that may follow between Japan and Soviet Russia will begin, in addition to air bombardments and air reconnaissance, with a landing on a large scale by Japanese expeditionary forces in Northern and Southern Korea and in Southern Manchuria, and possibly at other points on the coast of the mainland.

No doubt the air-arm will play an incomparably greater part in the next war than in earlier wars. But we cannot at the moment regard aircraft at the present stage of aerial development as a reliable factor in strategy, not only because it is beyond our powers to foresee even the next stage of that development, but because no offensive technique is absolute, but is conditioned by the technique of the defence against it. For this reason we cannot agree with the sanguine view, not shared, incidentally, by all Russian experts, that the near proximity of the Russian air bases constitutes an insurmountable obstacle to Japanese strategy. It may be accepted that the Russian air-arm is quantitatively and even qualitatively stronger than Japan's, that the Soviet Government has concentrated in the coast province, i.e. within a distance on an average of a thousand miles of the vital centres of the Japanese industry, a sufficient air force, and that that force has adequate, well-protected, and well-armed bases.[38] The menace to Japan is clear, but nothing can be said on the seriousness of the menace so long as we are ignorant of the counter-factors—weather conditions and Japan's air defences. On the atmospheric and weather conditions in the Sea of Japan, Captain N. L. Klado, one of the best-known Russian naval strategists of the old navy, who for many years held high posts in the Russian Navy in those waters, says that there is heavy frost from December to April and fog from May to July, with the result that naval operations are much impeded during those months.[39] Aircraft, naturally, is even more seriously handicapped by such weather conditions, and the period left for air action, and especially for bombing, is limited to four to five months. As to the Japanese air defences, these, in the view of Russian experts, are excellent and well organized.[40] Therefore it may be accepted that a raid by Russian bombers on Japan's vital centres at the outbreak of the war would not materially affect the general situation. But the situation would definitely alter if the Russian air forces were able seriously to challenge the Japanese Navy, and to threaten Japan's supremacy at sea. Moscow is convinced that relatively soon Russia could act against the Japanese Navy with a strong air fleet.[41] In theory, a battle between a well-armed air fleet and a navy is perfectly possible, and has been tried out in manœuvres (especially in the United States), but it would be idle to advance any definite opinion on its outcome without having actual war experience. Taking into account the present technical development, the Russian air forces can hardly be said to constitute a serious menace to Japan's supremacy at sea.

The Russian naval forces in Far Eastern waters, according to German sources, consist of two torpedo boats, one mine-layer, and a few submarines—a recent (June 1936) Japanese estimate talks of about fifty submarines. It would certainly be a waste of time to discuss the "chances" of such a navy against the powerful Japanese fleet. The Russian flotillas on the River Amur and on Lake Hanka (to the west of Spask) may, however, be of positive service to the Russian operations on land. As far as naval warfare is concerned, they may be left out of consideration. Thus it may be accepted that Japan's supremacy at sea will remain as undisputed as it was in the second period of the Russo-Japanese War of 1904–5, or throughout the whole course of the Sino-Japanese War of 1894–5. But the picture may be modified as a result of the activity of Russian submarines which in all probability will be brought in great numbers by railway to Vladivostok, and of the attacks by Russian air forces on the Japanese fleet, which might well interfere with Japanese troop transports overseas. On the other hand, we must remember that the Japanese possess four aeroplane carriers of a total tonnage of 69,370 (two more are under construction) and three aircraft tenders which can take on board two hundred machines. Besides that, all the Japanese battleships and battle-cruisers carry aeroplanes as part of their armament. These moving air bases which Russia altogether lacks in the Far East may play a great part in repelling air attack at sea, and in protecting troop transports against the bomber.[42]

The extreme importance to Japan of supremacy at sea in the event of war with the Soviet Union may be realized by any student of the two earlier wars fought by Japan on the continent. Japanese strategy on the continent, the landing operations, the deployment and concentration of her armies were possible only because of her undisputed control of the sea routes. Certainly the Japanese victory was the result of the battles on the mainland, but the essential condition of victory on land was supremacy at sea. And there is one other lesson to be learned from those two wars: only at sea can Japan be vanquished. There was a party at Russian general headquarters, including the Commander-in-Chief, Kuropatkin, which shortly before the cessation of the hostilities strongly maintained the view that the Russian army was now strong enough to undertake a successful offensive against the Japanese. That may have been correct from the standpoint of land strategy, but without a fleet strong enough to wrest from the Japanese fleet the supremacy at sea, or at least seriously to injure that fleet, ultimate victory was impossible. That has been irrefutably demonstrated in the brilliant pamphlet by the Russian naval strategist, N. L. Klado, from which we have already quoted.[43] The arguments he then advanced are equally valid to-day.

The deployment and concentration of the Japanese armies will be considerably facilitated by the fact that they have in Northern Manchuria a magnificent, already prepared field of deployment, while at the beginning of the war the Russian forces will be spread in a long curve from Vladivostok to Verkhne-Udinsk. The Japanese will have all the advantages of "interior lines," both in the broad and the narrow meaning of that term. On the one hand the sea routes are open to them, and so they are able to effect movements of troops on a large scale to the right wing operating in the Vladivostok region, or to the left advancing on Mongolia or vice versa. Such movements will be naturally made easy by co-operation between transport by sea and the Korean and Manchurian railway system, while by using sea transport for troops the railways will be freed to continue their necessary work behind the front line.

That in itself illustrates the value of "interior lines" in the broad sense of that term. But in the narrow sense, too, the Japanese have the advantage of "interior lines" in that the Manchurian railway system enables them to move troops at will to and from any part on Russia's common frontier with Northern Manchuria.

As supremacy at sea assures more or less absolute safety of sea transport, the Japanese, as a result of their experience in the last two wars, will be able by a series of mobilizations and landing operations to concentrate very swiftly a formidable army in Northern Manchuria, whose mere presence there will constitute an extremely serious menace to the lines of communication of the Russian forces in the Coast province. Whether the Russian command is prepared to let Vladivostok stand a siege and play in the next war the part which Port Arthur played in the last, that is, to tie down a considerable part of the Japanese Army, is still a matter of controversy in Japan. But one may take for granted that the Russian command will never make the blunder of making the raising of the siege the main, or even a secondary, object of its strategy.[44]

There is equal speculation in Japan whether the Russian command will seek to defend the Coast and Amur provinces, and, if so, with what forces. It appears that lately a large force had been concentrated in the region assigned to the Special Army of the Far East, with headquarters probably at Habarovsk. The Japanese military expert, Hirata, from whom we have already quoted, estimated the strength of the Russian Far Eastern Army at the end of 1933 at ten infantry divisions, two cavalry divisions, and a special cavalry brigade, with corresponding strength in artillery, tank sections, squadrons of aeroplanes and various technical troops. This means roughly 90 battalions and 45 to 55 squadrons. Russia has then concentrated in her Far Eastern provinces an army which is considerably more numerous and much better equipped than the army which she concentrated there just before the outbreak of the last war in 1904 (according to Kuropatkin, 63 battalions).[45]

The Japanese Army in the Kwantung peninsula and in Manchuria is estimated by Russian writers at four infantry divisions and two cavalry brigades. The newly organized Manchurian army, under Japanese officers, comprises 18 infantry divisions and 12 cavalry brigades, but it could only be employed on the lines of communication. In peace time the 19th and 20th Divisions are stationed in Korea, and would be immediately available for service in Manchuria. Japan then would have at her disposal on the mainland at the outbreak of the war six infantry divisions, or 72 battalions, that is roughly one-third of the whole active army.

The rest of the active army is stationed in the southern region of Japan itself, in the island Kyû-shû (6th and 12th Divisions) and in the south-western district of the main island Hondo (5th, 10th, and 16th Divisions). These five divisions could be brought in a few hours to Shimono-seki, Sasse-bo and Maisuru, ports which are either actually on the Straits of Korea or in the southern area of the Sea of Japan. Here everything will be ready for their transport overseas, and here the necessary shipping will be supplied by the mercantile marine. Japan's commercial fleet to-day is over 4,000,000 tons, while in 1904–5 she had available only one-quarter of that tonnage.[46] A part of these transports will cross the Korea Strait, a matter of a few hours—there is a regular ferry service between Shimono-seki and Fuchan—and disembark the troops at Fuchan, the main Japanese port in Southern Korea; thence they will be sent forward by the Korean railway lines (at the beginning of 1932 the total length of this system in operation was 4,150 km. while 1,600 km. were under construction) to Manchuria. Another part will convey troops to Northern Korea, to Yuki, Rashin, and Seiskin, ports recently constructed in the immediate neighbourhood of the Russian frontier. From these ports they will go by rail by the line Yenki–Tunhua–Lafa–Kirin, westwards to the region served by the South Manchurian Railway, and northwards by the line Tumen–Mutang–kiang, opened for traffic at the end of 1932, which is linked to the Chinese

Eastern Railway. In the course of 1935 the line Tumen–Mutang-kiang was to be extended to the Sungari valley. It is hardly necessary to point out the strategical value of this line which runs parallel to the frontier of the Russian Coast province, some 120 km. from it. The third part of the transports will disembark troops either at Antung at the mouth of the Yalu river, the port of North-West Korea, from which the troops will be directed towards Mukden, or at the South Manchurian ports (Newchwang, probably, or Halutao) and from there the troops will advance via Taonan and Solun towards the Mongolian frontier. Thus within a short period, the Japanese armies will be concentrated on a line roughly from the Great Hingan to the Ussuri valley, based on a net of strategic railways, which will enable operations to be begun in any direction which the Japanese command may choose.[47] During this initial period, that is, during the first few weeks after the outbreak of war, the Russian Army will have to be spread over the gigantic arc extending from Trans-Baikalia through the Amur Province to the Coast province. The Russian front will thus in a sense envelop the Japanese lines, a position which has distinct disadvantages for the Russians. Such a situation is a source of strength only to an army of overwhelming numerical superiority; if it does not enjoy such superiority the "enveloped" army has excellent chances of success as may be seen by the heavy defeat of the Russian Northern Army in East Prussia in 1914. Under the conditions prevailing in the Far East—great distances and inadequate means of transport—the Russian high command will have to change such a situation as rapidly as possible if it is to avoid disaster.

It is probable that the Japanese gains during this initial phase of the war will not be strategical but only tactical. The Russian high command after several unimportant actions will probably succeed in concentrating the Russian forces to the rear and in forming a new and more suitable line of defence. This movement in retreat will be a difficult undertaking, particularly for the Russian left in the Coast province, for the only line open to them on the right bank of the Ussuri river and the left bank of the Amur river is directly threatened by the Japanese.

The Russians' strategy here will be one of defence—a strategy of which they are traditionally masters—and the probability therefore is that the retreat will be successfully accomplished and a new defensive front stabilized behind the Great Hingan, with the left wing on the Upper Amur and the right in the valley of the Kerulen river. Japanese military writers agree that the second phase of the war on this front will begin with the Russians standing to fight on roughly this new front.[48]

As far as transport and supply are concerned, the new Russian position with only one railway line connecting it with the west will still be far from favourable, particularly as compared with the Japanese, who can now, besides the three railway lines in their rear, make use of the Amur railway line.

It would be idle to speculate on the probable numerical strength of the two armies. It may be assumed that, simply as a result of the experience gained in the last Russo-Japanese war, both belligerents will develop their strength on the field as swiftly and fully as possible, so as to have available at least the forces which faced each other in the last phase of the earlier war, in the autumn of 1905. The Russians had at that time 600,000 to 650,000 men, and the Japanese 500,000, in the field.[49] It is obvious, however, that the (comparatively) well-developed Manchurian railway system constitutes an instrument of reinforcement and supply much more efficient than does the one available railway line at the disposal of the Russians. This disadvantage to the Russians will not be radically remedied even by the doubling of the Transsiberian line which was finished some time ago. It may be taken as certain that the Japanese will concentrate in Manchuria at least their entire active army of 17 divisions, and it is very probable that at the same time at least half their reserves, or eight reserve divisions, will also be concentrated there. That gives a total of roughly 25 divisions, or 500,000 men, to which must be added cavalry and technical troops. The Russian forces which will face the Japanese can hardly exceed 20 divisions. Military writers regard this as a maximum because of the distances and unfavourable transport conditions which are indeed the two outstanding difficulties which Moscow must face in contemplating a campaign thousands of miles away.[50]

The Japanese Army has still another advantage. That is the existence close at hand of a fertile country—Manchuria. Between the Russian Army entrenched in its second positions and fertile Western Siberia there is, on the other hand, a distance of several hundred miles.

It would be, however, a mistake to deduce from the fact that the general position of the Japanese Army is on the whole stronger that a Russian defeat is inevitable. The Japanese line behind the Great Hingan is secure against any frontal attack, but it could be, if not rolled up, at least seriously menaced from the left flank. It may be taken for granted that from Outer Mongolia, which is entirely under Russian influence, the Russians will attempt, by advancing along the line roughly, say Urga–Ude–Dolon-nor, to turn the Japanese left. The effects of such an attack, considering the distances that must be covered over sparsely populated steppes which are difficult to cross in winter and in midsummer, should not, of course, be over-estimated. None the less, military history shows that raids of this kind have often great moral effect and produce, if they are at all successful, a feeling of insecurity.

Nor must we forget that the duel between Japan and the Soviet Union will be fought out in the presence of a third party, and its attitude must of necessity influence the course of the struggle. Both the Japanese and the Russians cannot but attach vital importance to having at least the sympathy of the Chinese nation. The tactical victories which the Japanese Army will probably win in the first phase of the war will naturally raise the prestige of the Island Kingdom in Northern China. It is all important for the Russians, therefore, to deal that prestige a serious blow. It is therefore likely that the Russian high command will create in Chinese territory Chinese formations which, under Russian officers, will threaten the Japanese left and the lines of communication with its base. Here the Russians can draw on the remnants of the soviet forces in Southern China, where the nuclei are available for guerilla war against the Japanese lines.

The Japanese on their part will certainly attempt to roll up the Russian front by outflanking it beyond the Great Hingan. The Japanese counter-offensive here will almost certainly be made also via Outer Mongolia. It seems, however, that the Russians have already used their protectorate over Mongolia to prepare there first-class defensive positions. The character of the Mongolian battle zone which can be described as "a land not yet touched by civilization" on the one hand, and on the other as dominated by the influence of the enemy will make Japanese operations unusually difficult.[51]

The Japanese will most certainly do their utmost to keep the war one of movement, so as to obtain rapid results. The conception of the Russian strategists, who in the Far Eastern theatre of war cannot count on rapid successes and are compelled to reckon with a long defensive war, is quite different. In the long run geography is stronger than sociology and technique—at any rate under the conditions in the Far East. The Russian strategy in the next Russo-Japanese War will be, in some of its fundamental principles, not so very dissimilar to that of Kuropatkin. "All these speculations," says the Russian writer Amiragoff, from whom we have already quoted, "leave no doubt possible that we must be prepared for an intensive, highly complicated war of long duration, a war, too, which cannot but be one of very varying forms when we consider the types of military operations and the way the forces on both sides are arrayed." In these words is expressed the fundamental idea of Russian strategy, as a strategy that is traditionally defensive. Strategical retreat with the least possible loss, drawing the enemy on into the vast Russian spaces, economy of one's own strength and the weakening of the enemy by continual threat to his lines of communication—all these elements of the old Russian strategy will once again come into their own.

It it natural to assume that the Japanese will do all in their power in order to extend their left wing westwards as far as possible, aiming on the one hand at placing their armies in a position outflanking the Russians, and on the other at cutting communications between Russia and China. Hence the endeavour of the Japanese to establish themselves in Inner Mongolia, in the valley of the Huang-ho river and still farther to the west. Japan's railway policy in the Huang-ho valley is intended to link up their old "sphere of influence" in Shan-tung across the Huang-ho with Ning-hsia (Irgai) via Pao-to. The great Japanese line of defence would probably stretch from Lan-tchou over Ning-hsia–Sui-juan–Dolon-nor, and so over the Great Hingan to the Upper Amur.

Although both general staffs in theory tend strongly towards a "war of movement," with full use of their motorized and mechanized armies, it seems more likely that in the Far East we shall have again, though perhaps with some variations, a war of positions like that of 1914–18. For the weaker party, in this case the Russians, would be always inclined to refuse to abandon ground, to entrench itself and to paralyse in this way the advance of the stronger adversary. The Japanese will in all probability have no more chance than they had in 1904–5 to administer on the enemy a decisive defeat in the sense of Cannae or Sedan. Russia cannot be conquered in Eastern Asia. So long as the political and economic foundations of Russia's strength in Western Siberia and in Europe are not destroyed, the Russians will be always able after every tactical defeat, after every retreat, to occupy new positions and to reconcentrate their strength. It is only in Europe that Russia can be defeated.

Japan has two chances. The first possibility is that the defeat of the Russian Army in the Far East will lead to revolution, or at any rate to a strong revolutionary movement and that such a situation at home would compel the Russian Government to seek for peace. The experience of 1904–5 must, however, have taught the Japanese that even in such a case it will be very difficult to make Russia capitulate and surrender all her positions in the Far East. It would be, indeed, very dangerous if Japan were to count on a complete collapse of the Soviet regime. The second possibility is that in Europe Russia may be assailed by a powerful enemy—as things are to-day this can only be Germany; that would most likely mean the capitulation of Russia in the Far East. But such a speculation takes us far beyond the limits of our speculation on the chances of a war between Russia and Japan alone. Apart from these, however, Tokio cannot but consider it most probable that the next Russo-Japanese War will be like that of 1904–5—great tactical successes in the first phase and then the deadlock of a war of positions. What is likely to happen after that can be prophesied by any Japanese politician who has read the history of the last forty years—the intervention of the Great Powers, a compromise peace, disillusioned public opinion at home and all that that involves, and above all the fact that Russia will still be a powerful factor in the Far East with whose hostility one must reckon and whose friendship will in the end have to be bought by concessions.

The Soviet Government, too, however, can count no more on a decisive victory and the elimination of Japan as a military Power in Eastern Asia. The limit of what they can reasonably hope to achieve is to maintain their positions in Trans-Baikalia and in Outer Mongolia. When in the early autumn of 1905 the Russian armies, after their serious defeat at Mukden (February–March, 1905), fell back to the prepared positions at Sypingai (170 km. from Mukden) and at last became in numbers and quality at least equal to their adversaries, there was a strong body of opinion in the Russian General Staff that the war should be continued, for they believed that there was sure ground for maintaining that a Russian offensive on a large scale would drive the Japanese armies back to the Pacific in decisive defeat. When the politicians and diplomatists with Witte at their head had finally carried the day for peace, attempts were made in Russia, too, to construct the legend of "the stab in the back," and to lay the responsibility for a "shameful peace" on the revolution and the civilians. In reality, however, not the generals, but the politicians were right. So long as Japan retained supremacy at sea it was completely impossible to defeat her decisively; it was not at Liaoyang and Mukden that Russia was beaten, but off Tsu-shima (May 27–28, 1905) when the second Russian Pacific Fleet, under Roshdestvensky, was sent to the bottom of the Sea of Japan.

Even if the Russians managed to concentrate an army a million strong in Eastern Asia and drove the Japanese from every position in Northern Manchuria and in the Russian provinces they had occupied, the Japanese could still maintain themselves in South Manchuria, in the Kwantung peninsula, and in Korea, from where they could not be evicted by the Russians without a strong navy. Russia cannot decisively defeat Japan unless there is a strong Russian fleet in the Pacific which can challenge successfully Japanese supremacy at sea. No victories on the mainland can bring the Island State to its knees; Japan can only be defeated at sea.

As it can hardly be imagined that the Russians, who actually have a very weak navy,[52] could—after the experience of Roshdestvensky's expedition—send into Pacific waters a strong fleet, the Soviet Union cannot count on a decisive victory over Japan unless, indeed, they get help in the shape of a strong sea Power as ally. This possibility, too, lies beyond the scope of our investigations on an isolated Russo-Japanese war. Without such a development the Russians can at the best hope only for tactical victories which will lead to a compromise peace.

Russia's superiority in the economic field is offset by the geographical and strategical position in the Far East, and it may be assumed that, in the event of a war of long duration,

Japan and Russia are approximately equal in strength. The initial Japanese successes which will be the direct results of their more favourable strategical position will come to an end if the war goes on, because of Russia's economic superiority. Thus neither Power can hope for a decisive victory in an isolated war. The strategist, in such a situation, will have to advise the politician to make peace.[53]

§ 3. SEA STRATEGY IN AN AMERICAN-JAPANESE WAR

Still more uncertain is the prospect of an isolated war between Japan and the United States. Every speculation on strategy in the Pacific must reckon with the tremendous distances in the theatre of war. There are 4,500 nautical miles between Yokohama and San Francisco. The most important American naval base and the one nearest to the Western Pacific—it is the Western Pacific which must be regarded as the theatre of war in a naval conflict between the United States and Japan—Pearl Harbour (Honolulu), is 3,440 nautical miles from Yokohama, 4,950 from Hong-Kong, and 3,750 from the island of Yap. Puget Sound, which is the most important point of concentration for the American Navy (in the State of Washington, close to the Canadian frontier), is 2,360 nautical miles from Pearl Harbour, and the latter is 2,080 nautical miles from San Francisco.

These distances alone make an offensive war extremely difficult for either Power. It can be scarcely assumed that the Japanese would attack the Americans in the Eastern Pacific. But how can the Americans carry on war against Japan without attacking her in the Western Pacific? Japan cannot carry the war into American waters, said Admiral Bristol as long ago as 1930, but unless America is able to carry the war into Japanese waters she will lose it.[54] The only sure way for the Americans to destroy the Japanese fleet would be to entice the Japanese fleet from its "entrenchments" in the Western Pacific into the dangerous waters east of Long. 180° E., that is, into the American quadrilateral, which is already famous; Dutch

Harbour (Aleutian islands)–Guam–Tutuila (Samoa)–Pearl Harbour. It is, however, hardly credible that the Japanese fleet would let itself be manœuvred into such a dangerous position.

Should the war, however, as most people believe, be fought out in the Western Pacific and begin with an American offensive, it is easy to show that the Japanese fleet would find itself in a position of superiority. A glance at the map is enough to show that the Japanese Navy has at its disposal in the Western Pacific a series of first-rate naval bases which considerably increase the strength of the fleet. Yokosuka in the east of the main island is the base of the squadrons which will operate on the arc Bonin–Vulkan island–the Mariannes. The distance between Yokosuka and the American base at Guam is indeed over 1,200 nautical miles, but throughout the islands there are a number of well-protected bases, Saipan group, Angaur, the Palau islands, etc., in which, as we shall show later, squadrons engaged in secondary operations, particularly on the way to Yokosuka, can find refuge. The two other main naval bases are Kure on the inner sea and Sasse-bo on the Straits of Korea. But the whole eastern shore of the Sea of Japan is well provided with second-class bases, so that ships can use it as if it were home waters.[55] All the entrances to the latter are also in Japan's possession, and thus the Japanese Navy is completely free to manœuvre in these waters. Just as has the Japanese Army in Manchuria, the Japanese Navy has all the advantages of interior lines, and can quietly assemble its units to concentrate them at a given point against an enemy attempting a blockade. Such a concentration is also made easier by the fact that between the main island Hondo and the two southern islands Kyû-shû and Shi-koku there is the so-called "Inner Sea," which has always been connected by three natural channels, both with the Straits of Korea and with the ocean, and has now a fourth and artificial channel leading directly to the Sea of Japan (across the Biwa Lake to Wakasa Bay).

But Japan's "sea entrenchments" extend right along the coast of the East Asian mainland far to the south and form a continuous, strongly protected line from the La Pérouse Strait to the Ballingtang channel south of Formosa. South of Kyû-shû as far as Formosa stretch the Ryû-kyû islands, which bar the way to a hostile fleet endeavouring to reach the Yellow Sea and the East China Sea (Tung-hai). From the south, via the Formosa channel, it is just as difficult to attack Japan's "sea entrenchments," for her Pescadore islands with the naval base Mako, and beyond them the heavily fortified Kilung Harbour (at the northern end of Formosa), bar the way.

It is safe to assume that the only two American naval bases in the Western Pacific, both weak ones, Guam in the Mariannes and Cavite in Luzon, Philippines, will be seized or destroyed by the Japanese immediately after war breaks out. The American fleet which will appear in the Western Pacific a few weeks after the outbreak of war will, whenever it passes east of Long. 180° E., come within the area of the first Japanese "quadrilateral of defence," south and south-west of the arc Bonin–Vulkan island–Saipan to the Palau isles, and thence east over the Caroline and Marshall islands as far as Long. 170° E. The end of this line, which probably, in spite of the Washington Treaty, is now well fortified, is a powerfully armed outpost in the Yaluit islands (in the Ralik group), 2,000 nautical miles distance from Pearl Harbour. The American fleet, if it takes the direct way from Hawaii to the Philippines, either to bring help to the American garrisons therein or to organize their naval bases for further operations against the Japanese islands, would already, when off Yaluit, be a long way behind it. And from that point onwards the American fleet would have to encounter real difficulties all along the 2,200 nautical miles from Yaluit to Angaur (Palau islands), via Panope in the eastern Caroline islands. The American ships would be unceasingly harassed by Japanese submarines and torpedo boats without having any possibility of repairing properly any damage suffered. It is obvious that the fighting strength of the fleet when it appeared off the Philippines would be substantially reduced, for there they would not find a first-rate naval base with dry-dock and well protected from attacks from the sea, from the land, and from the air, but would have to fight for such a base or rather would have to make one.[56]

The American fleet, however, could take the other, the northern, route to the Western Pacific which goes via the Midway islands (about 1,500 nautical miles from Pearl Harbour) which could probably be made to serve as a base for the American ships. This route, though, from the standpoint of safety, it is undoubtedly preferable as far as the largest part of it is concerned—these regions of the Pacific are practically "empty," and thus the Japanese submarines have no place for ambush—leads straight into the Japanese defensive line running north-south, and a little farther on into the zone of the "sea entrenchments." Even on this course, which is much longer, the American ships will finally be exposed to attack by Japanese submarines, and, besides, will have possibly to accept battle in the neighbourhood of the Japanese main naval bases.

Let us assume that the American fleet, after a more or less successful crossing, has reached Western Pacific waters and has secured an adequate and well-protected naval base. What then? How will the naval war develop? The main question here is the relative strength of the two navies.

Any comparison between two navies which seeks to estimate their comparative strength in the event of war is vitiated by the fact that no one can tell at what time war will break out. The pre-war preparedness of the belligerents, i.e. the construction and launching of new ships, the repair of old ships, the modernizing of guns and engines, is not attained at the same speed by both. It is not only possible, it is very probable, that the relative strengths of the two navies are very different at different times. In fact, there is no doubt that the choice of the moment for declaring war will be to a great extent influenced by considerations as to the respective states of preparedness. The relative strength of both navies to-day is not in itself sufficient basis for estimating the relative strength of these navies when war breaks out.

To get a true ratio—what to the bewilderment of the layman is called a "visible coefficient"—for tonnage, guns, speed and the like on which there is such detail in technical naval books, useful though it may be, actually helps very little to get at the truth of the real relative strength of the two navies. When one remembers on the one hand the extreme complexity of modern technique and on the other the secrecy preserved regarding everything concerned with new constructions, it is very possible that this or that detail in armour, guns, or machinery, a detail of the existence of which even the experts have at the moment no inkling, may give the navy of one belligerent an overwhelming superiority over the other. For that reason it is really superfluous to go into the detail of the bases of official data, for any comparison thus made has only very relative value. It will be enough to place before the reader a rough picture of the relative strengths so that any difference between them may broadly be realized. (See tables on pages 247 and 248.)

Quite apart from the political considerations, it is naturally not to be assumed that the whole American Navy would be risked in a campaign in the Western Pacific. This implies a modification of the comparative figures there given. As far as artillery is concerned the American battleship is on the whole about 50 per cent stronger than the Japanese of the same class. In super-heavy guns the superiority is more than 50 per cent, about 45 per cent in heavy guns, while in light guns the strength is about equal. The guns in the aeroplane-carriers and the submarines are roughly equal in both navies. American superiority in battleship guns is, however, completely compensated for by the fact that the Japanese cruiser in super-heavy and heavy guns is about 68 per cent stronger than the American ship of the same class, while in light guns the Japanese ship is two and a half times as strong as the American. Equally significant, when we consider the nature of a modern battle at sea, is the superiority of the Japanese Navy in torpedo-tubes; the Japanese battleship possesses three times and the Japanese cruiser two-and-a-half times as many torpedo-tubes as the

AMERICAN AND JAPANESE NAVIES AT THE END OF 1933[57]

	Ships		Tonnage	
	U.S.A.	Japan	U.S.A.	Japan
Battleships and battle-cruisers	15	10	455,400	298,220
Aeroplane-carriers ..	6	4	131,300	68,000
Cruisers	30	45	273,150	313,072
Submarines	88	67	75,270	79,137

Guns in the Battleships

	Calibre in mm.	Number	
		U.S.A.	Japan
Super-heavy guns	406	24	16
	356	124	78
	305	12	0
		— 160	— 94
Heavy guns	152	0	96
	140	0	80
	127	264	4
		— 264	— 180
Light guns	78	48	40
Total	—	472	314
Torpedo-tubes ..	—	16	52

Guns in Aeroplane Carriers

	Calibre in mm.	U.S.A.	Japan
Super-heavy guns	203	16	20
Heavy guns	140	0	4
	130	0	12
	127	52	0
	120	0	32
		— 52	— 48
Light guns	76	0	2
Total	—	68	70

Guns in Cruisers

	Calibre in mm.	Number	
		U.S.A.	Japan
Super-heavy guns	254	0	1
	230	92	130
		— 92	— 131
Heavy guns	155	0	15
	152	111	80
	140	0	112
	127	48	0
	120	0	48
		—159	—255
Light guns	76	40	103
Total	—	291	489
Torpedo-tubes ..	—	120	290

Guns in Submarines

Cailbre in mm.	Number	
	U.S.A.	Japan
152	6	0
140	0	14
127	2	0
120	0	14
102	47	11
76	31	46
Total ..	86	85
Torpedo-tubes	351	380

corresponding American ships. Their submarines, too, have more tubes than the American. It is generally believed that the new Japanese cruisers, the so-called "Washington cruisers," are stronger than the American and English ships of the same class. The average speed of Japan's Grand Fleet and of her cruiser squadrons is rather greater than that of the American ships. Her squadrons composed of ships built in series are more homogeneous in type than those of the adversary. All these factors are of great importance when we remember that modern operations at sea are *par excellence* manœuvre operations.[58]

The Russian Rear-Admiral, A. D. Bubnoff, who saw service in the Russo-Japanese War as a naval officer, and in the Great War as head of the naval department at Russian General Headquarters, in 1922, immediately after the Washington Conference, estimated the relative strengths of the American and Japanese Navies in the event of war in the Western Pacific at four to three.[59] We believe that since then the ratio has not changed to America's advantage. Taking into consideration, however, the strategical conditions affecting either side in a war in the Western Pacific, which necessarily reduces the fighting strength of the American Navy, it must be admitted that in that case the American fleet must be regarded as the weaker.

Since a landing on the main islands of Japan is out of the question, there are but two chances for the Americans to destroy Japan's sea-power: either to compel the Japanese fleet to accept battle and to defeat it decisively, or to enforce a blockade which would make impossible or at least very difficult imports of raw materials and food-stuffs and starve Japan out.

The first chance depends entirely on the decision of the Japanese High Command. Entrenched as it is behind its "sea entrenchments," the Japanese fleet has full freedom of choice as to the moment when the decisive naval action will be fought. It can bring the American fleet to battle when and where it will, while the American fleet is not in a position to attack it in its lurking-places.[60] It is therefore most probable that the Japanese admirals would first try seriously to weaken the American squadrons. Meantime the Americans could do no more than try to establish an effective blockade. Now the naval bases, Guam and Cavite, which would be used here, are 1,500 nautical miles from the Straits of Korea. It can, of course, be assumed that the Americans would seize some other islands in the Southern Pacific to organize bases there. In the spring of 1933 the French Government occupied several islands belonging to no one which control the sea-way from the north to the Philippines and Borneo. In the Press the opinion was expressed that the French were merely keeping the islands warm for a new owner—the Americans.[61] Something of this kind might well happen during the war and probably will happen. But it is very doubtful whether such future bases will be any nearer to Japan than are Guam and Cavite.

A "distant" blockade of this sort can hardly achieve its purpose. The Japanese in their "sea entrenchments" will undoubtedly continue fully to control the sea-ways to the Asiatic mainland. Here the American blockade is bound to be ineffective. The only practical task which the American fleet could undertake would be to shut off the Japanese from the Southern China Sea (Nan-hai) and so from the Dutch East Indies and the Indian Ocean. This would be a severe blow to Japanese raw materials import, especially mineral oil and rubber. But one may well ask whether America would have a sufficiency of force to carry out that task. It is difficult to be precise here, but it must be remembered that the Japanese can reach the Dutch East Indies from the east by the Celebes Sea, as well as via the Southern Chinese Sea, and that this latter route is to a certain degree protected by Japan's defensive sea-line, Marianne islands–Palau.

Because of the vast distances in the Western Pacific and of the very strong strategical position of the Japanese Navy, already very strong simply as a fleet, any American blockade would have only one chance of success, and that is if it were maintained by much stronger forces than those which America now possesses. Otherwise the American fleet runs serious risk of becoming worn and weakened by the long duration of the blockade and finally being forced to fight a decisive battle at the most unfavourable moment. But when we seek to estimate the chances in such a war, we must keep in mind above all the simple fact that the American fleet will have on the theatre of war no first-class bases and that every serious damage done to one of the ships means sending the ship home.

An American-Japanese war would be the first real ocean war to be fought out with *modern* technical instruments. In it the operations at sea would not be secondary operations; they would be the main operations. The result is that it is extremely difficult to judge of the prospects of such a war, because we have to all intents and purposes no previous experience to guide us. But clearly such a war would last many years and would end with the complete exhaustion of both sides. America would at any rate be obliged to throw into the balance its whole industrial strength and to double or even treble its present naval strength if it is to defeat the Japanese decisively.

The position of the United States would, of course, be much improved should it find an ally on the Asiatic mainland. It is highly probable that the naval war in the Western Pacific would develop simultaneously with a war on land or would cause the latter sooner or later. It can be easily understood that certain elements in China would sympathize with the United States, and would indirectly aid America's campaign. This would be of great importance, as it would enable the Americans to find naval bases on the mainland, and also would seriously endanger Japan's import of raw materials from China. Japan, however, to prevent anything of the kind, would probably immediately after the outbreak of war occupy more or less effectively the most important Chinese ports as she could do with her command of Chinese waters. The Yang-tse valley would at any rate be exposed to the attack of a Japanese army of Occupation, and in such circumstances the Nanking Government would be extremely chary of abandoning neutrality in favour of the United States. Only in the later stages of the war at sea, if the Americans succeeded in driving the Japanese fleet out of Chinese waters or out of part of them, would any active intervention of the Chinese on America's side be possible. It is just as possible, however, that if the war at sea was unduly prolonged, the Japanese would be compelled to carry out a complete occupation of all the Chinese eastern provinces, or to attempt in some other manner to compel the Chinese people to join "the Asiatic front." But as far as the intervention of a third State is concerned, Russia is a much surer candidate. There is, however, one great handicap to strategical co-operation between America and the Soviet Union, namely the difficulty of communications. The supplying of guns, munitions, and engines of war to the Russian Army, which would be the first task of the Americans, would encounter great difficulties. Transport over the Atlantic, and then by the railways in European Russia and in Siberia, would certainly be possible, but it would put a tremendous strain on the Transsiberian line. There is another possible route over Behring Straits and the Kamchatka peninsula. But here distances are really too great. From the back areas behind the lines, which the Russians would take up in Trans-Baikalia, or between the Russian frontiers and the Great Hingan to Northern Kamchatka on the Behring Sea, is a distance of about 3,000 km.—a distance equal to that between Madrid and Leningrad; from Petropalovsk, which would probably be the port for American shipments across the Behring Sea to the northern end of Kamchatka, the distance is 1,500 km., and from here the line of communications with the Russian Army in Trans-Baikalia, a line made necessary because of the Sea of Okhotsk, would be certainly unsafe because of the activity of the Japanese cruisers, is another long 1,500 km. There are neither railways nor motor roads and the only possible communication is by air. It is therefore possible to conceive that, to secure military co-operation between America and the Soviet Union, a regular air service would be established via the Aleutian islands and Kamchatka to Trans-Baikalia. Such a service would be of great value for the transmission of information and for the transport of those products which are particularly needed in war, but it would be premature to consider seriously in the strategical sense such a connection as would ensure mass transport between America and Russia via the Behring Sea. For the present we must reckon with the fact that the Russian Army in the Far East is obliged to rely on the Transsiberian railway and Russia's own economic bases.

It seems, however, that the American War Office is already contemplating a certain strategical shifting to the north. The post-war strategy of the American naval staff used to be based on the famous "quadrilateral": Dutch Harbour (Aleutian islands)–Pearl Harbour (Hawaii)–Tutuila (Samoa)–Guam (Marianne islands).[62] The greatest disadvantage of this combination of bases, as is known, is the fact that Guam is separated from the other three bases by the Japanese mandated zone, while Tutuila lies far distant from the future theatres of war. It seems that now the American naval staff attaches less importance to the "quadrilateral"; that is not unconnected with the fact that the Philippines are no longer considered as a naval base. Instead new bases are now being built on the Pacific coast of the United States, and a new "quadrilateral" will probably be created. The strategic naval bases of the new "quadrilateral" are the zone San Pedro–San Diego in the south of California, Puget Sound, Dutch Harbour in Unalaska (Aleutian islands), and Pearl Harbour. This new combination of naval bases will be on the one hand linked up through Pearl Harbour with the defensive line Dutch Harbour–Pearl Harbour–Tutuila, and on the other through Dutch Harbour with the new line of defence of the Aleutian islands. This last line conjointly with the Russian fortified bases in the Commodore isles, will completely protect the Behring Sea against any Japanese attack, and so will secure direct communication with

Russian North-Eastern Asia. The construction of a base at Nome (on Norton Sound) in Alaska, which will be used both as an air as well as a naval base, is intended to serve the same end.

Thus we can visualize something in the nature of an enveloping of Japan by sea from the north. But this new combination does not bring the American fleet effectively near the islands of Japan. It must not be forgotten that Japan also has strong naval bases in the north. One need only mention Ominato on the Tsugaru Strait and also Hakodate and Muroran (in Yezo). These bases can be used not merely to defend the northern entrances to the Sea of Japan, but also as a base for offensive operations in the Sea of Okhotsk (see Map 9).

This short strategical survey of the incompleteness of which we are well aware is, however, quite sufficient to establish the fact that a war in Eastern Asia, however we may envisage its course, cannot be one of those wars which end, after a few months of speedy victories, in the overthrow of the enemy. A war in the Western Pacific, whether it is purely a continental war or purely a sea war or a combination of both, will last not months but years. Victory will be won only through the extreme economic and social effort of the belligerents. In the course of it there will be mighty changes in the whole economic and social structure of the nations directly participating in it. For them it will be destiny itself. Such a war could cause revolution in Japan and even in America, and counter-revolution in Russia—apart altogether from the fact that it is scarcely possible that a war in Eastern Asia could be an isolated two-Power war. The classes which to-day hold power in Japan, America, and Russia know well its risks.

NOTES TO CHAPTER III

1. Alfred Fabre-Luce, *Caillaux*, Paris, 1933.

2. V. Batrak, "Tjashelaja promyschlennostj Japoniji" (Russ.: "The Japanese Heavy Industries") in the Russian military review, *Voina i Revolutsija*, December 1934, p. 107: Tokio's arsenals during the World War employed 30,000 hands.

3. Batrak, *l.c.*, p. 103; cf. J. E. Orchard, *Japan's Economic Position*, New York, 1930, p. 267.

4. *Armaments Year Book*, 1934 (League of Nations), p. 844.

5. The material on the plans for the economic mobilization of Japan is taken from the collection *Japonia* ("Partisdat," Leningrad, 1934), pp. 235–6. A special chapter (pp. 231–320) describes in detail "the military resources of Japanese imperialism." The difficulties of accurate estimate are obvious. What is said by Japanese and Russians alike on their own state of preparedness would, if taken literally, probably lead to serious under-estimation. On the other hand, what each says of the other is so clearly exaggerated that the figures have to be used with great caution.

6 The figures are taken from the latest (1935–6) *Statistical Year-Book of the League of Nations*. These figures do not tally with those in other books of reference—the reader may be referred to these, e.g. *U.S.S.R. Handbook* (London 1936), *Statesman's Year Book* (London 1936), *Japan-Manchukuo Year Book* (Tokyo 1936), and the last editions of the *Statistisches Jahrbuch für das Deutsche Reich* (Berlin). What matters here, however, is the comparison not the accuracy to a ton or two of the estimates.

7. The two coalfields in Manchuria, which supply coal suitable for coking, are situated in the neighbourhood of the Russian frontier, in the lower Sungari valley (Hegan), and in the Mishany district, in the valley of the Mulin-he river. If war breaks out both are exposed to cavalry raids. Batrak, *l.c.*, p. 103.

8. Orchard, *l.c.*, p. 294.

9. Cf. Edwin L. James, "Oil is the Weak Point in Tokyo's Strategy," in *The New York Times*, February 3, 1935.

10. Batrak, *l.c.*, p. 100.

11. Batrak, *l.c.*, p. 104.

12. Orchard, *l.c.*, p. 282.

13. Batrak, *l.c.*, p. 102.

14. A group of Japanese business men contracted in 1928 to deliver to Japan (shipping from Yampi Sound on Timor Sea, West Kimberley, West Australia) large quantities of iron ore (10,000,000 tons within 12 years) (*Far Eastern Review*, November 1928). The Japanese are anxious to secure all available supplies of iron ore in the Southern Pacific. The main source, however, is in the Malay States, where the Japanese possess concessions in Johore and some other States.

(Orchard, *l.c.*, p. 331). Japan itself lacks sufficiency of aluminium, lead, tin, and zinc, all of them most important for the munition industry; 100 per cent of the aluminium used is imported; lead 94·6 per cent, tin 80·6 per cent, and zinc 55·1 per cent (Document B *Les Relations du Japon avec la Manchourie et la Mongolie*, 1932, Juillet, pp. 195–200.

15. Batrak, *l.c.*, p. 104; Orchard, *l.c.*, pp. 310, 333.

16. *Sozialistitscheskoje Strojitelstwo SSSR*, Moscow, 1934, p. 50, contains the figures for 1932. The prospective figures for 1933 and the effective production, January–July 1933, are taken from *Rüstung und Abrüstung. Eine Umschau uber das Heer- und Kriegswesen aller Länder*. Edited by K. L. von Oertzen, Berlin 1934, p. 268, which adds: "The construction of motor-cars is strongly influenced by economic and military considerations, which have determined the increase in production. The producing capacity of the factory "Stalin" has, for instance, been raised to 80,000 cars, while this spring a new tractor factory has been set up in Cheliabinsk "

17. Batrak, *l.c.*, p. 105.

18. "The productive capacity of Japan's chemical industry is strong enough to meet the requirements of the army and navy as far as the most essential war explosives are concerned" (Batrak, *l.c.*, pp. 106–7); cf. *Rustüng und Abrüstung*, Berlin, 1934, p. 278.

19. Batrak, *l.c.*, p. 104.

20. *Rüstung und Abrüstung*, Berlin, 1934, p. 301.

21. Orchard, *l.c.*, p. 116. Orchard, who is on the whole a rather friendly observer of Japan's economic development, is not inclined to believe that Japan is likely to become a first-rate industrial Power (p. 260). He points out that the technical standard is low and that an original technical culture is lacking (p. 264).

22. Karl Justrow, *Feldherr und Kriegstechnik, Studien über den Operationsplan des Grafen Schlieffen und Lehren für unseren Wehraufbau und unsere Landesverteidigung*, Oldenburg, 1933. Justrow, who is regarded in German military circles as an outspoken representative of the school which regards technique as supreme, sums up his views on the part played by technical experiment in the World War in the following manner: "In this way it was necessary, under the compulsion of events, to try to make up for lost opportunities in the field as rapidly as possible, and even to extemporize. The German technicians, too late, alas! achieved an amazingly great deal in this field. The advice of the technician had to be taken and comprehensive cooperation with him was an urgent necessity" (p. 133).—"It was during the course of the war itself that—very often unexpectedly for the generals and for the army itself—new weapons came into existence" (A. Volpe, "Thoughts on the Dialectic of War," in *Voina i Revolutsija*, 1929, 6, p. 36).

23. Rocco Morreta, *Come sarà la guerra di domani?* German version by Theodor Lücke: *Wie sieht der Krieg von morgen aus?* Berlin, 1934, pp. 221–2. This work by a well-known Italian soldier is a very valuable

summary and criticism of the *strategical* theories of the post-War period. The author is a representative of the "golden mean" school, which to-day dominates general staffs everywhere.

24. Quoted by Morreta, *l.c.*, p. 220.

25. We have taken for Japan as well as for the Soviet Union as "man-power reserves," the male population between the ages of 18 and 44. All Japanese males between the ages of 17 and 40 are liable to military service; in Russia the age limits are 17 and 40. Cf. *Annuaire Militaire*, Geneva, 1934, pp. 8, 486. The male population between 18 and 44 years of age is 38·8 per cent of the total Russian population; of Japan's 38·0 per cent. The Russian figures will be found in *Sozialistitscheskoje Strojitelstwo*, Moscow, 1934, p. 360. Those for Japan, in the *Résumé Statistique de l'Empire du Japon*, Tokio, 1934 (p. 7).

26. D. S. Amiragoff, "O charaktere budustschej wojny" (Russ: "What the Coming War Will be Like") in the review *Voina i Revolutsija*, Moscow, 1934, September–October, p. 10.

27. General A. Bilderling in the *Russkij Invalid*, 1906, No. 166, quoted by A. N. Kuropatkin, *Zapisky o russko-japonskoj wojne. Itogy wojny* (Russ: "Memoirs on the Russo-Japanese War"), Berlin, 1909, p. 419.

28. Kuropatkin, *l.c.*, p. 416.

29. Kuropatkin, *l.c.*, p. 470.

30. Leo Trotzky, "Die Kriegsstärke der Roten Armee," in *Europäische Hefte*, 1934, Nr. 11, p. 293. The former Commissary for War and creator of the Red Army in articles published in this Prague review (1934, Nos. 9–11) throws a light on the material and psychological bases of the problem of the "Red Army" with great knowledge and sufficient objectivity. Cf. St. Ivanovitch, *Krasnaja Armija*, Paris, 1931 (Russ: "The Red Army"), which is a critical and well-documented study on the sociological structure of the Red Army from the anti-Bolshevik standpoint. In the German Year Book, *Rüstung und Abrüstung*, Berlin, 1934, there is the following: "When on duty severe discipline prevails in the Red Army. When not on duty the rank and file's relations with their officers are the normal ones between civilians. Off-duty saluting is not compulsory. The spirit of the Red army must be recognized as good. The uniformity of training interest and ideas creates a solid bond which holds the army together and increases confidence in the leaders. Attempts to win the army over to opposition views have so far been successfully defeated" (p. 168).

31. Trotzky, *l.c.*, p. 237. Cf. *Rüstung und Abrüstung*, p. 167, where "military education before active service" and "military education outside the army" is described.

32. The former Russian general, now an *émigré*, N. N. Golowin, regards anti-Bolshevik risings behind the front as inevitable if war breaks out (N. N. Golowin, *Sovremennaja strategitscheskaja obstanovka na Dalnem Vostoke*) (Russ: "The Present Strategical Position in

the Far East"), Belgrade, 1934, p. 11. All such prophecies, however, rest on a series of assumptions which cannot be proved.

33. Amiragoff thinks on the whole that, in the event of war, that part of the proletariat which is class-conscious in any country engaged in a war against the Soviet Union, will play the part of a Red Army detachment whose function it will be to destroy the enemy State from within (*l.c.*, pp. 12–13). But Moscow, however, is quite aware that these sanguine hopes have no immediate practical significance. "It must be observed, however, that this (anti-militarist) spirit so far has assumed a politically active form only among a minority of Japan's workers and peasants. Wide strata of the working labour masses are still passive and are not politically organized. The growth of the anti-militaristic sympathies in the country is obvious. The army and navy, however, are on the whole obedient agents of Japanese imperialism" (O Tanin and E. Jogan, "Krisis i obostrenije klassovich protivoretschij v Japoniji", Russ: "The Crisis and the Clash of Class-Interests in Japan," *Japonija*, Leningrad, 1934, p. 82).

34. According to the Japanese statistical year book, there were in 1931 64,436 industrial concerns with 128,887 salaried employees and engineers and 1,661,502 workers (*Résumé Statistique de L'Empire du Japon*, Tokio, 1934, pp. 96, 99). It is added (p. 103) that in 1932 there were 870 strikes, involving 53,338 workers.

35. Tanin and Jogan, *l.c.*, p. 78.

36. *Résumé Statistique de l'Empire du Japon*, Tokio, 1934, says that in 1932 there were 3,414 disputes between landlords and tenants, involving 16,706 estates and 61,499 tenants (p. 101).

37. Cf. Chapter II, p. 142; Mahan's *Influence of Sea-power Upon History* contains numerous examples of the importance of sea-power for the issue of a war.

38. It is hardly necessary to say that there is no possibility of getting reliable information as to the strength of Japanese or Russian air forces. The *Annuaire Militaire*, 1933, says that on January 1, 1931, there were 750 Russian and 1,440 Japanese military aeroplanes (pp. 355, 486). *Rüstung und Abrüstung* estimates the figures as 2,700 Russian and 2,050 Japanese (pp. 223, 219). In either land the air strength of the other is put considerably higher than its own. Cf. the remarks of the well-known military writer, Shinsaku Hirata, in his work *How Shall We Fight?* Tokio, 1933, of which a shortened Russian version (Part 2) has been given in *Japonija*, pp. 292, 315. A well-documented article by L. Dvorzov ("Japonskij vojennij vosdushnij flot," "The Japanese Military Air Fleet") in *Vojna i Revolutsija*, 1934, May–June, pp. 67–91, contains a detailed study and appreciation of the strength of the Japanese air fleet. Japanese industry is now in a position to meet the full demand for aeroplanes which is likely to arise in the event of war. But so far they have failed to bring out a native type of aeroplane engine and are content for the time being to copy foreign engines. In the course of the last two years the Japanese have made

great progress in organizing effective air defence, and especially so in the central industrial area, Osaka–Kobe–Kyoto. According to reports in the Japanese Press, the great air manœuvres in July 1934 showed that passive defence against aircraft was effectively organized, and that the civil population was thoroughly trained in discipline. Cf. N. Nikolajev, "Vosdushnije utchenija i manevry Pvo v Japoniji" (Russ: "Air Manœuvres and Air Defence in Japan") in the *Krasnaja Zvezda*, November 1, 1934. (This paper is published by the Commissariat for Defence.)

39. N. L. Klado, *Posle uchoda vtoroj eskadry Tichovo Okeana* (Russ: "The Departure of the Second Pacific Fleet"), Petersburg, 1905, p. 16.

40. The chief of the Japanese air defence staff stated two years ago that an air attack on Japan would inflict only insignificant damage on the country (Nikolajev in *Krasnaja Zvezda*, December 27, 1933). It is to be assumed, too, that the Japanese air forces—to-day at least 2,050 front-line planes (v. Note 38) will not be idle while the Russian planes attack Japan's vital centres. It is much more likely that the Japanese, based on the fifty air ports in the triangle Harbin–Mukden–Tsitsikar, will try right at the beginning of the war to attack the Russian air bases in the Coast Province and destroy them. In any case, the struggle for the mastery of the air will be carried on *actively* by both sides (cf. Golovin, *l.c.*, p. 45).

41. Cf. Amiragoff, *l.c.*, p. 17.

42. On the strengths of the Japanese and Russian Navies v. *The Annuaire Militaire* and *Rüstung und Abrüstung*, Japanese aircraft carriers, cf. Streshnevsky, "Vosduschniy Flot Japonii" (Russ: "Japan's Air Fleet") in *Krasnaja Zvezda*, December 18, 1933. On the manœuvres, experience gained by the American Navy against air attack, cf. F. Ogorodnikoff, "Vosduschnaja vojna po sarubeshnim vsgljadam" (Russ: "War in the Air and the Foreign Views Upon It"), in *Vojna i Revolutsija*, 1934, May–June, p. 108.

43. Klado, *l.c.*, pp. 18–19, 25–9, 86.

44. Hirata, *l.c.*, p. 299.

45. Hirata, in the December number of *Kai-zô*, quoted in *Revue du Pacifique*, 1934, Nr. 3 (March 1934), pp. 96–9. These estimates of the present strength of the Russian Army in the Far East are, of course, only of relative value. The Russian and Japanese effectives concentrated here naturally change constantly. According to the most recent information, the Russians have concentrated in the Far Eastern provinces forces much superior to the Japanese Army in Manchuria.

46. *Rüstung und Abrüstung*, 1934, p. 103. According to other sources four infantry divisions are stationed in Northern Manchuria and two infantry divisions in Inner Mongolia and on the Great Wall (spring, 1934). Cf. N. N. Golowin, *l.c.*, p. 26. Besides the ports mentioned there is also the important ports of Hiroshi-mâ (on the inner

sea), which was formerly the central port for all Japanese military transports to the continent, and of Tsuruga (on Wakasa Bay). The latter will be linked to the inner sea by a canal from Osaka across the Biwa Lake, now under construction, and capable of admitting even battleships. Thus the Sea of Japan and the inner sea which is so important as the centre of the whole war economy will be joined up. For the Japanese mercantile marine vide *Résumé Statistique de l'Empire du Japon*, p. 89.

47. "To-day operations carried on by railways, motor transport and aircraft over a wide front, and aided by long-range weapons will be decisive. Envelopment to-day is infinitely more difficult unless there is adequate transport, and the army using interior lines is as a rule superior because it can better dominate the war area with its technical resources" (Karl Justrow, *Feldherr und Kriegstechnik*, Oldenburg, 1933, p. 294).

48. Hirata, *l.c.*, pp. 32–3. The development of strategical operations as portrayed in the text is only one of the possible developments. In war naturally anything may happen. The advantage of the "interior lines" which in our account are held by the Japanese would find their real significance when the Japanese succeeded in cutting off the Russian Eastern Group in the coastal province from the Western Group in the Trans-Baikalia region, and particularly if they succeeded in cutting all the lines of communication of the Eastern Group. It is, however, possible that the Russian forces in the coastal provinces, instead of relying on the Amur railway, which would be exposed to cavalry and air attacks, would use some other line of communication. They might choose the line running over the southern slopes of the Stanovoi Mountains to the Aldan–Maja region (where the Lena river rises). During summer a great supply base could be established at the mouth of the Lena. These supplies could be forwarded during the summer months up that mighty stream and its tributaries to the Aldan Plateau. In the winter such transport could be done by motor-sledges. This northern base might well become of essential importance in the event of a military alliance between the Soviet Union and the United States. The Russian Eastern Group would then be completely independent of the Amur railway (vide Map 8). Nor should it be forgotten that the present lack of railways in Siberia could be made good to some extent by using aircraft. A day's supply for an infantry division of fifteen thousand men means five railway truckloads of food, or fifty tons. Twenty-five large transport planes, with a carrying capacity of one net ton each, could easily cover twice daily a total distance of 600 kilometres, and could comfortably supply a division.

49. Adolf von Horsetzky, *Kriegsgeschichtliche Uebersicht der wichtigsten Feldzüge seit 1792*, Vienna, 1913, p. 674.

50. According to the estimates of the Russian General Staff, 1·1 to 1·6 railway trains a day are needed to meet adequately the daily requirements of a division. The general staffs of the Western European

armies estimate that 2·7 to 3·3 trains a day are needed. According to the estimates of N. N. Golovin (*l.c.*, p. 35), the Japanese would bring the number of the trains on the northern Manchurian railway network to three trains to one army division, in agreement with the Western European estimates. There is a wide difference of opinion as to the transport capacity of the Transsiberian railway. In the summer of 1905 the then not completed Transsiberian railway succeeded in running twelve trains a day (A. N. Kuropatkin, *l.c.*, p. 241), To-day a capacity many times this would certainly not be an overestimate.

51. Cf. W. Kangelari, "Mongolija kak malo kulturnij teatr" (Russ: "Mongolia as a Theatre of War Untouched by Civilization") in *Vojna i Revolutsija*, 1928, pp. 3–22.

52. Russia in 1935 possessed four battleships, seven cruisers, twenty-seven destroyers, ten torpedo boats, and about twenty-five submarines of a total tonnage of 184,333 (*Rüstung und Abrüstung*, p. 210; cf. *Annuaire Militaire*, p. 871).

53. As to the prospects of the Red Army in the event of war with Japan two diametrically opposite opinions are expressed in the Russian military reviews. The leading strategist of Soviet Russia, the ex-Czarist general, A. Svetchin, after a very objective appreciation of the merits and shortcomings of the Japanese Army—he reproaches the Japanese with military conservatism and a lack of originality—comes to the conclusion that, though the way to victory over the Japanese is not an easy one, it is possible, and, provided there is careful preparation to repel the Japanese attack, the military defeat of Japan is inevitable. On the other hand, General Golovin (anti-Bolshevik), also an ex-Czarist general and the author of several books on tactics, thinks that a crushing defeat of the Soviet Russian armies is inevitable. The analysis Golovin makes of the strategical situation in the Far East is a fundamental, well-documented one, but strangely enough he deals only with the situation in which the Russian forces in the Coast province are separated from those in Trans-Baikalia, and arbitrarily assumes that only the Coast and Amur provinces will be the main theatres of war. It is, however, much more probable that the Russian commanders would prefer to concentrate the whole of the army west of the Great Hingan, and regard the defence of the Coast province as secondary. Some of the Japanese experts, including Hirata, assume that the decisive battles will take place west of the Great Hingan and in Outer Mongolia. It is taken for granted in Japan that the Russians will organize to wage a defensive campaign in Trans-Baikalia. As the extreme western objective of the Japanese strategy, Hirata chooses Krasnojarsk (on the supper Yenissei river), and frankly confesses his fear that the farther the Japanese armies get drawn into Siberia the more difficult will their position become (Hirata, *l.c.*, pp. 302, 313–14). The weak point of Golovin's thesis is just the fact that he docs not take into consideration the possibility of an *active* Russian defensive

on a large scale, cf. A. Svetchin, "Japonskaja armija v 1904 godu i na sovremennom etape" (Russ: "The Japanese Army in 1904 and To-day") in *Vojna i Revolutsija*, 1934, March–April, pp. 86–101; Golovin, *l.c.*, pp. 5, 21 sq.

54. Quoted by K. Haushofer, *Japans Werdegang als Weltmacht und Empire*, Berlin and Leipzig, 1933, p. 100.

55. Lebeneff in *Krasnaja Zvezda* of September 17, 1933.

56. Another possible development of the naval campaign is that the Americans would choose first to clean up Japan's eastern sea-defences and to capture as a temporary base one of the islands under Japanese mandate. In this case, too, however, the Americans would have to be prepared for heavy losses.

57. The tables are compiled from the official information in the *Annuaire Militaire*, pp. 264, 497. *Rüstung und Abrüstung*, p. 202, gives somewhat different and later figures, but gives no information on guns. The new additional building programmes have not been taken into account, because the information so far available is of very relative value. What we are concerned with here is simply to arrive at an approximate estimate of what the relative strength of the two navies may be.

58. Lebeneff, *l.c.*

59. Golovin, in *The Problem of the Pacific in the Twentieth Century*, London, 1922, p. 141. Quoted from the Russian version (Prague, 1924). Chapters VII, VIII, IX and X of this work are by A. D. Bubnoff.

60. "A great military leader of antiquity is said to have challenged an opponent thus: 'If you are the great warrior you boast you are, why don't you come down and fight me?' To which came the retort: 'If you are the greater leader you claim to be, why don't you make me come down and fight you?' " (Mahan, *Influence of Sea-Power Upon History*, 1890; German version, Berlin, 1899, vol. ii, p. 677).

61. *Ostasiatische Rundschau*, 1933, p. 363. Cf. *Poslednija Nowosti*, a Russian newspaper published in Paris, issue of December 27, 1933.

62. Isaiah Bowman, *The New World*, London, 1923, p. 522.

EPILOGUE

Let us look once again at the map of the old world which has been before us throughout this investigation. On it Europe appears as a small, highly organized peninsula of the great Asiatic continent; beside the other peninsulas—India, Asia Minor, and Indo-China. The fortunes of the European peninsula have always been and still are, in fact, to-day perhaps more than at any time in the past, inseparably connected with those of the motherland of Asia.

The more closely we study the map the more clearly is revealed the peripheral character of our world, "Europe proper," which lies between the North Sea and the Dnieper, for neither the British Isles nor the Soviet Union can be regarded as parts of "Europe proper."

The farther the axis of world politics shifts toward the Pacific region the greater becomes the significance of such entities as the Soviet Union and the British Empire. Both the British and the Russians are at one and the same time Europeans and Non-Europeans. Their interests are divided between Asia and Europe, and hence their special and very complicated position in European politics.

From the standpoint of a continental European, Germany is to-day the central political entity which is exposed to pressure from all sides and which in reaction exercises counter-pressure in every direction. From the standpoint of world politics, Germany is on the periphery, and it is rather Russia which can lay claim to be considered a central Power, Russia, which since Peter the Great has been exposed to pressure from Europe in the west and from Asia in the east.

Similarly hybrid is the position of England which is to no greater extent a European than an Indo-Pacific Power. England's sphere of domination envelops Eurasia from the south and from the Indo-Pacific region, just as Russia encircles Eurasia from the north. The pressure exercised by these two dominations on one another is one of the most important—perhaps the most important—elements in world politics throughout the last century. Britain and Russia are the great rivals in Eurasian politics, but in that rivalry there is always present the possibility of a mutual understanding, a possibility which lies in the fact that both empires occupy a peculiar Asiatic-European position. Both States are particularly concerned to maintain a balance of power in Europe which would be based on a balance of power in Asia.

"The balance of power" is not an English invention, nor is it the invention of diplomatists and politicians. Certainly the maintenance of the balance of power is an old tradition in British politics. Henry VIII boasted that he had maintained the balance between Charles V and François I. In the days of Queen Elizabeth, just as much as in the period of the two Pitts, with Beaconsfield as well as with Salisbury, and even to-day the idea of the balance of power has been the point to which the compass of English policy has steadily pointed. That, however, proves only the fact that English policy in its empirical instinct has grasped the meaning of the most significant element in historical evolution.

So long as there are conflicts between nations and conflicts between classes there is throughout history a constant sequence of dynamic and static periods throughout history. There is no need to "explain" that statement, world history is there to prove it. Perhaps this sequence is the result of a physiological necessity to obtain some balance between the expenditure and accumulation of natural strength. The conservative instinct is at any rate as much innate in man as the revolutionary instinct. The result of the struggle between these two tendencies is what we call history. The endeavours to secure the "balance of power" to secure a static position in which the scales are held even as between classes and States, is just as "justified" just as much characteristic of humanity as the effort towards change, a revolution, or "revision."

There are times when "continental" politicians believe that

if necessary the balance in Europe can be achieved without England and without Russia. That is sheer phantasy. For the main difficulty in securing a European balance of power is just the fact that Russia and England, that is to say the two States which are at once European and more than European, are the essential elements in that balance. In the course of the last 350 years England, and in the course of the last 200 years Russia, has taken part in every European combination, and both have been constantly concerned in all European developments. But for both England and Russia, participation in the affairs of Europe has been a means to an end, the end being the spread of their influence outside Europe.

Any attempts to bring about a balance of power in Europe on a purely continental basis is as futile as that to square the circle. The balance of power in Europe can never be more than a part of the problem of a world balance of power. America, Asia, and Africa are to-day just as important factors in European problems as Austria, Italy, or Germany.

The isolation of the United States as regards Europe is to-day a mere phrase which may still have some electioneering value in the States of the Middle West or in the speeches of backwoods senators in Washington, but every serious politician on either side of the Atlantic knows that the United States is just as interested in the fact of Austria as in that of Panama. Conversely, America with all its problems has to-day become an essential part of the European political system. To re-establish the balance of power in Europe which was upset on the battlefields of Flanders and of Northern France by the German guns, our part of the world used American industry and the American Army. The same thing will happen again.

Forty and fifty years earlier it was in Africa that the balance was upset. In 1935 France buried with pomp and circumstance General Marchand, whose name is for ever associated with one of the most serious international crises of last decade of last century (Fashoda). Then France and England were on the brink of war over the solution of the problem of the partition of the African continent. Since then the African balance of power has been secured by the Anglo-French condominium: England, France, with Italy as a third partner whose rôle is to be that of perpetual "dummy" in the game. Little is heard of Africa to-day, and so it is possible to forget that Africa is one of the main bases of the European system.*

The correlative of the static-dynamic development of Europe is in the Asiatic system. The tensions within the pentagon Great Britain–the United States–China–Russia–Japan are still of the same significance as during the last hundred years for the shaping of European policies. Britain, the most conservative and at the same time the most flexible political system of our planet, is obviously most concerned in preserving the stability of the world. As a consequence of her far-flung world interests and of her complicated internal condition, Britain is so deeply concerned in the maintenance of the stability in the world as a whole, that she is prepared to accept a disturbance of the balance of power in this or that part of the globe, perhaps even in Europe, provided that such a change serves to preserve the larger balance of power. The "continental" politician who as a rule is obliged to be "European only" finds it difficult to understand the British viewpoint.

To England the East Asian and the European problems are inseparable parts of one and the same system. The least certain area in this system is, in English opinion, the Soviet Union. The economic development and consolidation of Russia, especially her industrialization and the shifting of the centre of gravity of the Soviet Union towards Asia, can in certain circumstances upset the balance in that part of the world and therewith the balance in the world as a whole. The Russian advance into Central Asia brings the Soviet Union into direct contact with the outposts of Britain's Indo-Pacific Empire. Here, then, the path of Russian expansion must be blocked in time. On the other hand, it is no more to Britain's interests

* These lines were written before the Fascist adventure in Africa, *vide* my Preface.

that Russia should be too seriously weakened. A German-Japanese alliance which would destroy Russian power in Europe and in Asia is not wanted by Britain; for on the day after the destruction of Russia, England would be faced with a powerful German Empire not only in Central Europe, but in the Mediterranean and throughout Hither Asia. The old problem Berlin–Constantinople–Baghdad would once again become a serious one. And in Asia, the spectre of Pan-Asianism under Japanese leadership would very seriously endanger the British position in the Indo-Pacific area.

British policy thus seeks to keep the Soviet Union in Asia within certain limits and at the same time to prevent the destruction of Russia by a German-Japanese alliance. London is prepared to be an intermediary between Tokio and Moscow in order to enable Russia to concentrate her forces in Europe. By doing so she sees it possible to keep Germany in check.

If, however, development becomes "dynamic," then she will seek as far as possible to localize the conflict. Then, at the worst, there would be only a war on the continent or an isolated Russo-Japanese war. In either case the two Anglo-Saxon Powers would be strong enough to intervene when the belligerents were exhausted and impose a peace upon them. In any case, however, an Anglo-American entente is a necessity which is more and more becoming the essential aim of British policy. It is from this point of view that the British efforts to mediate between the United States and Japan must equally be viewed.

The United States, which is more "dynamic" than England, is to-day equally concerned in maintaining the world balance, and so is prepared to make considerable sacrifices to maintain the balance in the Western Pacific. For it is quite recognized in Washington that a balance of power in East Asia is a necessary condition of a balance of power in Europe and that in spite of the professed "aloofness" in Atlantic-European as well as in Pacific-Asiatic developments there is a risk that America will by necessity be involved. It would be a fallacy also to think that Washington is very desirous to allow the Communist

Soviet Russia to become a power in Eastern Asia at the cost of Japan.

Seen through European eyes, there is to-day but one problem: Germany. But it is often forgotten that the German plain is but a continuation of the Russian steppes and that the latter stretch to the Pacific. The French *bourgeoisie*, which seems to be so afraid of the new German barbarism, is still more afraid of a European revolution. A Franco-Russian alliance? By all means, but what will become of Europe if the victorious Red Armies reach Berlin or even Warsaw? France seeks rather to use her Russian ally to give Germany a salutary fright than to provoke any real danger of war. Balance of power in Europe based on the "armed peace" is still the ideal of the French *bourgeoisie*. But it will not let itself be manœuvred into being involved in a Russo-German war. In short, France does not want either a Germany or a Russia which is too strong. France needs Britain not only to protect her eastern frontiers against Germany, but also to make Russia capable of pursuing a European policy, that is, to be sufficiently strong to check Germany on Russia's western frontiers, and yet at the same time to be sufficiently embroiled in Eastern and Central Asia to prevent her being dangerous either to European peace or to European capitalism.

From the European point of view, the decisive political tensions are those between Russia and Germany and between France and Germany. Actually, however, these tensions are merely two particular aspects of the world political problem whose centre of gravity does not lie in Europe at all. If one looks at the political chessboard as a whole, the situation is very different than if we look merely at the European sector. Just as there is no eternal compulsion for France and Germany to be enemies, so there is no inevitability about the conflict between Germany and Russia. We have sought to show that in world politics there are no such things as eternal friendships and eternal enmities. The conflict between Britain and Russia and between Britain and Germany is certainly much more serious and from the geopolitical point of view much more likely than the conflict between France and Germany and between Germany and Russia. To-day Germany and Russia are kept apart by the very different conceptions of life. But what would happen if both these authoritarian States found *rapprochement* possible on the compromise conception of "national bolshevism"? A German-Russian block in certain circumstances supported by Japan—we do not say that such a conception is actual, but what realist statesman, particularly what Anglo-Saxon statesman, could leave such a prospect, however distant, completely out of his calculation? If the dynamic forces get free play, and if the conservative elements in London, Paris, and Washington are unable to keep the fields in which they will play isolated, it is highly probable that the friendships and enmities within the field of the eternal world-conflict will be very different from those existing to-day.

The conservative elements in Britain, France, and the United States, whose interest chiefly lies in preserving the world balance of power and maintaining the *status quo*, i.e. the "static" elements in world politics, will they be supple enough to find a new balance of power in the world and so a new one in Europe? For the art of maintaining the balance—an old and yet ever new art—consists in finding and constructing new forms of it. Conservatism has got to be progressive or disappear.

Or will the new balance be attained by the means of the world revolution which do not alter the old forms but destroy them?

But the choice between these two ways is conditioned less by man's will than by his destiny.

BIBLIOGRAPHY

AJAX, *Anglo-japonskoje soglashenije:* in Russ ("The Anglo-Japanese Alliance") in *Novy Vostok*, vol. xxv (1929).

AMIRAGOFF, D. S., *O haraktere budustchej Vojny*: in Russ ("The Character of the Coming War") in *Vojna i Revolutsija*, Moscow, September–October 1934.

ANDREE-HEIDERICH-SIEGER, *Geographie des Welthandels*, Vienna, 1930, Bd. 3.

Annuaire Militaire, Reseignements généraux et statistiques sur les Armements terrestres, navales et aériens. Tenth Year. League of Nations, Geneva, 1934.

Annuaire Statistique de la Société des Nations, 1933-1934 (Statistical Year-Book of the League of Nations), Geneva, 1934.

Australia, Commonwealth of. Year Book, 1933.

BARDOUX, JACQUES, *L'Angleterre et l'Asie* (in the *Temps*, January 1, 1935).

BATRAK, W., *Tjaschelaja promyshlennostj v Japoniji*: in Russ ("The Japanese Heavy Industries") in *Vojna i Revolutsija*, Moscow, December 1934.

BERG, L. S., *Otkrytija russkih v Tihom Okeane*: in Russ ("The Russian Discoveries in the Pacific) in *Tihij Okean. Russkija Nautchnyja issledowanija. Akademija Nauk*, Leningrad, 1926.

BIENSTOCK, GREGOR, *Einführung in die Weltwirtschaft*, Berlin, 1927.

BILDERLING, GENERAL A., in *Russkij Invalid*, 1906, No. 166, quoted in A. N. Kuropatkin, *Zapiski o Russko-Japonskoj wojne. Itogi wojny.* In Russ ("Memoirs of the Russo-Japanese War"), Berlin, 1909.

BLAKESLEE, GEORGE H., *The Recent Foreign Policy of the United States*, New York and Cincinatti, 1925.

BOWMAN, ISAIAH, *The New World. Problems in Political Geography*, London, 1923.

British Documents on the Origin of the War, 1898-1914, London, 1927, sq.

Bulletin d'Informations économiques et financières, Paris. Edited by Balet. June 1934.

CHAVANNES, E., *Documents sur les Tou-kioue (Turcs) occidentaux*, St. Petersburg, 1903.

China Year-Book, 1933. Edited by H. G. Woodhead. Shanghai.

Chinese Economic Journal, No. 7, 1927, "Chinese Labour Migration to Manchuria."

CLARK, GROVER, *Economic Rivalries in China*, New Haven, 1932.

Le Conflict Sino-Japonais. Memoranda du Gouvernement Chinois, présentés à la commission d'Etude de la Société des Nations, Nanking and Peiping, April–August 1932.

COURANT, MAURICE, *La Sibérie, colonie russe, jusqu'a la Construction du Transsiberien*, Paris, 1920.

CURZON, GEORGE N. (Marquis Curzon), *The Problems of the Far East*, London, 1894.

Persia and the Persian Question, London, 1892.

DENNET, TYLER, *Roosevelt and the Russo-Japanese War*, New York, 1925.

Americans in Eastern Asia, New York, 1922.

DIETRICH, BRUNO, and LEITER, HERMANN, *Produktion, Verkehr und Handel*, Vienna, 1930.

DOCUMENT B., *Les Relations du Japon avec la Manchourie et la Mongolie*, July 1932.

DODD, WILLIAM E., *Woodrow Wilson and His Work*, New York, 1920.

DUBOSCQ, ANDRÉ, *D'Extrême Orient en Asie centrale* (in the *Temps*, October 23, 1934).

DVORZOV, L., *Japonskij Voennyj Vozdushnyj flot*: in Russ ("The Japanese Military Air Fleet") in *Vojna i Revolutsija*, May–June 1934.

Eastern Siberia, London, 1920 (No. 55 of the handbooks prepared under the direction of the Historical Section of the Foreign Office. Edited by G. W. Prothero.)

EGERTON, H. E., *The Origin and Growth of the English Colonies and of their System of Government*, Oxford, 1903.

FABRE-LUCE, ALFRED, *Caillaux*, Paris, 1933.

The Far Eastern Review, November 1928, April 1930.

FILCHNER, WILHELM, *Sturm über Asien. Erlebnisse eines diplomatischen Geheimagenten*, Berlin, 1924.

FIRSOV, N. N., *Tchtenija po istoriji Sibiri*: in Russ ("Lectures on the History of Siberia"), Moscow, 1920.

FISCHER, LOUIS, *The Soviets in World Affairs*, London and New York, 1930, 2 vols.

Forward or Backward in China? Discussed by Dr. Hu Shih, Mr. Grover Clark and Dr. Stanley K. Hornbeck. A Stenographic Report of the Ninety-Sixth Luncheon Discussion, February 26, 1927, of the Foreign Policy Association in New York.

FOX, FRANK, *The Mastery of the Pacific. Can the British Empire and the United States Agree?* London, 1928.

FRIEDJUNG, HEINRICH, *Das Zeitalter Des Imperialismus, 1884-1914*, Berlin, 1919, 2 vols.

GOLOVIN, GENERAL N. N., *Sovremennaja strategitcheskaja obstanovka na Dalnem Vostoke*: in Russ ("The Present Strategical Position in the Far East"), Belgrade, 1934.

The Problem of the Pacific in the Twentieth Century, London, 1922. Russian edition, Prague, 1924. Chapters vii, viii, ix and x are by A. D. Bubnoff.

GREENHOW, R., *History of Oregon and California*, Boston, 1847.

GRIFFIS, W. E., *Corea, the Hermit Nation*, London, 1882.

GRONSKI, P. A., *Les Russes aux Îles Hawai au début du XIX Siècle* (in *Le Monde Slave*, Paris, 1928).

Die grosse Politik der europäischen Kabinette, 1871–1914, Berlin, 1920, esp. vol. xvii.

GROUSSET, RENÉ, *Histoire de l'Asie*, Paris, 1922.

HALPHEN, L., *La Place de l'Asie dans l'Histoire du Monde* (in the *Revue Historique*, 1923, vol. cxlii, p. 13).

HART, ALBERT BUSHNELL, *The Monroe Doctrine: An Interpretation*, Boston, 1916.

HAUSHOFER, KARL, *Japans Werdegang als Weltmacht und Empire*, Berlin and Leipzig, 1933.

Geopolitik des Pazifischen Ozeans, Berlin, 1924.

The Secret Memoirs of Count Tadasu Hayashi, edited by A. M. Pooley, London, 1915.

HAYES, A. A., *China and the United States*, in the *Atlantic Monthly*, vol. lix.

HIRATA, SHINSAKU, *How We Shall Make War*: in Jap. Tokio, 1933. An abbreviated version in *Japonija*, Leningrad, 1934.

in the December number of the Japanese-Russian review, *Kai-zo*, quoted in the *Revue du Pacifique*, No. 3, 1934.

HORSETZKY, ADOLF VON, *Kriegsgeschichtliche Uebersicht der wichtigsten Feilzüge seit, 1872*, Wien, 1913.

IVANOVITCH, ST., *Krasnaja Armija*: in Russ ("The Red Army"), Paris, 1931.

JAKUSCHEV, I., *Rajonizovannaja Sibirj v zyfrah*: in Russ ("Some Figures on Siberia") in *Volnaja Sibirj*, Prague, No. 8, 1930.

Die Zukunft Sibiriens, Prague, 1928.

JAMES, EDWIN L., *Oil is the Weak Point in Tokio's Strategy*, in the *New York Times*, February 3, 1935.

JAMES, HERMAN G., and MARTIN, PERCY A., *The Republics of Latin America*, New York and London, 1923.

The Japan Year-Book, Foreign Affairs Association of Japan, 1933.

Japonija, "Partisdat," Leningrad, 1934. Particularly the chapter "The Military Resources of Japanese Imperialism."

JASCHNOV, E. E., *Kitajskaja Kolonisazija severnoj Manjuriji i ee perspektivy*: in Russ ("The Chinese Colonization in Northern Manchuria"), East China Railway Co., Harbin, 1928.

Journal de Genève, August 25, 1934.

Journal of the Iron and Steel Institute, II, 1885.

JUSTROW, KARL, *Feldherr und Kriegstechnik. Studien über den Operationsplan des Grafen Schlieffen und Lehren für unseren Wehraufbau und unsere Landesverteidigung*, Oldenburg, 1933.

KANGELARI, W., *Mongolija kak malo kulturnyj teatr*: in Russ ("Mongolia as a Battle Ground Untouched by Civilization") in *Vojna i Revolutsija*, 1928.

KAWAKAMI, K. K., *Manchukuo, Child of Conflict*, New York, 1933.

KLADO, N. L., *Posle unhoda vtoroj eskadry Tihovo Okeana*: in Russ ("The Departure of the Second Pacific Squadron"), St. Petersburg, 1905.

KNOWLES, L. C. A., *The Economic Development of the British Overseas Empire*, London, 1928.

KOROSTOVETZ, I. J., *Von Chinggis Khan zur Sowjetrepublik. Eine kurze Geschichte der Mongolei unter besonderer Berücksichtigung der neuesten Zeit*, Berlin, 1926.

KRAUSE, F. E. A., *Geschichte Ostasiens*, Göttingen, 1925, 2 vols.

KULISCHER, A. and E., *Kriegs- und Wanderzüge. Weltgeschichte als Völkerbewegung*, Berlin and Leipzig, 1932.

LACHIN, MAURICE, *Japon, 1934*, Paris, 1934.

LATTIMORE, OWEN, *Mongolia*, in *The China Year Book, 1933*.

LEBENEFF, in *Krasnaja Zwezda*, September 17, 1933.

LEROY-BEAULIEU, PAUL, *De la colonisation chez les peuples modernes*, Paris, 1891, 4th ed.

The United States in World Affairs: An Account of American Foreign Relations, 1931, edited by Walter Lippman and William O. Scroges, New York and London, 1932.

LJUBIMOV, L. J., *Kitajskaja Emigrazija*: in Russ ("The Chinese Emigration"), Harbin, 1932.

LOSOVOJ, J. G., *Voprossy Peresselenija i kolonizatsiji Sibiri*, in *Volnaja Sibirj*, No. 3, Prague, 1928: in Russ ("Colonization and Migration Problems in Siberia").

MACMURRAY, J. V. A., *Treaties and Agreements With and Concerning China, 1894–1919*, New York, 1921 (vol. i).

MAHAN, A. T., *The Interest of America in Sea-Power, Present and Future*, Boston, 1898.

Influence of Sea-Power Upon History, 1890.

Influence of Sea-Power Upon the French Revolution and Empire, 1893.

MICHAILOV, M. J., *K voprosu o transportnoj probleme v Kitaje*: in Russ ("The Transport Problem in China"), in *Vestnik Mandchuriji* ("The Manchuria Monitor"), Harbin, organ of the management of the Chinese Eastern Railway, Nos. 6 and 7, 1932.

MILIOUKOV, P., *La Politique Extérieure des Soviets*, Paris, 1934.

MILLARD, THOMAS F., *Conflict of Policies in Asia*, London: George Allen & Unwin Ltd., 1924.

Democracy and the Eastern Question, London, 1919.

MORRETA, ROCCO, *Wie sieht der Krieg von morgen aus?* Berlin, 1934 (German translation).

MORSE, H. B., *The International Relations of the Chinese Empire* (3 vols., esp. vol. ii), London and New York, 1918.

MOSOLF, HANS, *Die chinesische Auswanderung. Uraschen, Wesen und Wirkungen*, Rostock, 1932.

MOSSDORF, OTTO, *Chinas entfremdete Aussenländer* in the *Ostasiatische Rundschau*, Nos. 3 and 4, 1932.

NAGAKURA, C. (New York Office, South Manchurian Railway), *Hsinking Speeding Railroad Building* in the *New York Times*, March 25, 1934.

The *New York Times*, January 6, 1935.

The New Zealand Official Year-Book, Wellington, 1934.

NIKOLAEW, *Vosduschnyje utschenija i manevry Pvo w Japoniji*: in Russ ("Air Manœuvres and Air Defence in Japan"), in *Krasnaja Zvezda*, November 1, 1934.

OGORODNIKOFF, F., *Vozdushnaja Vojna po zarubeshnym Vzgljadam*: in Russ ("War in the Air and the Foreign Views Thereon"), in *Vojna i Revolutsija*, 1934, May and June.

ORCHARD, J. E., *Japan's Economic Position*, New York, 1930.

Ostasiatische Rundschau, 1929, No. 22, 1932–33, and esp. *Luftverkehr in Ostasien*, in Nos. 21–2, October–November, 1934, Hamburg.

PARKER, E. H., *A Thousand Years of the Tartars*, London, 1875.

PAVLOVITCH, M. (M. P. WELTMANN), *Sovetskaja Rossija i imperialistitscheskaja Japonija*: in Russ ("Soviet Russia and Imperialist Japan"), Moscow, 1933.

Sovetskaja Rossija i kapitalistitscheskaja Amerika: in Russ ("Soviet Russia and Capitalist America"), Moscow and Petrograd, 1922.

The Poslednija Nowosti, Paris, December 27, 1933.

DE QUATREFAGES, *Les Polynésiens et leur migration*, Paris, 1860.

RADEK, K., *Portrety i Pamflety*: in Russ ("Portraits and Pamphlets"), vol. ii, Moscow, 1934.

RATHGEN, KARL, *Die Entstehung des modernen Japans*, Dresden, 1896.

Résumé statistique de l'Empire du Japon, 47th year, Tokio, 1933–4.

Revue de la situation économique mondiale, League of Nations, Geneva, 1934.

Revue du Pacifique, No. 9–10, 1934.

ROBERTS, STEPHEN H., M.A., *Population Problems of the Pacific*, London, 1927.

ROBINSON, EDGAR E., and WEST, VICTOR J., *The Foreign Policy of Woodrow Wilson, 1913–1917*, New York, 1918.

Rüstung und Abrüstung. Eine Umschau über das Heer- und Kriegswesen aller Länder, edited by K. L. von Oertzen, Berlin, 1934.

SAVICKY, P. N., *O zadatschach Kochevnikovedenija*: in Russ ("Problems in the Study of Nomads"), Prague, 1928.

SEARS, LOUIS MARTIN, *A History of American Foreign Relations*, London, 1928.

Sowjety w Kitaje. Sbornik materialow i dokumentow. Perewod s nemezkogo. Nautschnoissledovatelskij institut po Kitaju pri Kommunistitscheskoj Akademiji: in Russ ("The Soviets in China"), Moscow, 1934.

Sozialistitscheskoje Stroitelstwo SSSR. Statistitscheskij Yeschgegodnik: in Russ ("The Socialist Reconstruction"), Moscow, 1934.

Statistical Year-Book of the League of Nations, Geneva, 1927.

Statistical Abstract of the United States, 1933, Washington.

Statistisches Jahrbuch für das Deutsche Reich (for 1930 and 1934), Berlin.

STRESCHNEVSKY, *Vosduschnij flot Japoniji*: in Russ ("The Japanese Air Fleet"), in *Krasnaja Zvezda*, December 18, 1933.

SWETSCHIN, A., *Japonskaja armija w 1904 godu i na sovremennom etape*: in Russ ("The Japanese Army in 1904 and at the Present Day"), in *Vojna i Revolutsija*, March–April, 1934.

TANIN, O., and JOGAN, E., *Krisis i obostrenije klassovych protivoretschij v Japoniji*: in Russ ("The Crisis and the Development of Class Conflict in Japan"), in *Japonija*, Leningrad, 1934.

T'ANG LEANG-LI, *The Foundation of Modern China*, London, 1928.

TEMPERLEY, HAROLD, *The Foreign Policy of Canning, 1822–1827*, London, 1925.

TEUBERT, WILHELM, *Die Welt im Querschnitt des Verkehrs*, Berlin, 1928.

THAYER, WILLIAM ROSCOE, *The Life of John Hay*, Boston and New York, 1915.

TOLL, V. P. *Skify i gunny*: in Russ ("Scythians and Huns"), Prague, 1928.

TROTZKY, LEO, *Die Kriegsstärke der Roten Armee* in *Europäische Hefte*, No. 11, Prague, 1934.

UYEDA, TEYIRO, *The Future of the Japanese Population*, 1933 (Jap. quoted in the *Revue de la situation économique mondiale*, League of Nations, Geneva, 1934).

PRINCE VARANAIDYA, *Le Statut International du Siam*, in the *Académie Diplomatique Internationale*, January–March 1933.

VERNADSKY, G. W., *Opyt istoriji Evrasiji*: in Russ ("Essay on the History of Eurasia"), Berlin, 1934.

WHATES, *The Third Salisbury Administration*, 1900.

WILENSKY, WL. (Sibirjakow), *Japonija*: in Russ ("Japan"), Moscow, 1923.

Die Wirtschaftlichen Kräfte der Welt, edited by the Dresdner Bank, Berlin, 1930.

WITTE, GRAF, S. J. *Vospominanija* (1849–94): in Russ ("Reminiscences"), Berlin, 1923.

WOLPE, A., *Einige Gedanken zur Dialektik des Krieges*, in *Wojna i Rewolutsija*, No. 6, 1929.

WONG CHING-WAI (Chairman of the Governing Committee of the People's Government of China), *China and the Nations. Being the Draft of the Report on International Problems Prepared for the International Problems Committee of the People's Conference of Delegates in Peking in April, 1925*, London, 1927.

WOO, T. C., *The Kuomintang and the Future of the Chinese Revolution*, London: George Allen & Unwin Ltd., 1928.

WOODWARD, W. H., *A Short History of the Expansion of the British Empire, 1500–1902*, Cambridge, 1907.

WOYTINSKY, WL., *Die Welt in Zahlen*, vol. i, Berlin, 1925.

ZÜHLKE, HERBERT, *Die Rolle des Fernen Ostens in den politischen Beziehungen der Machte, 1895–1905*, Berlin, 1929.

George Allen & Unwin Ltd. are the official agents in Great Britain and the Crown Colonies for the publications of the League of Nations, of which many are mentioned in this book.

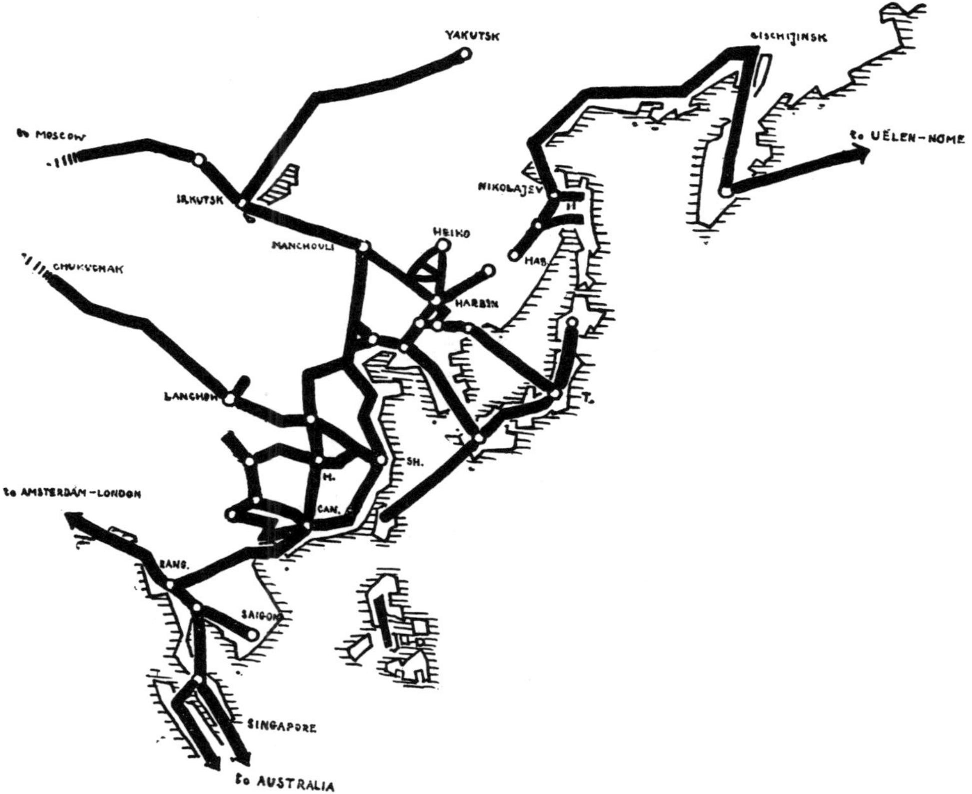

FIG. I.—THE EAST ASIAN AIR SERVICES

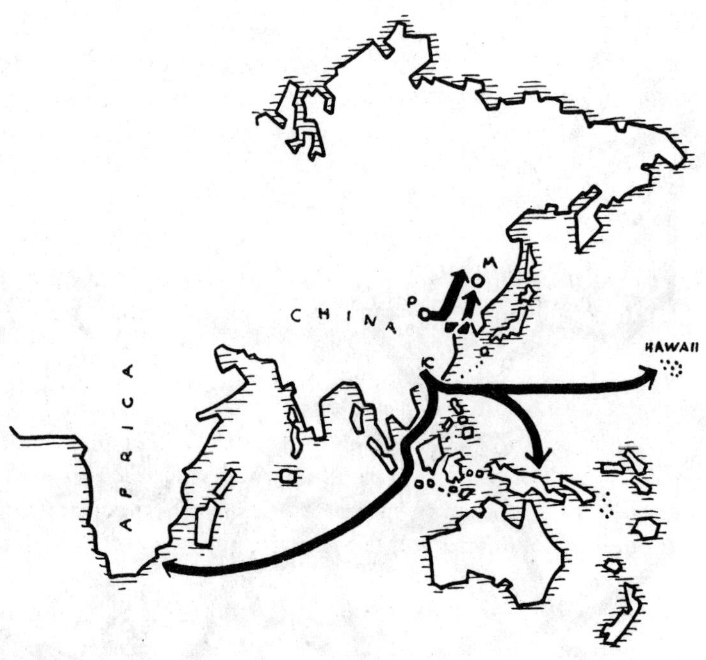

FIG. 2.—CHINESE COLONIZATION

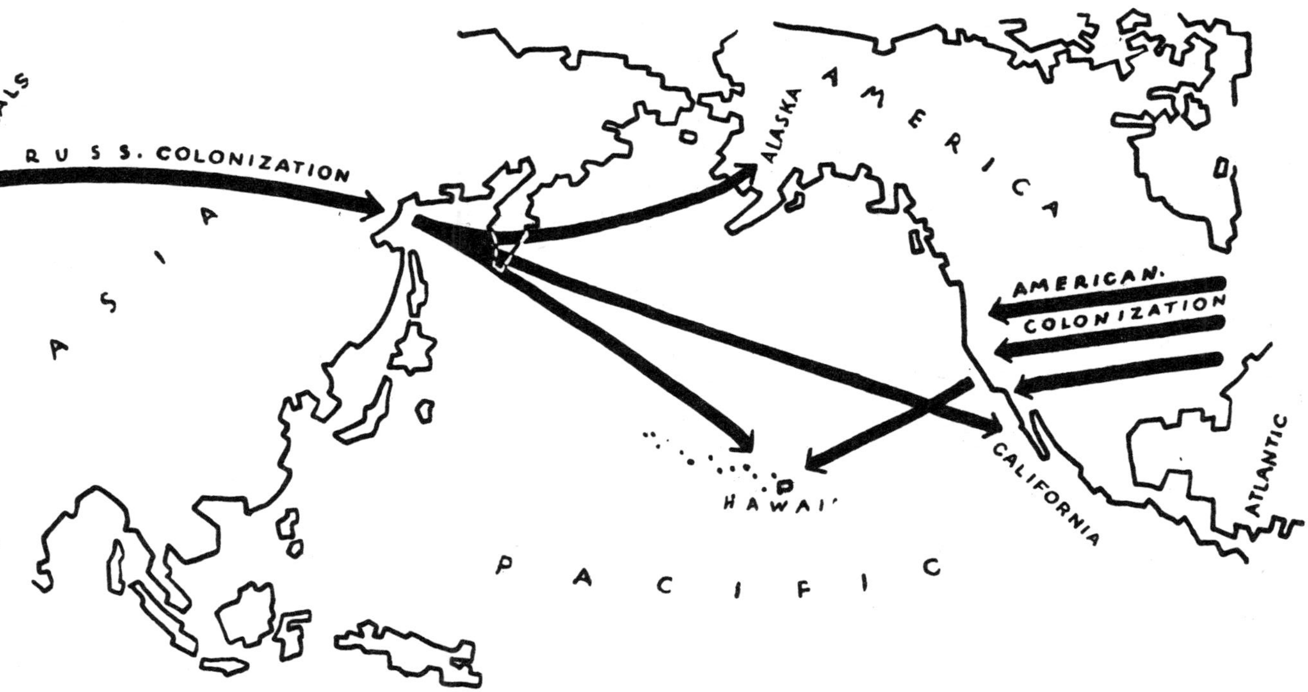

FIG. 3.—RUSSIAN AND AMERICAN COLONIZATION.

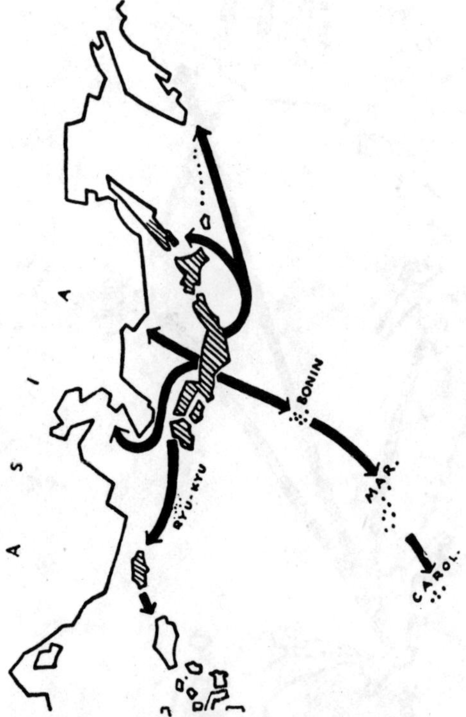

FIG. 4.—JAPANESE COLONIZATION

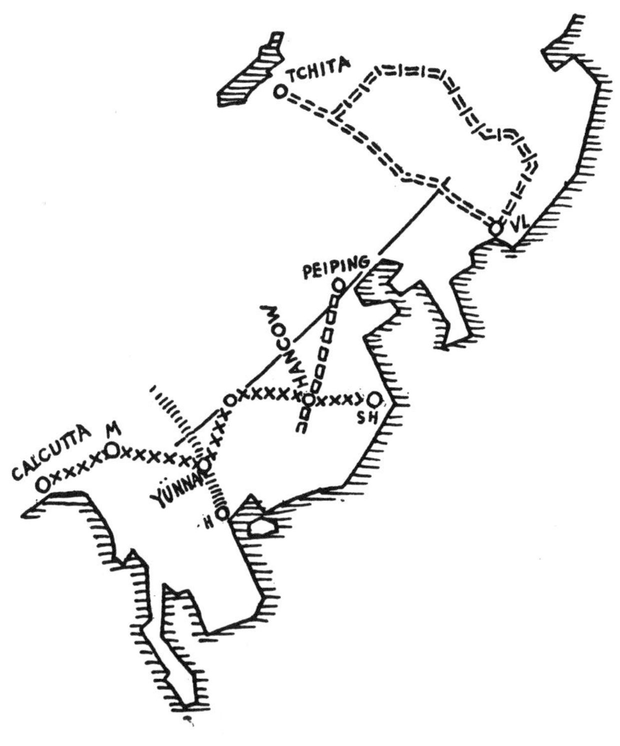

××××× The projected English railway from Calcutta to Shanghai.

ııııııııı The projected French railway.

==== / =ı=ı=ı= } The Russian railways.

▫▫▫▫ The projected Belgian railway from Peiping to Hankow.

—— The planned connection between the Russian and French railways.

FIG. 5.—THE RIVAL RAILWAY INTERESTS AT THE END OF THE NINETEENTH CENTURY

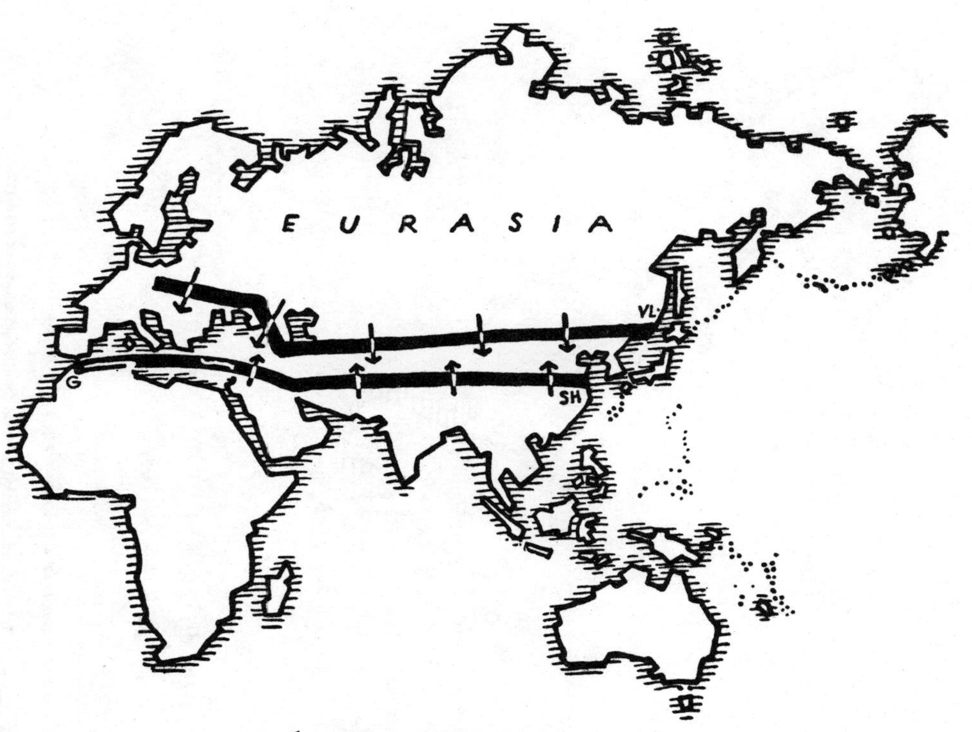

FIG. 6.—ANGLO-RUSSIAN RIVALRY IN EURASIA

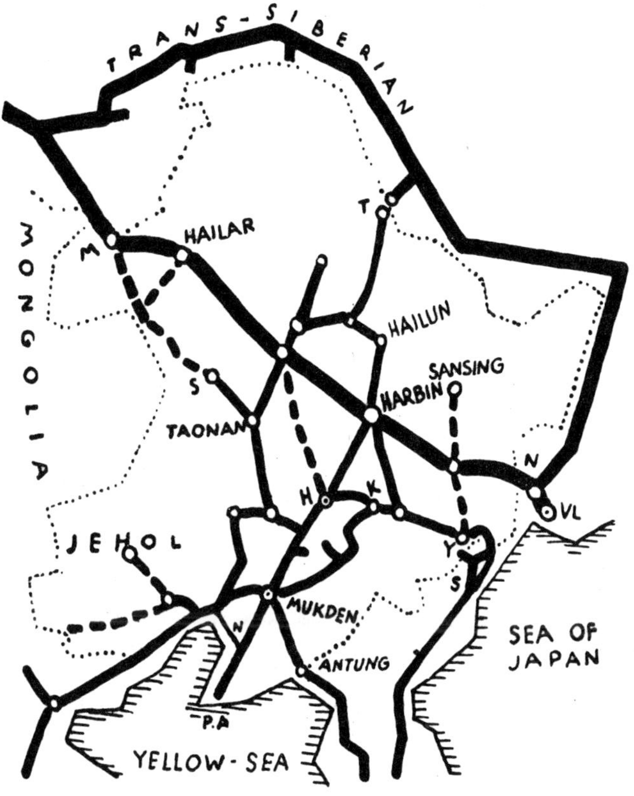

FIG. 7.—THE RAILWAY SYSTEM IN MANCHURIA

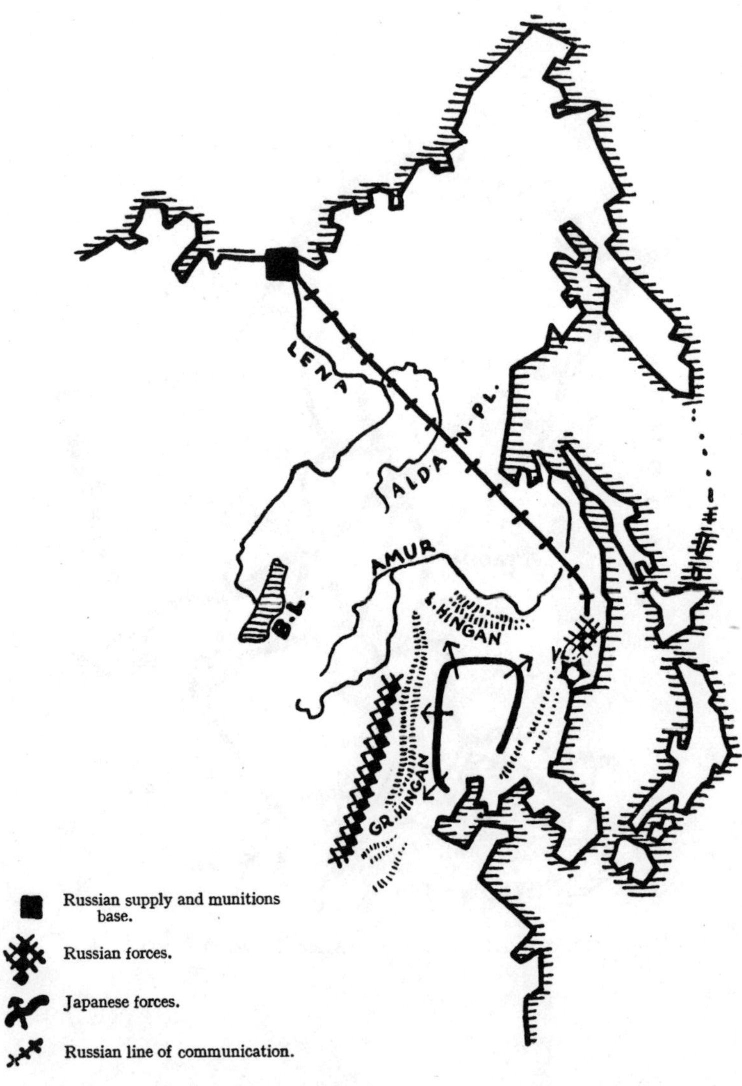

FIG. 8.—STRATEGICAL MAP FOR A SECOND RUSSO-JAPANESE WAR

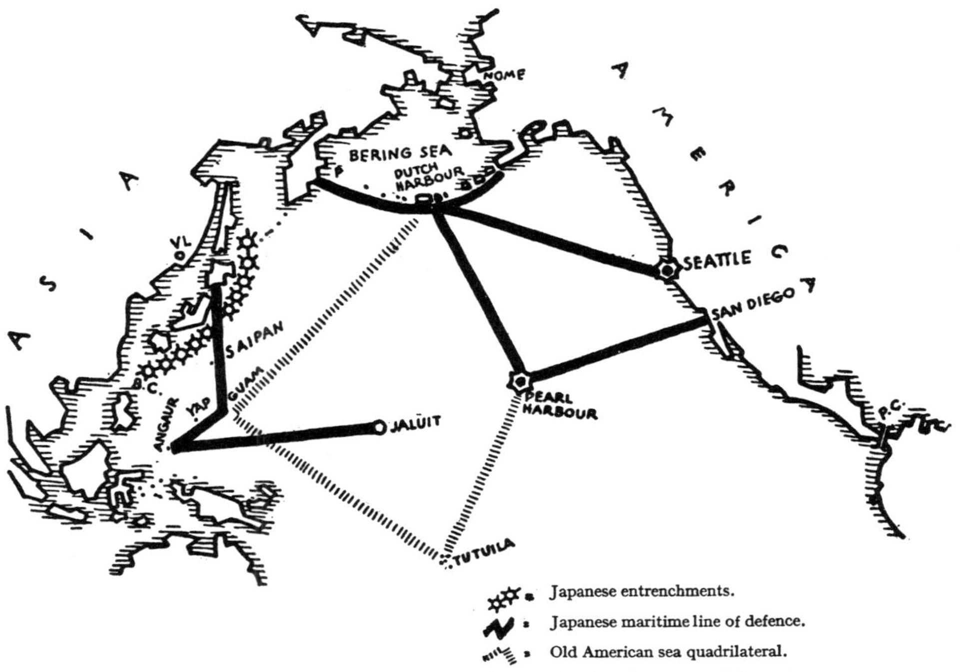

FIG. 9.—AMERICAN AND JAPANESE NAVAL BASES

INDEX OF NAMES

GEOGRAPHICAL INDEX